New Englanders in a New Land

Ceres
RUTGERS
STUDIES
IN HISTORY

Ceres:
RUTGERS STUDIES IN HISTORY

Lucia McMahon and Christopher T. Fisher, Series Editors

New Jersey holds a unique place in the American story. One of the thirteen colonies in British North America and the original states of the United States, New Jersey plays a central, yet underappreciated, place in America's economic, political, and social development. New Jersey's axial position as the nation's financial, intellectual, and political corridor has become something of a signature, evident in quips about the turnpike and punchlines that end with its many exits. Yet, New Jersey is more than a crossroad or an interstitial "elsewhere." Far from being ancillary to the nation, New Jersey is an axis around which America's story has turned, and within its borders gather a rich collection of ideas, innovations, people, and politics. The region's historical development makes it a microcosm of the challenges and possibilities of the nation, and it also reflects the complexities of the modern, cosmopolitan world. Yet, far too little of the literature recognizes New Jersey's significance to the national story, and despite promising scholarship done at the local level, New Jersey history often remains hidden in plain sight.

Ceres books represent new, rigorously peer-reviewed scholarship on New Jersey and the surrounding region. Named for the Roman goddess of prosperity portrayed on the New Jersey State Seal, Ceres provides a platform for cultivating and disseminating the next generation of scholarship. It features the work of both established historians and a new generation of scholars across disciplines. Ceres aims to be field-shaping, providing a home for the newest and best empirical, archival, and theoretical work on the region's past. We are also dedicated to fostering diverse and inclusive scholarship and hope to feature works addressing issues of social justice and activism.

For a complete list of titles in the series, please see the last page of the book.

New Englanders in a New Land

Newark in the Proprietary Period, 1666–1702

Timothy J. Crist

Rutgers University Press
New Brunswick, Camden, and Newark, New Jersey
London

Rutgers University Press is a department of Rutgers, The State University of New Jersey, one of the leading public research universities in the nation. By publishing worldwide, it furthers the University's mission of dedication to excellence in teaching, scholarship, research, and clinical care.

ISBN 978-1-9788-4689-0 (cloth)

ISBN 978-1-9788-4688-3 (paper)

ISBN 978-1-9788-4690-6 (epub)

Cataloging-in-Publication data is available from the Library of Congress

LCCN 2026008453

A British Cataloging-in-Publication record for this book is available from the British Library.

∞ The paper used in this publication meets the requirements of the American National Standard for Information Sciences—Permanence of Paper for Printed Library Materials, ANSI Z39.48-1992.

rutgersuniversitypress.org

Contents

Note on the Text

In citing primary texts, I have retained original spelling, but removed archaisms such as the long *s*, interchangeable *u/v* usage, and thorn/*y* for "th"; I have also corrected or expanded superscript abbreviations.

Until 1752, March 25 was considered the legal start of a new year in England, Wales, Ireland, and the colonies. In the text, I have followed modern practice in considering January 1 as the beginning of the calendar year. In the endnotes, however, I have cited both years for events that took place in the period between January 1 and March 24. For example, I discuss the meeting listed in the Newark town records for February 3, 1669, as having taken place on February 3, 1670, but the endnotes cite the date of the meeting as February 3, 1669/70.

Most Dutch provinces used the Gregorian calendar ("new style") in the seventeenth century while the English still used the Julian calendar ("old style"), resulting in a ten-day gap in how the Dutch and the English dated their documents. For the period of the Dutch reconquest of New York and New Jersey in 1673–1674, I have cited both dates in my discussion. For example, I refer to an order by the Dutch Council of War issued on August 19, 1673 (Gregorian calendar) as having been made on August 9/19, 1673.

New Englanders in a New Land

Introduction

New Englanders from the former New Haven Colony settled Newark in 1666. To organize the new township in the New England way, they entered into two bargains, or compacts. The first was among themselves, in what they called fundamental agreements. The second was a set of articles negotiated with Philip Carteret, proprietary governor of New Jersey. With these compacts in place, they drew on skills honed in several New England towns over the previous two and a half decades to the daunting task of forming a township.

Seven years later, despite their methodical planning and hard work in developing the new settlement, Newarkers faced an existential crisis. To protect their community-based control over admitting new inhabitants and allocating land within the township, they had joined other New Englanders in Elizabethtown and Piscataway in a rebellion challenging Carteret's authority as governor, believing he had reneged on his promises. Now, in the spring of 1673, they waited for news from London that they hoped would confirm their carefully negotiated rights and privileges. They would be sorely disappointed.

At the end of April, James Bollen, secretary to Governor Carteret, reached New York with London's response to the rebellion in New Jersey a year earlier. He brought hard news for the settlers of Newark and others who had challenged the governor. Most ominous was King Charles II's letter calling them "turbulent and disaffected persons." Scarcely less favorable was the news that Sir George Carteret, one of two proprietors of New Jersey, was "much incensed" against those who had participated in the rebellion. Bollen also carried the proprietors' response to a petition from "the pretended Representatives" of Newark, Elizabethtown, and Piscataway with their "pretended grievances and complaints." The proprietors advised the petitioners to "yield due obedience to our Government and laws within the Province of . . . New Jersey" but softened their rejection by inviting the petitioners to "send over any person to make good your allegations in your petition."[1]

Grasping hopefully at this straw, Abraham Pierson, Newark's minister, and Jasper Crane, Newark's magistrate, drew on their long and mutually respectful relationship with Connecticut governor John Winthrop Jr., the most influential ally among their many friends in New England. Two weeks after Bollen's return, Pierson and Crane wrote to Winthrop that "some ill-affected towards our people have given out a report to our honorable lords proprietors, that [we] are of unquiet and troublesome behaviour, which tends (as they conceive) to their advantage, and our disparagement and damage." They asked Winthrop to send a letter to the proprietors on their behalf "to remove the ill report that some have given, and gaine credit to what we shall truly and honestly say toutching our estate." They also suggested that Samuel Wyllys, senior magistrate in Connecticut, should sign the letter, "he having bin sometimes with Sir George Carteret."[2]

A month later, in a second letter to Winthrop hurriedly scrawled by Pierson, they repeated their request for a testimonial to the proprietors. They explained that their fundamental disagreement with governor Philip Carteret was grounded in their conviction that New England–style townships provided the best way to distribute land and organize their lives together, as opposed to living on widely separated farms or estates granted to individuals in the headright system favored by the proprietors and Governor Carteret. As Pierson wrote to Winthrop, Newarkers believed nothing less than their "civil society, safety, learning and religion" were at stake: "Also if you please give some hint of your judgement touching the planting of the countrie whether in townships where accommodations ly conveniently for such purposes or els in farmes which tend to the spoyleing of cohabitation, civil society, safety, learning and religion. Capt: Philip Catteret did much lean that way." As New Englanders, Winthrop and Wyllys understood and shared Pierson's assertion about the importance of townships. On the same day they received Pierson's second letter, they wrote to Sir George Carteret, wishing him "all prosperity in the well Settlement of this your American province" but recommending that it would be "very expedient that your Colony be Branched out into Convenient Townshipps which we find Best Conducinge to Safety and the advansinge of Civill Societyes."[3]

Historians have ascribed the rebellion of 1672 in New Jersey to the controversy over the payment of quitrents to the proprietors and disputes over land titles, or to the meddling of James Carteret, Sir George Carteret's son, but not to a fundamental disagreement about how the province should be settled and daily life organized in townships. In the nineteenth century, William Whitehead, a stout defender of the proprietary government and an admirer of what he considered Philip Carteret's manly struggle "against the spirit of anarchy," blamed the rebellion largely on settlers' opposition to paying quitrents.[4] John Pomfret adopted Whitehead's analysis in *The Province of East Jersey, 1609–1702*, concluding that it "was precipitated in large measure over the payment of quitrents."[5] John Latschar, in his well-documented discussion of the rebellion of 1672, instead emphasized the role of James Carteret in encouraging the rebellion.[6] Richard P. McCormick offered the most measured, but very brief, analysis of the rebellion in his *New Jersey from Colony to State, 1609 to 1789*, concluding "it was caused primarily by the confusion over land titles . . . but it was undoubtedly influenced as well by the fact that the people of the towns since their arrival in New Jersey had assumed that they were to manage their own affairs."[7]

Those were all certainly important factors, but Pierson and Crane's letter suggests that the fierce determination by settlers from New England to distribute land and govern themselves in townships in the New England way was at the heart of their ongoing challenge to Governor Carteret. Rather than just "assuming" that they were to manage their own affairs, as McCormick suggested, Newarkers were convinced they had negotiated articles with Carteret that spelled out their township rights. Although the text of these articles is not extant, traces survive in several references to articles in the Newark town records.[8]

The articles no doubt spelled out how Newarkers would be responsible for their militia and town courts, how they would choose their representatives to the general assembly, and how they would pay the proprietors' quitrent. In addition, the articles would have made provision for Newarkers to implement their form of Bible-based "godly government," for which the New England township was essential. Newark's articles would have been at least as clear on these points as the articles the founders of Woodbridge and Piscataway signed with Governor Carteret in May 1666—at the same time when Newark's founders were negotiating with Carteret. The Woodbridge articles provided the town with "liberty to lay out every mens proportion of land according to their Judgement and discretion" if the allocations did not exceed the limits laid out in the proprietors' concessions. They also explicitly gave the town meeting "the power to admit of their own Inhabitants" and "make all such orders as shall be thought necessary for the prudential ordering and governing" of the town if they were not contrary to provincial laws.[9]

For these reasons, the township theme, with its associated method of distributing land, provides a crucial lens for interpreting both the early history of Newark and the continuing friction between Newarkers and the proprietary government. With this perspective, it is evident that Governor Carteret backtracked on assurances he had provided New Englanders and then asserted his power and authority over the townships when they protested. He shunted to the side key leaders of the different groups of New Englanders—John Ogden in Elizabethtown and Daniel Pierce in Woodbridge, both of whom served briefly on Carteret's council before being dismissed, as well as Robert Treat in Newark—and aimed to govern with the support of major landowners and others to whom he could assign favors. The extraordinary instability of New Jersey's government during the proprietary period, not least the rebellion of 1672, was largely due to New Englanders' continuing advocacy for their "right and privileges," as negotiated in their township articles or expressed in the proprietors' concessions. Among New Englanders in New Jersey, Newarkers were the most persistent for the longest period in holding firm to the founding principles of their New England township.

In New England, groups of households could form a new township by taking three foundational steps: securing a large tract of land by purchase from Native Americans and acknowledgment from the colonial government, with the costs of development financed by a group of associates; covenanting together in a gathered

Congregational church; and adopting a political structure for dealing with township matters. Newarkers took great care with each of these steps. The minimum number of households for a new township, or "plantation," was generally twenty to thirty families. Newark was planned with the expectation of eighty to one hundred households making the move; in the end, sixty-four men subscribed on behalf of their households to fundamental agreements establishing Newark.

New England townships implemented the most egalitarian method of distributing land used in the American colonies. Home lots large enough for gardens and orchards were allocated first. Divisions of upland and meadow for cultivation of crops, timber, and grazing of animals followed in due course, with the order in which settlers selected their parcels of land usually determined by drawing lots. Average landholdings were generally small enough to be worked by a household, without the need for indentured or enslaved laborers but large enough to sustain each family and perhaps generate a surplus for trade or barter with each other. Each township selected its own recorder to maintain careful records of land titles and subsequent transfers and conveyances; Newarkers chose Robert Treat to fill that role in addition to his service as magistrate. As a township grew to a certain size, usually two hundred households or when there was no longer sufficient land to distribute to existing or new households, a group of settlers (often including younger sons) would hive off and start a new township with its own association of investors, church covenant, and political arrangement. Newark attempted, unsuccessfully, to allow for this expansion by acquiring Nathaniel Kingsland's New Barbadoes tract in 1673 during the brief period when the Dutch regained New York and New Jersey, and then by negotiating for the Acquackanonk tract to the north of the Newark tract in 1674.[10]

It is perhaps not surprising that Philip Carteret did not appreciate the fundamental importance of townships to settlers from New England. As historian John Frederick Martin pointed out, "There had been no such thing as a town before New Englanders invented it, no English precedent, no guide to instruct the colonists. In creating the town, colonists came up with a wholly new institution. It was part land company and part borough, part joint-stock company and part village. The entrepreneurial aspect of towns helped overcome the tremendous organizational and financial difficulties presented by settling the wilderness. The borough qualities helped establish public order in the wilderness."[11] On the other hand, Richard Nicolls, the first English governor of New York, quickly grasped the importance of townships in attracting New Englanders to settle in what became New Jersey. When he circulated his *Conditions for New-Planters* throughout New England in 1665, Nicolls made it clear that "the Purchasers [of land from 'Indian Sachims'] are to set out a Town, and Inhabit together." In addition to allowing "liberty of Conscience . . . in the exercise of the Protestant Religion," Nicolls spelled out two further conditions designed to appeal to New Englanders: "The several Townships have liberty to make their peculiar Laws, and Deciding all small Causes within themselves," and "Every Township hath the free choice of all their Officers both Civil, and Military." Nicolls laid out these conditions even though he found it frustrating to deal with stubborn New Englanders, whom he considered "a sort of People of such refractory & peevish dispositions as are not knowne in old England," but he recognized that New Englanders would not settle in a new area unless these conditions were in place.[12]

Philip Carteret would learn just how refractory and peevish New Englanders could be when he worked to establish the new proprietary government in New Jersey. When Sir George Carteret and Lord John Berkeley, proprietors of New Jersey, named the then twenty-six-year-old as governor, they required that he reserve one-seventh of each tract of land for themselves and collect a half-penny per acre quitrent from all landowners starting in 1670, so they could begin to earn a return on their investment. The proprietors' concessions, dated February 10, 1665, laid out parameters for the roles and powers of the governor, council, and assembly within the provincial government. The document allowed for liberty of conscience "in matter of religious concernments," although not from an enlightened view of religious tolerance but rather to broaden the pool of potential settlers.

The proprietors also charged Governor Carteret with implementing a headright land distribution system, adapted from the West Indies and Carolina, in which land grants of prescribed size would be made to each head of family, with larger grants available if a settler brought indentured servants and/or enslaved persons with him to New Jersey. The proprietors listed the headright incentives for attracting new settlers in their concessions, "that the Planting of the . . . Province may be the more speedily promoted." These incentives encouraged the development of separate manors and farms, often larger than one family could manage on its own and thus requiring indentured servants or enslaved persons to cultivate the land. Each settler arriving in the province before January 1, 1666, with provisions for six months and a supply of arms and ammunition, would receive 120 acres on his own account, plus an additional 120 acres for each "able servant" accompanying him and sixty acres of land for "every weaker servant, or slave, male or female, exceeding the age of fourteen years." "Christian" indentured servants, in turn, were promised a grant of sixty acres for their own use at the expiration of their service, but no allowance was made for enslaved persons to eventually receive land.

The land grant incentives declined over a three-year period to sixty acres for every free man and free woman settling, plus sixty acres for each able servant and thirty acres for every weaker servant or slave. Land was to be surveyed and divided "by general lots" ranging in size from 2,100 acres to 21,000 acres, making it straightforward to set aside a one-seventh part for the proprietors. The proprietors also exercised their prerogative over managing property records: They required that all land grants carry a warrant from the governor, a certificate by the surveyor general noting the boundary of the tract, and registration in the proprietary land records so that quitrents could be collected starting in 1670. This headright system of allocating land, potentially resulting in widely separated farms and estates, was fundamentally at odds with the New England township model. It assumed, as historian Claire Priest put it, that "land policy was a central prerogative of the King and his deputies," implemented through top-down government directives.

However, the proprietors' instructions were honored more often in the breach than not in the early years of the province, leading to years of disputes over land titles and, as Abraham Pierson asserted in his letter to Governor Winthrop, the spoiling of civil society.[13]

Neither Sir George Carteret nor Lord John Berkeley ever visited the eighty-seven hundred square miles of territory that James, Duke of York, granted them in June 1664 and named in honor of Sir George's ties to the Isle of Jersey.[14] Sir George had gained royal favor in 1649 by hosting King Charles II, his brother James, Duke of York, and their entourage in exile on the Isle of Jersey, the last Royalist stronghold, as Oliver Cromwell tightened his control over England.[15] An experienced sailor with a reputation for brilliant naval tactics, Sir George gained further royal favor and newfound wealth in the early 1650s from privateering in the English Channel, where his ships disrupted and seized Cromwellian trade. After the Restoration of Charles II to the English throne in 1660, Sir George became vice-chamberlain of the Royal Household, a member of the Privy Council, and treasurer of the Navy. All were powerful positions and, at least in the case of treasurer of the Navy, highly remunerative; he was entitled to three pence out of every pound spent from Treasury accounts.

Immensely wealthy, Sir George became a key player in developing the British Atlantic and extending England's imperial reach by investing in chartered companies and proprietary provinces. His investments included the Company of Royal Adventurers into Africa and its successors that developed the English slave trade (chartered in 1660 and renewed in 1662 and 1672 under slightly different names), the Royal Fishing Company (1664) and indirectly, the Hudson's Bay Company (1670). He also invested in the province of Carolina, where, with Lord John Berkeley, he was among eight proprietors (1663), the Bahamas, where he was one of six proprietors (1670), and, of course, New Jersey in 1664.

In proprietary provinces—Maryland, Carolina, New Jersey, New York, and Pennsylvania—the Crown granted proprietors authority over both land and government within their province, including the right to determine how land would be allocated and the power to name a governor to oversee the province in their absence. In contrast, the Crown appointed the governors in royal colonies like Virginia, New York (after 1685) and New Jersey (after 1702); in New England colonists themselves selected their governors. The headright system of land distribution installed in Carolina and the Bahamas, and intended for New Jersey, was designed not just to attract planters and indentured servants to the new provinces but also to serve the proprietors' private interests and investment goals. New Jersey's proprietors aimed for current income from quitrents and future gains from the sale of acreage reserved for them each time land parcels were allocated and patented. Since both were investors in the Royal African Company, they would also benefit from any increase in the English slave trade, although this played out more in Carolina and the Bahamas than in New Jersey.[16]

Thus, two models for development were at play in the early years of New Jersey: the headright system with potentially large estates favored by the proprietors, and the township model insisted on by settlers from New England. The contest between these two visions for the future of the province, one more individualistic and authoritarian and the other more community-based, informs much of the history of both early Newark and New Jersey as a whole.

In undertaking this detailed study of early Newark, I have looked to archival sources, especially the rich collections at the New Jersey Historical Society, New Jersey State Archives, New York State Archives, and UK National Archives. There are crucial gaps in the archival record, however. For example, Governor Carteret's memorandum book from the earliest years of the province has not survived, although some items were copied in various legal filings by attorneys in eighteenth-century suits and countersuits over land titles. Other records were lost in April 1686, when James Emmot, provincial secretary of East Jersey, suffered a "dreadfull fire" at his house with "the original Concessions . . . amongst other writeings bookes and papers was there burnt and consumed."[17] Similarly, the records of Newark's church were lost when British forces ransacked the Reverend Alexander MacWhorter's house in late 1776. However, Newark town records and early land records are extant. Woodbridge town records allow for comparisons in how different towns settled by New Englanders responded to events and challenges, as do, to a more limited degree, Piscataway town records; both are held by Rutgers University Special Collections. The extensive correspondence in the Winthrop Papers at the Massachusetts Historical Society, never explored by historians of Newark or New Jersey, provides critical insights. Two future governors of Connecticut, Robert Treat, founding magistrate of Newark, and William Leete, an investor, were among the many leaders of the former New Haven Colony involved in the settlement of Newark, so it is no surprise that Governor Winthrop's correspondents included not just Abraham Pierson but Winthrop's contacts in New Haven, Milford, and elsewhere who were keen to pass along news of the new township. The North Lanarkshire Archives in Scotland holds letters of Scottish Covenanters briefly resident in Newark in 1686. I have drawn on these and other archival sources with the aim of providing a fresh interpretation of the founding and settlement of Newark and adding context and nuance to the larger history of both New Jersey and New England. The periods when Newark's interests diverged from those of Connecticut, notably during the Dutch reconquest of New York in 1673 and the later stages of Leisler's rebellion, are especially revealing.

I have benefited from many studies of early New Jersey and New England, particularly Maxine Lurie's decades-long scholarly engagement with New Jersey's proprietary government and Brendan McConville's insights about the origins in the proprietary period of the eighteenth-century struggle in New Jersey for property and power.[18] I have also reviewed unpublished dissertations for important insights. In 1977, Edward P. Rindler undertook a demographic study of Newark's founding households and the formation of Newark, modeled on earlier studies of Dedham, Andover, and Sudbury in Massachusetts, although gaps in the records hindered his analysis, and he did not explore the town's relationship with the proprietary government.[19] Taking a different tack, John A. Latschar studied Philip Carteret's tenure as governor with close attention to original sources, but he did not examine individual townships.[20]

Part One of this study is composed of five chapters that provide a fresh interpretation of the founding and settlement of Newark as a self-contained New England community, including interactions with Natives, the formation of godly self-government, the allocation and farming of land, and the spread of slavery. The eight chapters in Part Two analyze Newarkers' relationship with the proprietary government in the seventeenth century, from early cooperation through resistance and rebellion—with a hopeful interlude of Dutch rule—and finally to an uneasy accommodation over land titles and political representation before Queen Anne imposed royal government on New Jersey in 1702. Conflict between the two systems of land distribution and two sources of authority, one scriptural and community-based and the other royal and proprietary, was predictable and perhaps inevitable.[21]

Newark was founded as a New England township with godly self-government and community-based land distribution, but Newark's leaders lacked the protective support of a Puritan colonial government that other New England townships benefited from in Massachusetts, Connecticut, and the former New Haven Colony. Newark's founders failed in their effort to acquire additional large tracts of land nearby for the formation of allied townships. They also did not recognize how difficult it would be to maintain self-government within Restoration England's imperial framework. Their tenacious conflict with the proprietary government brought into sharp relief their different objectives for extending political representation and distributing land—and anticipated by a decade or more the issues Massachusetts townships faced when Sir Edmund Andros, as governor of the Dominion of New England, challenged township government and local land titles in the late 1680s. Newarkers were prepared to resist to the point of rebellion to implement their vision of godly self-government, but despite their determination they were unable in isolation to sustain a full measure of New England township governance throughout the proprietary period.

PART I

A New Township

CHAPTER 1

Before Newark

On May 21, 1666, Robert Treat and Samuel Swaine, with about two dozen others, met "near to Elizabeth Town, and the Town Plotts on Passaic River" and agreed to "make one township," soon called Newark, to be "settled by them and their associates." Most of those who took part came from Milford in the former New Haven Colony, but representatives from the neighboring towns of Guilford, Branford, and New Haven also joined them. Their aim, as they put it, was "through God's blessing" to carry on "civil and town affairs according to God and a Godly government."

The founders of Newark brought long and varied experience with New England townships to their new settlement. Individually, they had taken part in developing townships in both the New Haven Colony and Connecticut, and on Long Island, over the prior two and one-half decades. They learned from both their successes and failures, and those lessons—clear title, strong leadership, sufficient capital, and shared religious beliefs—informed their careful preparation for establishing their new township on the Passaic River. They recognized many decisions would need to be made in the first weeks and months, even before a church was gathered and the first town meeting took place, including acquiring land, laying out and assigning home lots, and determining who would be permitted to settle with them and under what conditions. So, at that meeting in May 1666 they chose eleven men to form a committee "for the speedier and better expedition of things then emergent to be done." Four committee members were from Milford, three each from Branford and New Haven, and one from Guilford. Together, they brought more than two hundred years of experience settling new towns and making decisions within the New England township model.[1]

New Haven Colony residents first explored settling in the area near present-day Newark following the Restoration of the monarchy in England. In November 1661, the colony's deputy governor informed New Netherland governor Peter Stuyvesant, on behalf of "a companie of Considerable persons" mostly from Milford, that they were considering "some adjacent parts of this American wilderness" for a new settlement where they could provide for their "outward comfortable subsistance" and their "soules welfare," as well as lands for their children. Assuring Stuyvesant that they were "true men and noe spies," the group asserted that the settlement could prove more for the "benefit & welfare of the Dutch nation In America and the honor of their principals in Europe" than any established to that point.[2]

This concern for the Dutch was extraordinary for English settlers, but it reflects the extent to which residents of New Haven Colony were unsettled by the Restoration of Charles II in 1660. With their strong Puritan views, they recognized immediately that the Restoration would turn their world upside down. They had formed the New Haven Colony in 1639 to demonstrate how biblical rules should guide the organization of both church and state. They expected to be the proverbial "city on the hill" showing God's way to England, and when the civil war broke out in England it seemed that events were playing out as they hoped. They strongly supported Parliament against the king, and they no doubt approved of the decision to put Charles I on trial in 1649. They had close personal ties to Oliver Cromwell, who, in turn, endorsed their ideas on church government. But their favored standing, as well as that of other New Englanders, ended in 1660. William Hooke, a minister of the New Haven church who had returned to England to become one of Cromwell's chaplains, went underground after the Restoration, living in concealed places in and about London. Hugh Peter, who took part in the ordination of Abraham Pierson in 1640 before returning to England, was hanged at Charing Cross in London in October 1660 for his involvement in the trial and execution of King Charles I eleven years earlier. Two other regicides, Edmund Whalley and William Goffe, escaped from England and made their way to New England before an act of Parliament excluded them from pardon. At the time the Milford group entered negotiations with Governor Stuyvesant in late 1661, Whalley and Goffe were hiding from the king's agents in the Milford home of Micah Tompkins, a founder of Newark and one of the first deacons of the Newark church. The willingness of the Milford community to protect regicides from the reach of the king underscores their determination to continue despite all odds to work for what they considered "the Kingdom of Christ in the Congregationall way." This resolve guided both their negotiation with Stuyvesant and their subsequent settlement of Newark.[3]

The New Haven Colony group, including Robert Treat, spelled out terms for their possible settlement in New Netherland in seven propositions sent to Stuyvesant. The first two propositions concerned religion and organization of their churches, reflecting both the fundamental importance of religion in their lives and their commitment to structuring a government in which only church members could vote and hold public office. In their first proposition, they requested approval to organize churches in the Congregational way "without any . . . Impositions of any other forms, orders or customes to be observed by them" and asked that the Dutch acknowledge their approval publicly. In their second proposition they sought consent to form associations of English churches for "mutuall helpfulness" and call a synod, as the need might arise, to suppress heresies, schisms, and false worship.

This second proposition suggests they anticipated the settlement of several towns, each with its own church "planted under the Dutch Government," or perhaps even the transfer of the entire New Haven Colony to today's northern New Jersey. Stuyvesant and his council had little objection to these propositions, since the Dutch "never practised restraint of Conscience" either in their home country or in New Netherland. They readily agreed that church congregations could seek advice from other churches or ministers; however, they indicated at first that the governor and council would need to approve the calling of any synod. Later, after receiving advice from directors of the West Indies Company keen to encourage the settlement, Stuyvesant "absolutely granted" the first two propositions.[4]

The third proposition, covering the authority settlers would have to govern themselves, required the most extensive negotiation with the Dutch. In essence, the New Haven group proposed transposing the colony's godly government to New Netherland and "ordering . . . all Judicature and . . . all their civill affaires within themselves," without interference from the Dutch authorities. They wanted to elect their own magistrates and all other officers, "make all . . . laws and orders as they shall find most sutable to their condition and welfare in that place," and constitute and keep courts with "sentences made & verdicts declared without appeales to any other Authority or jurisdiction." They also proposed that all persons would be subject to their laws and orders while within "their precincts." In addition, they noted that the laws of New Haven Colony, which they would draw on "as we shall finde it will alike suite Christ's ends and our conditions there," were in print and could be reviewed by the Dutch. They supplemented this third proposition with a fifth proposition that each township would retain control over who would be permitted to settle within its bounds: "that we have the sole power of disposeing our lands and entertaineing or rejecting all Inhabitants." That Stuyvesant and the directors of the Dutch West India Company would entertain these proposals suggests how much they wanted to develop New Netherland beyond the trading entrepôt of New Amsterdam by attracting settlers to their territory "back of Staten-Island on the Raritan's Kil," since they could serve "as a strong outpost against the Raritan and Nevesink savages."[5]

In their fourth proposition, the New Haven Colony group emphasized their desire to gain a clear title to the land so that it could become the "proper Inheritance of the English Planters and their posteritie for ever." They recognized that this would require the purchase of the land from the Native American owners. To this end, they requested a deed showing the lands "clearly and undeniably purchased of the Indians." They wanted to retain a copy of the deed in their custody, "subscribed and soe owned" in the presence of English, Dutch, and those "Indians that have the natural and civill right" to the lands, demonstrating that it was "lawfully bought and sould" and now belonged to the English planters. A few years later, the founders of Newark followed the same approach in seeking a clear title to their new settlement on the Passaic. The sixth and seventh propositions posed no difficulties. The group wanted the same access to trade as Dutch settlers in New Netherland, but they were willing to pay "all lawfull dues and customes as the

Du[t]ch doe" for the privilege. They also requested the final agreement negotiated with the Dutch be ratified by appropriate powers in Holland, and a copy of the document "signed sealed and Authentically Attested" be provided to them so they could keep it among their public records.

Negotiations between the New Haven Colony group and the Dutch continued for two years, with Robert Treat taking the lead in communicating with Stuyvesant. They reached an agreement on most matters due to extensive concessions by the Dutch. By the middle of 1663, Stuyvesant went so far as to approach the Sachem Oratam to inquire if the Hackensack would sell a hook of land behind Kill Van Kull for the use of the settlers. Oratam deflected the request. At the same time, the settler group appears to have fragmented, with some members distracted by the fierce dispute between Connecticut and New Haven Colony over whether and how the new royal charter for Connecticut subsumed New Haven's lands within it. Treat and Stuyvesant exchanged final letters in June and July, with the latter asking a last time whether the group intended to proceed. If Treat responded, it is no longer extant. A year later, the English took New Amsterdam, and the matter was moot.[6]

Their failure to conclude negotiations with Stuyvesant did not end the interest of residents of the New Haven Colony in lands to the south. In December 1664, as the decision whether towns in New Haven Colony would submit to Connecticut's new royal charter came to a head, William Jones, deputy governor of New Haven Colony, wrote to Richard Nicolls, English governor of New York, to lay a fresh claim to land along the Delaware River. After informing Nicolls about "the great wrong and injury this Colony have suffered from the Dutch at Delaware Bay, about 14 yeares ago, being violently repulsed with great damage out of theire just purchases and possession there," Jones claimed "the Indians of whome we purchased the land, doe still owne our right & much desire the coming of the English."[7] Six months later, when Philip Carteret arrived in the newly created province of New Jersey, leaders of New Haven Colony negotiated in earnest with him about settling along the Delaware River. Documents were exchanged, and Jones reported to New Haven Colony's General Court about "the busines of Delaware, & the Articles."[8] Meanwhile, Carteret sent the articles to the proprietors for their review. These articles, at least fifteen in number, are not extant, but Carteret's response to them in February 1666, addressed to William Jones "and the rest of the undertakers of the Plantation upon Delaware bay or River," gives a sense of how tenaciously the New Haven Colony group insisted on managing their proposed new townships in the New England manner. The propositions that the New Haven Colony group had negotiated with Stuyvesant a few years earlier most likely made up the core of the fifteen articles. They wanted assurances about town courts and the right of appeal, laws, and punishments guided by scripture for offenses such as theft, provisions for setting aside common land for cattle and other livestock, input into the selection of council members, and confirmation that they could transfer land titles to heirs and successors. Carteret compromised on the number of acres to be set aside for the proprietors, but he insisted on not less than five hundred acres. He also did not relent on either imposing a half penny quitrent per acre or requiring individuals to record their grants of land within one year.[9]

A few weeks later, representatives from Milford and New Haven sailed to the Delaware River to jointly inspect possible sites, but as Carteret reported to the proprietors, they did not find places suitable for "the settling of such great townes as they Intended." New England townships required sufficient land not only for home lots but also for upland and meadows that could be divided among settlers for growing crops and grazing livestock. Essentially, they concluded that townships in the New England manner could not be developed, only small "townes of 20 or 30 families" or perhaps "plan[ta]tions in the manner of Virginia and Meriland"—larger tracts allocated through a headright system or granted as estates and farmed in this period mostly by indentured servants from England or enslaved persons—rather than larger townships of eighty to one hundred households gathered in a tightknit community. New Englanders did not view the Virginia and Maryland model with favor; only one town of any size had been formed in each colony (Jamestown in Virginia and St. Mary's City in Maryland), and local government took place at the county level. As a result, they abandoned their plans for the Delaware.[10]

As they sailed away from the Delaware, the settler group likely reviewed their reasons for leaving their homes and settling in a new land. Undoubtedly, they felt the strong pull of securing new land for themselves and their children. Like other New Englanders, they had emigrated from England in family groups. Gender balance between males and females was close to parity, unlike the sharp disparity between the sexes in the Chesapeake, with the result that in due course new households were formed and large families started. By the mid-1660s, sons needed land of their own so they could support new households. To keep New England, in historian Alan Taylor's description, "the healthiest, the most populous, and the most egalitarian in the distribution of property" among all the English colonial regions, it was essential to have continuing access to land. However, good land within easy reach of home lots had become scarce in Milford and other nearby towns. In addition, New Haven had proved a disappointment, as one contemporary observed, with "the land very barren, the Merchants either dead or come away, the rest gotten to their Farmes, The Towne is not so glorious as once it was." Starting over again in a new location was a tempting proposition.[11]

In addition to the pull of new land, there was the push of their intense disappointment about New Haven Colony being subsumed within Connecticut's patent. Fierce disputes broke out between Connecticut and New Haven Colony residents about political and theological matters, leading to suspicion and alienation even among longtime friends. Nearly eighteen months lapsed between the time John Winthrop Jr. returned from London, bringing the royal charter for Connecticut with enlarged boundaries that encompassed New Haven Colony, and the time when New Haven, Milford, Branford, and Guilford finally submitted to the government of Connecticut. Connecticut's general assembly rubbed salt in fresh wounds by laying a disproportionate tax on the four towns, which they strongly resisted. As Jasper Crane protested to Governor Winthrop, "Men will doe there most to vindicate and to recover the takeing away there estates without law . . . if it be forceably caryed in this disproporsinate way, of Rateing."[12]

Fundamental theological disagreements compounded their alienation. While Congregational churches—separately gathered congregations of visible saints governed by lay leaders with advice from well-educated clergy—were the rule in both New Haven Colony and Connecticut, New Haven Colony had restricted the vote and therefore the right to participate in town government to church members, while Connecticut did not. Also, New Haven Colony churches restricted the sacrament of baptism to church members and their infant children. In contrast, the minister of the Hartford church favored the so-called Halfway Covenant that allowed for baptism of children whose grandparents had been church members but whose parents had not experienced saving grace and thus had not been accepted as church members. Employing the rolling cadences that must have characterized his preaching, Abraham Pierson wrote to Governor Winthrop that it grieved him that leaders of the Hartford church should be so "easiyly turned aside from the good old way [of baptizing only children of church members] that was discovered by persons of so much honor, and respect, of so much learning and acquaintance in the word of God; who with much labour, study and piety with so many prayers and fastings layd the foundation of ther church-fellowship, yea, and with order in the church." He emphasized that the founders of the Hartford church decades earlier had solemnly pledged to maintain church order "when they entered into a civil Society, and government;" the new leaders were now breaking that promise.[13] John Davenport, New Haven's minister, also wrote to Winthrop. He worried that townships would shift from the Congregational way of selectively admitting church members and be instead "brought into a parish-way" of including all who lived in a particular location in church membership, as practiced by the Anglicans in England and Presbyterians in Scotland, undermining the foundation of godly government. Davenport added that "most of the churches, in this jurisdiction, are professedly against this new way, both in judgement and practice, upon Gospel grounds, viz. New Haven, Milford, Stratford, Branford, Gillford, Norwalke, [and] Stamford."[14]

New Haven Colony had been united in exploring options for settling on the Delaware, but after the collapse of that plan, they split into two groups, what Carteret called the New Haven men and the Milford men. Several of the New Haven men apparently lost enthusiasm for creating a new township. The original idea was that the entire town would move, but that fell apart, as Governor Carteret explained in his letter to the proprietors in August 1666, "They not agreeing with their Church Conserning their removing," perhaps due to the serious illness in this period of John Davenport, the minister of New Haven's church.[15] However, Carteret reported that a number of New Haven men on their own account still "resolved to Come and settle about these parts." To that end, he offered "to purchase a neck of Land" on the east side of the Passaic River, later called Barbadoes Neck, but lamented to the proprietors that he lacked the resources to clear the Indigenous title to the land:

"There is nothing Wanting butt Comodities for the satisfying of the Indians without Which there is nothing to be donn."[16]

The Milford men were more determined. Having considered their options, they recalled the land for which they had negotiated extensively with Governor Stuyvesant a few years earlier. They likely sailed directly to Elizabethtown to report to Carteret about their assessment of the Delaware River lands and to discuss alternative sites for a new township. In this fresh negotiation, they were no doubt guided by insights gained in the extensive prior exchanges with Stuyvesant and the Dutch authorities. They likely also consulted with several men from New Haven Colony who had settled in Elizabethtown about their experience and prospects for the area.[17] In addition, they had the advantage of recent experience with Carteret and knew that he was keen to attract large groups of settlers.[18] By holding firm to their demands, the Milford men secured key concessions in the terms under which they would acquire a large tract of land with plans to "settle a towne of 80 or 100 families"—what became Newark. They insisted on articles documenting the conditions allowing them to organize their new township in the New England way, including provisions related to town courts, the election of magistrates, and common lands. Indeed, once they acquired the land, they confidently took steps entirely consistent with implementing godly government within the township. In the coming years, when Carteret challenged or ignored their tenets of godly government, they returned to these articles to buttress their case.[19]

Shortly after this negotiation, Carteret explained to the proprietors that it had been "impossible" for him "to Reserve the 1/7 or any part" of the land for them as required in their concessions, because the settlers insisted on living "so Close together" as they had in their New England towns. He argued that in the long run the arrangement would be "more advantageous" for the proprietors, not only because there were other parcels of land nearby that were just as good, but also because the most important objective in their current situation was "to Strenghten our selves and keep possession and Nott to be beaten off by the Indians as formerly the dutch have bene." Carteret was also quick to assure the proprietors that each settler would pay a quitrent "for somuch land as they doe pattent."[20]

Newark was taking shape. The next step was to acquire legal title to the land.

CHAPTER 2

True Owners of the Land

In late May 1666, a band of Hackensack Natives confronted a group of settlers unloading goods from their vessels to the banks of the Passaic River in present-day Newark. Robert Treat, the leader of the settlers, recalled later that the Hackensack "seem'd troubled and angry that we landed [any] of our Goods there." Insisting the land belonged to them and had not been sold, the Hackensack persuaded the settlers to "put [their] Goods on board the Vessels again" and sail back down the Passaic.[1]

The Hackensack were a woodlands tribe within the Munsee Lenape nation, living in small bands in the eastern half of northern New Jersey. At the time of the European settlement of North America, the homelands of Munsee-speaking Natives covered a vast area that included today's western Long Island, Manhattan, Staten Island, northern New Jersey across to the Delaware River, and up the Hudson River as far north as today's Kingston, where the Esopus tribe was centered (see Figure 1). Munsee sovereignty over this area was largely recognized by other Indigenous groups. What the Munsee lacked in technological skills compared to Europeans, skills like metalsmithing, they more than made up for in their knowledge of their natural environment and ability to live off the land by fishing, hunting, gathering, and cultivating crops like corn, beans, and squash.[2]

Anthropologist Robert Grumet estimated there were about fifteen thousand Munsee-speaking Natives spread thinly through their lands when Henry Hudson and his crew sailed up the river now named for him in 1609. For the next few decades, Munsee outnumbered the European colonists, but disease, war, and the growing settler population took an awful toll. Munsee still outnumbered European colonists through the 1650s, keeping them penned in small settlements, including at the southern tip of Manhattan and along the west side of the Hudson River. During the Peach War in 1655, hundreds of Munsee warriors came down the Hudson in canoes to defend their homeland; they burned settlements at Pavonia and Staten Island, killed several colonists, and took several dozen others captive.[3] Hostilities soon ended, however, and Hackensack and other Munsee tribes renewed a peace

Figure 1. The territory of Munsee-speaking peoples, including the Hackensack, ranged from today's western Long Island, Manhattan, Staten Island, northern New Jersey across the Delaware River, and up the Hudson River valley.
Map of Lenape languages and tribes, created by Nikater—File: Delaware01.png, CC BY-SA 3.0, Wikimedia Commons, https://commons.wikimedia.org/w/index.php?curid=27384249

treaty with the Dutch in 1660. Another smallpox epidemic followed. By the time the English captured New Amsterdam from the Dutch in 1664 and renamed it New York, the Munsee population had declined to about three thousand, and they had "already lost political control over the region."[4] When the Newark settlers sailed up the Passaic in 1666, it was probably near the crossover point in population, and perhaps at the inflection point in terms of the Munsee shaping their own long-term destiny (see Figure 2). Twenty years later, settlers outnumbered the Munsee by as

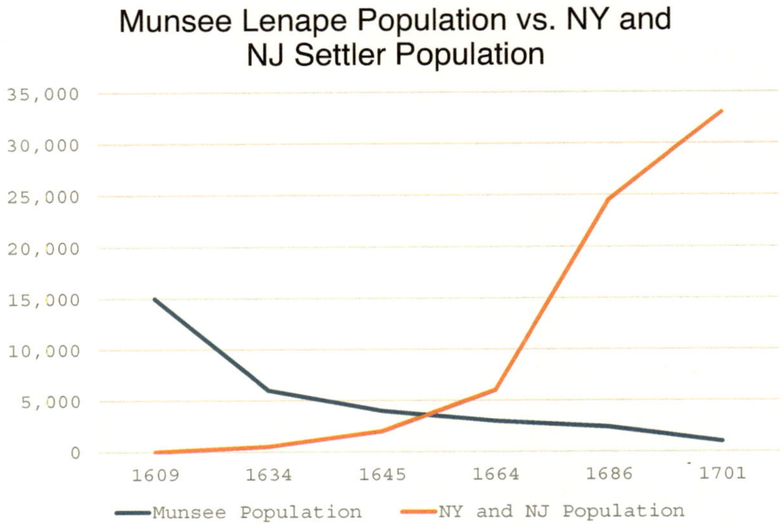

Figure 2. The population of Munsee Lenape collapsed by about two-thirds in the first twenty-five years after encountering European settlers as exposure to new diseases took an awful toll, and then continued to decline through the rest of the seventeenth century. The number of European settlers in New York and New Jersey increased sharply after the English captured New Netherland from the Dutch in 1664.
Source: R.S. Grumet, *The Munsee Indians* (2009), https://www.census.gov/history/pdf/colonialbostonpops.pdf

much as ten to one. At the turn of the eighteenth century, Munsee numbered only about one thousand, a decline of about 95 percent in less than a century.[5]

By 1666, Munsee had gained experience dealing with the Dutch and English about the use and sale of lands, although transactions were likely subject to misunderstandings common in negotiations between one party steeped in oral culture and the other party accustomed to written contracts. Like other Native tribes, the Munsee had a different concept of property than the Europeans. They held land in common, sometimes letting other groups camp, plant, fish, and hunt so long as their local customs and concerns were respected.[6] That practice of sharing the use of the land while retaining sovereignty no doubt informed the first Hackensack land sales in 1630 of Staten Island and part of today's Jersey City.[7] However, by the 1660s, they had likely gained a better understanding of how Europeans viewed land sales as final.

Historian Paul Otto argued that the Munsee took a strategic approach to land dispossession and resisted "wholesale alienation of their lands." He also maintained that they did not "quickly or naively" sell their lands. Communal ownership of the land required communal decision-making about its possible sale. This consultative approach to making decisions was at work in July 1663, when Oratam, the most senior and most experienced Hackensack sachem, stalled governor Peter Stuyvesant's request to purchase land for settlers from New Haven Colony. Through an interpreter, Oratam told Stuyvesant that he had not been able to speak with the young men of his tribe because they were out hunting, and the old men did not want to sell, preferring to keep a portion for planting and not wanting to "go further inland for fear of being robbed by their enemies." However, he left the door open for the future, saying that there was land enough for both the colonists and Hackensack.[8]

Three years later, Robert Treat and the first Newark settlers pushed on that open door. The confrontation on the banks of the Passaic surprised them, because they had no doubt asked Governor Carteret for assurances that he had "cleared the Plantation from all Claims and Incumbrances" of the Hackensack and therefore could give "quiet Possession" of the land. In their negotiation with Stuyvesant three years earlier, the settlers acknowledged that Natives had both a "natural and civill right" to the land and insisted on a deed of sale subscribed not just by the Dutch and English but also by the "hands of those Indians" who "soe owned" it. From the settlers' perspective, the sale negotiation was an essential step in removing Natives from their lands so the settlers could then replace them and impose their own laws and cultural practices. Under the European Doctrine of Discovery, in New Jersey and elsewhere, Natives retained title to their land with a continuing right to occupy and use their lands that could last in perpetuity if they did not consent to sell the land, but they could only sell their land to parties approved by the government that claimed "discovery." For New Jersey in 1666, that was governor Philip Carteret. That is why the first settlers had expected Carteret to have cleared the tract from "all Claims and Incumbrances," or at least given them permission to negotiate with the Hackensack for the land.[9]

The Newark settlers were no doubt frustrated with this turn of events. They had already been to the Delaware River to scout a possible site for settlement and had not found one. Now Carteret had failed to clear title to the Newark tract, leading to the confrontation with the Hackensack on the banks of the Passaic. But rather than give up and return to their homes in Connecticut, they decided, with Carteret's encouragement, to meet with the Hackensack and determine if they could negotiate the purchase of the Newark tract. Carteret provided Treat with a letter of introduction to Oratam and gave instructions to two Dutch interpreters, Captain Post and Captain Cornelius, to facilitate the meeting.[10] In the event, Treat and several settlers went instead with "John Capteen . . . a good Indian interpreter" to meet with Oratam and other sachems at their village up the Hackensack River. During the meeting, a Hackensack named Perro laid primary claim for his clan to the land west of the Passaic River but apparently agreed to negotiate its sale. Treat, who had gained a reputation for his skill in negotiating with Natives from his frequent contact with the Quinnipiac in New Haven Colony, secured permission from Oratam to hold a second meeting with a group of sachems, this time on land in present-day Newark, to complete the sale and mark out the boundaries. Oratam did not take part in the second meeting because he was too ill to travel. As Treat later recalled, "Soon after they came, viz Perro, and his kindred, with the Sagamores [i.e., sachems] that were able to travel; Oraton being very old, but approved of Perro's acting."[11]

At this second gathering, Perro confirmed that the land had not been sold, and Hackensack leaders agreed with Newark settlers on the boundaries and terms for the land sale. Samuel Edsall, an Englishman experienced with land acquisitions involving the Hackensack, facilitated the negotiation. The process of trust-building likely took a few days and may have required generous amounts of food and strong spirits to reach an initial agreement. For example, a decade later when Carteret negotiated with Navesink for the purchase of a tract on the Raritan River, he incurred substantial expenses for food and drink at four different negotiation sessions. Once an agreement for the Newark tract was reached, Hackensack and settler representatives jointly set the boundaries; eighty years later, a relative recalled that Samuel Harrison was among those "sent by the People of Newark to go with the Indians to mark out [the] Purchase."[12]

As was the custom, after "enlarging and perfecting" terms, the deed of sale was confirmed and signed a year later by ten sachems and five similarly senior leaders from among the settlers. The most senior sachem was Wapamuk, whom Grumet identifies as Taptawappamund, a Navesink leader; several of the other sachems may also have represented other bands, including Minisink and Raritan, but the deed calls them "Indians belonging now to Hakinsack." Pierwim, "the Sachum of Pau," whom Grumet identifies as Perro and as Oratam's designated successor, was one of the witnesses to the deed, along with Samuel Edsall, who presumably interpreted the terms for the Hackensack and three others.[13] Obadiah Bruen, formerly of New London, signed "in behalf of the Inhabitants now being or to be the possessors of the Tract of Land;" Micah Tomkins (signing as "Michael"), John Browne, and Robert Denison, all from Milford, and Samuel Kitchell of Guilford also signed. Elsewhere in the deed, the five men are called "townsmen and Agents for the English Inhabitants of Pesayak." They likely provided much of the capital for acquiring the land, with the stipulation that they would be reimbursed by other settlers through a town tax.[14]

The written deed of sale was, of course, for the use of the settlers. The Hackensack would have transmitted the agreement orally among their people; if they created a wampum belt to record the transaction, it has not survived. In the deed of sale, the settlers were careful to refer to the Hackensack as the true owners of the land, or as they put it, "the true proprietors," and in another place, "the known acknowledged proprietors" of the land. By emphasizing that the Hackensack had original title to the land, the Newark settlers assured themselves that the Hackensack also had standing to transfer a clear title to the land. Thus, while the land deed notes that the sale took place with "the consent and advice" of Governor Carteret, the Newark settlers believed their title to the land resulted from their purchase, not from Carteret's assignment on behalf of the proprietors of New Jersey. They did not involve Carteret in the negotiations for the purchase or ask him to witness the deed of sale, as was later the custom. Indeed, they waited ten years before entering the deed in the official records kept by Carteret's government.[15]

The Newark tract encompassed the area from Weequahic Creek or Bound Creek on the south to Watchung or First Mountain on the west, Yanticaw Brook or Third River on the north, and the Passaic River on the east. Today, those lands include Newark, Irvington, some of the Oranges and Maplewood, Montclair, Glen Ridge, Bloomfield, Belleville, and Nutley (see Figure 3). Under the terms of the deed, Newark settlers secured use of the land and its timber and mineral resources, hunting and fishing rights, and free range for their cattle, horses, and hogs, even if they strayed beyond the boundaries of the tract. In a striking provision, apparently added almost as an afterthought as the last sentence of the deed of sale, settlers claimed "free liberty to take what timber and stones they please" in any areas where the Hackensack retained ownership of the lands, even those not included in the sale. All members of the Hackensack tribe retained fishing rights in the Passaic River, and those who had been living on the tract before the sale retained hunting rights in the area. In addition, Hackensack sachems negotiated compensation consisting of a variety of goods, ammunition, and alcohol that they could then distribute among the different family groups and clans, as well as a large amount of wampum—the de facto currency for trade in that period. The goods included twenty axes, twenty coats, ten kettles, four blankets, ten pairs of breeches, twenty hoes, fifty knives, and three trooper coats. The ammunition and weapons consisted of ten guns, twenty pistols, ten swords, and fifty double hands (i.e., two cupped hands) of powder, as well as one hundred bars of lead that presumably could be made into bullets, while the alcohol consisted of "four barrels of beere [and] two Ankors [i.e., twenty gallons] of Licquers or something Equivolent." In addition, the Newark settlers paid 850 fathoms—that is, more than 5,000 feet or nearly a mile—of wampum. By the time the deed of sale was signed in July 1667, the Newark settlers had delivered almost all these items, with "only a small remainder" yet to be paid.[16]

It does not appear that the Hackensack were coerced into relinquishing their title to the Newark tract, although they likely negotiated from a trauma-informed position of weakness.[17] They had adapted to the challenges of colonization and showed increasing agency in their dealings with Stuyvesant and others. Oratam successfully deflected Stuyvesant's desire for a similar sale a few years earlier, and a decade later the Hackensack declined offers from Newark settlers to acquire additional land at the northern end of their township. Why the Hackensack proceeded with the sale of the Newark tract is not known. Perhaps they wanted good relations with the English following the displacement of the Dutch two years earlier.[18] Or, perhaps they recognized their declining numbers and power in the face of continuing European settlement and wanted to extract value while they could. What is clear is that the Newark settlers were motivated buyers. Governor Carteret, for one, thought the Newark settlers agreed to a price that was much too high. In his opinion, they paid more than four times the value of the land.[19]

The deed of sale explicitly refers to the Hackensack living on "the upper commons" when the settlers first arrived. This campsite was most likely on today's Harriet Tubman Square, until recently called Washington Park. The actual phrase in

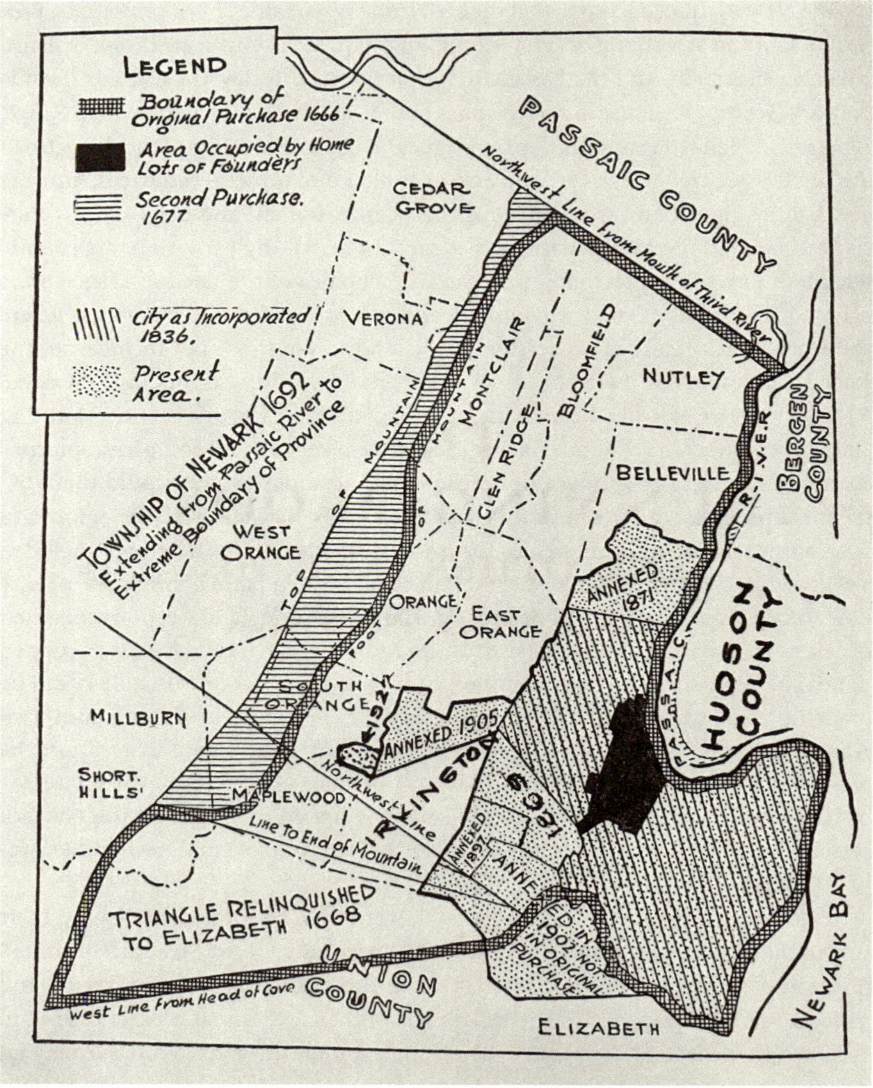

Figure 3. Historical map of Newark showing the boundary of the original Newark tract and subsequent changes to the City of Newark's borders. Drawn by Edward S. Rankin as the frontispiece to his *The Running Brooks*, 1930. Author's collection.

the deed is "liberty of hunting for the above said proprietors that were uppon the upper commons." The term "proprietors" was defined in the deed as the "Indians belonging now to Hakinsack, the known acknowledged proprietors" of the tract of land being sold. If the band of Hackensack, perhaps including Perro, were indeed camping on today's Tubman Square, just a couple hundred yards from the landing place of the Newark settlers, then there can be little surprise that they soon spotted and confronted settlers unloading their goods. That it had been a

Hackensack campsite may also be why the area was kept open as a town common when surveyors laid out the original homesites.[20]

Newark settlers tried several times over the next decade to make additional land deals with the Hackensack but succeeded on only one occasion. In August 1674, the Newark town meeting formed a committee "to treat with the Indians" about Acquackanonk, or "that Tract of Land as lieth above our Town, by the River," as the town records put it. However, the Newark committee failed to reach an agreement, and several years later the Sachem Captahem, who had joined other Native leaders in signing the deed of sale for the Newark tract in 1667, sold the Acquackanonk tract, comprising today's Passaic and Clifton, to a consortium of Dutch settlers instead. Frustrated, the Newark settlers claimed to have been "hindred and deprived," but it was probably their own unwillingness or lack of resources to meet the demands of the Hackensack that prevented the acquisition. Their failure had lasting repercussions, not only for the size of Newark but for the eventual boundary between today's Essex and Passaic counties. It also demonstrated the leverage the Hackensack had in land negotiations: They were not forced to sell the land if the buyers did not meet their needs or demands.[21]

However, in 1678 Newarkers successfully acquired a strip of land on the western border of the township. At their town meeting on March 1, after "much Debate," they voted to negotiate with the Hackensack for seven square miles of land from the foot to the top of First Mountain that had not been included in the original purchase. This time the negotiations moved quickly, and for the consideration of just two guns, three coats, and thirteen cans of rum, Winocksop and Shenocktos, "Indians and owners of the said Great Mountaine," agreed on March 13 to the deed of sale with John Ward and Thomas Johnson, justices of the peace for Newark, in the presence of Governor Carteret. A short time later, John Curtis and John Treat met with members of the Hackensack tribe to run the west line of the purchase; Edward Ball and Daniel Dod did the same thing with Hackensack for the north line, and the two groups met on First Mountain to complete marking the new tract.[22]

Once Newarkers secured title to land, they asserted their property rights and enforced their own rules and customs on the Hackensack regarding livestock, trading goods, and the sale of alcohol.[23] In an act of erasure, Newark settlers quickly assigned their own names to geographic and natural features of the land, and for the most part Munsee terms were lost. Newarkers retained the name Passaic for the river on their eastern boundary, most likely because their purchase did not encompass the full length of the river, let alone its eastern bank. That is more than settlers in Elizabethtown did, since they renamed the river flowing past their settlement the Mill River (later, Elizabeth River). The original Munsee name Watsessing, for a section in today's Bloomfield and East Orange has continued in use throughout the centuries.[24] However, Weequahic was renamed Bound Creek, since it formed much of the boundary with Elizabethtown; Watchung became First Mountain, and Yanticaw became Third River.

Hackensack continued to live on the Newark tract for at least the next couple of decades after the Newark settlers arrived, although their presence declined rapidly toward the end of the seventeenth century. They retained plots of land for planting, as well as the right to hunt and fish away from settler home lots and farms. They had a campsite well away from the Newark town lots, known to settlers as Perro's campsite, located where today's Monte Irvin Park is in Orange.[25] At the time Newark was settled, the Hackensack may have been most numerous in the Weequahic area near the boundary with Elizabethtown. The first settlers of Elizabethtown, fearing for their safety so long as they were outnumbered by Indigenous people, urged the first settlers of Newark to establish their farms nearby. Into the 1680s, encounters between the Hackensack and settlers were frequent enough, likely due to regular trade in goods, that Newarkers learned enough of the Munsee language to converse and make deals.[26]

Settler Control and Fear of Natives

During the proprietary period, the general assembly passed various laws regulating settler interactions with Indigenous people. Representatives of Newark took part in all the discussions and debates. In November 1668, the general assembly named Robert Treat to a five-person committee, including Governor Carteret, to develop methods for handling potential disputes that might stem from settler livestock straying onto Native lands. To protect settler property and perhaps to discourage theft, the general assembly also passed a law prohibiting settlers from buying any hogs, cattle, or horses, alive or dead, from Indians.[27] In October 1675, a time of heightened tensions, Carteret issued an order prohibiting "the Carying of goods & merchandize to the Indian plantations to trade with them," due to his stated concern that insults and abuse by Native groups might "cause a disturbance & breach of the public peace." He made it clear, however, that it remained "lawfull for any person or persons to trade with the Indians they bringing theire Corne or Goods to any man's house or plantations of Christian Inhabitants."[28]

Throughout New Jersey, relations between Indigenous people and settlers were tinged with suspicion and occasionally morphed into fear, at least among settlers. That settlers and Natives did not engage in raids or skirmishes after the creation of New Jersey is probably due more to restraint by Natives than reluctance by settlers. Newark men underwent regular militia training from the beginning of the township. On at least eight occasions in the first fifteen years after Newark was settled, Newarkers prepared to defend their town from possible attack. Samuel Swaine, captain of the Newark militia, likely felt a visceral need for preparation since his two sisters had been captured and one of them killed by Pequots in 1637, when his family lived in Wethersfield.[29] In 1668, a Newark inhabitant informed a former neighbor in Connecticut that "an Indyan servant to an Englishman that kept the towne Cowes att Elesabeth towne was latly killd in the woods and Fownd with his head Chopt of," raising settler "feers of the Indians plotting mischeefe against the English plantations about Carterets govrment." This incident may also suggest tension between Natives who worked for settlers and those who wanted to remain separate.[30] Five years later, after a series of thefts, the Newark town meeting voted, if requested, to join other towns in sending "men to the Indians to demand the Robbers" and scheduled another day of training "in consideration," as they put it, "of the present Danger, and fear of what may ensue."[31]

In 1675, as reports of King Philip's War in New England reached New Jersey, settler fear of Natives reached new levels. In July, having "received Information of an Insurrection made by the Indians . . . by burning houses and murdering several Christians," Governor Carteret commissioned militia companies in each of the towns, captained by members of his council. All men between the ages of sixteen and sixty were required to muster. Separately, Newarkers agreed at their town meeting in August 1675 to add "flanckers . . . at two Corners of the Meeting House with Palisades or Stockades." Carteret ordered the province into a "postyure of defense" in late October, after news reached New Jersey of the ambush of colonists at the Battle of Bloody Brook in Massachusetts, "not Knowing," he claimed, "how soone theire fury and rage may Extend against us." Militia officers were ordered to prepare fortifications and make "provision for the defense and safety of the Inhabitants." In December, the general assembly outlawed the sale of guns or ammunition to Natives and prohibited blacksmiths and locksmiths from repairing any guns already owned by Natives. After receiving news of the Great Swamp Fight in Rhode Island in December 1675, when New England forces, including Mohegan, Pequot, and Connecticut soldiers under Robert Treat's command, attacked the massive winter fortification of the Narragansett and Wampanoag and killed several hundred Natives, including women and children, Newarkers voted to "consider about and contrive for the Fortifications belonging to our Town." Two years later, when the assembly repealed the prohibition on selling guns or ammunition to Natives, Thomas Johnson of Newark and Henry Lyon of Elizabethtown were among the five members of the assembly who wanted the prohibition kept in place.[32]

Tensions subsided, but three years later, in April 1679, the town again felt threatened. The town meeting voted, "upon the News concerning the Indians rising," to ask Carteret to convene the general assembly "to consider what may be meet to secure ourselves, in Case of such Danger." Three months later, the town strengthened procedures for the night watch. Feeling especially vulnerable on the Sabbath when all were at church, they "agreed that one fourth Part of the Town at a time, and so taking their Turns, shall carry Arms to Meeting on the Lord's Days—and two to Ward, and one to stand Centry." In 1681, they perceived a new threat and again ordered "every Soldier [to] bring his Arms every Day of Public Worship, well fixed, and also Am'unition." Again, the danger subsided without conflict. By 1684, deputy governor Gawen Lawrie could write, perhaps hopefully, to the Scottish proprietors of East Jersey that "there are but few Indian Natives in the Countrey. Their strength is inconsiderable, they live in the Woods, and have small towns in some places far up in the Countrey."[33]

Abraham Pierson and Natives

While he lived in the New Haven Colony, Abraham Pierson Sr., the first minister of Newark's church, had been active in efforts to convert Native groups to Christianity. He learned the Eastern Algonquian dialect spoken by Quiripi and served as an interpreter in mediating a dispute when settlers in the colony failed to maintain a fence around an Indian planting ground.[34] To supplement his work as minister of the Branford church, Pierson undertook missionary work among Native Americans on behalf of the London-based Society for the Propagation of the Gospel in New England, in the same period when the Mayhews were active on Martha's Vineyard, and John Eliot was working in Massachusetts. Pierson made hundred-mile circuits of "Indian Towns" as often as eight times a month, reaching as far as Wethersfield, preaching to Native Americans in their language. He had little success, and he found them "very slow, and sleight=spirited." However, he thought some of them were "convinced of the errour of their way," noting that a local sachem attended sabbath services, "and another Indian is industrious in reading & is desirous that his Children may attain it."[35] As one of the few ministers who gained even a partial mastery of an Eastern Algonquian language, Pierson gained notice. In 1658, Thomas Mayhew wanted him to move to Martha's Vineyard to assist his efforts to engage Native Americans there, and in 1662 commissioners of the United Colonies "seriously and solemnly" urged him to move to Southertown, at the border of Connecticut and Rhode Island, and take on "the worke of preaching the gospel to the Pequotts"; Pierson declined and remained in Branford until his move to Newark in 1667.[36]

Like other New Englanders, Pierson considered English civilization and Christianity superior and viewed Natives as "other" and inferior. Pierson prepared *Some Helps for the Indians*, a catechism interlineated in English and Quiripi, printed in 1658.[37] He translated the Lord's Prayer, explained the Ten Commandments, and propounded a dense version of Calvinist theology. His experience with the Quinnipiac is evident in the catechism:

> Ob[servation]. If the Indians receive Gods Word will it not take away the honour and riches of the Sachems, and Liberty of the Indians?
>
> An[swer]. No in noe wise, yea this would quickly increase the honour and Riches of the Sachems . . . By humilitie and the feare of God are Riches honour, and life, and this will inlarge the liberty of the Indians by freeing them from the bondage of Sin and Sathan.
>
> Qu[estion]. What is the eight Commandement?
>
> An[swer]. Thou shalt not steal.
>
> Qu[estion]. What is the stealth here forbidden?
>
> An[swer]. To take away another man's goods without his knowledge, without his gift, to spend our own goods without profit to our selves, or others gaine. As Bad Indians do spend their estates when they want whores and play at strawes.[38]

Despite his experience, Pierson did not continue his missionary work among the Hackensack after moving to Newark, perhaps due to bouts with kidney stones that made travel difficult. He also lost the incentive of extra income, because the Society for the Propagation of the Gospel in New England stopped subsidizing his work once he moved to Newark. However, Newarkers long retained an interest in converting Native Americans to Christianity. Samuel Treat, Robert Treat's son, was noted for preaching to some five hundred Nauset Indians on Cape Cod in their own language in the 1680s and 1690s. David Brainerd, missionary to Native Americans, was ordained in Newark's church in 1744. His brother John Brainerd, who carried on his work among the Lenape in New Jersey for years, filled Newark's pulpit after Aaron Burr Sr. moved to Princeton in 1756 with the College of New Jersey. And at the end of the eighteenth century, Alexander MacWhorter, long-time minister of Newark's First Presbyterian Church, preached at the organizational meeting when the New York Missionary Society was formed with "the great object . . . to send the gospel to the Indian tribes."[39]

Surviving documentary records for Newark from the colonial period were, of course, created by settlers or English and Dutch governments, and not by the Hackensack, so an understanding of Natives is refracted through settler perspectives and actions.[40] There are also significant gaps in the records. If early court records survived, it might be possible to learn how settlers and Hackensack understood and worked through incidents that caused friction. A mechanism was set up for handling disputes, but it is not known how it worked in practice. If Governor Carteret's minute book for the first years in New Jersey or more of his correspondence with the proprietors survived, it might be possible to know as much about his meetings with Indigenous tribes as is known about similar meetings during the earlier Dutch period. However, it is evident that Carteret was frustrated that he did not have a larger supply of goods that he could "present to the Indian Kings or Sachems," as he put it, which slowed his efforts to establish contact. In 1666, Carteret pleaded with the proprietors to send him a supply of gunpowder, ammunition, and trade goods, noting the Natives "are much afected and drawne on by trade."[41] In some cases, archival silences may convey important insights. There is no record of captured settler women or children in Newark, as happened in New England, or any record of either settler-on-native assault or native-on-settler assault for Newark in this period. Despite frequent suspicions among the settlers, particularly during King Philip's War in New England, there is no record of skirmishes between natives and settlers in Newark, underscoring the peaceful reputation of the Hackensack.

There were continuing interactions between the two groups after the initial land transfer, primarily for trade. Sometimes settlers would go to Hackensack or Raritan encampments to engage in trade, perhaps out to Perro's campsite or other places where the Hackensack had their planting grounds, and sometimes Natives would come to the settlers. Interactions were extensive enough that settlers learned at least pidgin versions of the Munsee language. Ebenezer Lindsley, who came to Newark as a two-year-old, claimed later that "he pretty well understood the Indian Language," while Jonathan Tichenor recalled in 1742 that he "was capable in his younger

Years to understand and talk the Indian Language."[42] However, settlers and Hackensack lived mostly separate existences; settlers quickly built a fence around their new town, both for defense and to control their livestock. Natives apparently mostly stayed away from the town; Joseph Harrison recalled decades later the time he saw "a Number of Indians pass thro' Newark" on their way to Elizabethtown and then return through the town again two or three days later—perhaps a delegation of Hackensack on their way to meet with Governor Carteret, coming down the Assunpink Trail or Hackensack Trail that crossed the Passaic River in Newark. If that had happened frequently, it would not have seemed remarkable to him.[43]

Nonetheless, Newarkers and Natives apparently stayed on good terms. In 1694, the Native leader Mengootecum, with consent from twelve other Natives, deeded the Whippany tract, a crescent-shaped tract bordering the Pequannock River on one end and the Whippany River on the other, along with permission to establish a highway running from Newark to the tract, to Daniel Dod and Samuel Harrison of Newark, "for the love, goodwill and affection . . . toward my very loving friends." Using similar language, another group of Natives transferred by deed of gift a smaller tract of upland and meadow on the north side of Canoe Brook and the east side of the south branch of the Passaic River (part of today's Livingston) to Theophilus Pierson in August 1700. In a third and remarkable deed of gift, the Sachem Taphow, "commander in Chief of all those Indians Inhabiting the North part of what the English Call the Jerseys," conveyed a tract of land in 1701 on the west side of the south branch of the Passaic River to a group of eleven men, all but two of whom were Newarkers. In the deed, Taphow noted the men had "in times of Greatest Necesity been our Benefactors," even as he complained about how representatives of the proprietors surveyed land and "after the English way take patents for it without asking our Consent, much less Compacting with us for it." In making this gift of land, Taphow and the eighteen other Native leaders who acknowledged the deed intended to gain favor with William III, "the Great King of England under the Shadow of whose wings we not only Expect to be preserved in the possession of our Just Rights in time of peace, but also protected in times of war against the Invasions of those who become Enemies to us."[44]

By the end of the seventeenth century, as demonstrated by these deeds, the Hackensack had been pushed toward the western end of Essex County. By 1740, most of those who had remained left to join the Six Nations in upstate New York. When rumors spread in 1745 that a hundred Natives would come to the aid of Newarkers following a land riot, one man dismissed the stories, saying "the whole Province of New Jersey had then scarcely half that Number of Indian men . . . residing in it, and not one of them within thirty miles of Newark." By tradition, the last Native to leave was "Indian John" in 1761, but others likely stayed but were not visible to the growing settler population. It took nearly a century, but settler colonists had indeed removed and replaced the Hackensack and other Natives.[45]

CHAPTER 3

Godly Government

Following their negotiation with the Hackensack for the Newark tract, Robert Treat and the Milford group, joined by agents from other towns in the former New Haven Colony, quickly moved to establish the new township within a framework of godly self-government. Several steps were involved: forming a civil covenant, including fundamental agreements; accepting associates in the enterprise; in due course a church covenant; and after more than a year of discernment and work, election of town officers. Through this long and essential process, the settlers followed New England practice—particularly the pattern established in New Haven Colony—in forming their township.

The Newark settlers acted like they had a clean slate. The Hackensack did not figure in Newarkers' plans once they had been dispossessed of the land. The proprietors' concessions, intended to guide the settlement of New Jersey, did not shape any of the organizational steps taken by Newark settlers or receive any acknowledgment in the first entries in the Newark town records. Governor Carteret did not object to their plans to create a New England township when he waived the requirement for setting aside one-seventh of the Newark tract for the proprietors and agreed to articles related to courts, elections, and land distribution. During his first years as governor, Carteret focused on attracting settlers to New Jersey; indeed, he dispatched his secretary James Bollen to Milford in June 1666 to help with any issues at that end. He likely thought he could deal with potential conflicts between his authority and township government in the future, little knowing the resistance he would stir up when he did assert his authority.[1]

Civil Covenant

Samuel Swaine and Samuel Kitchell, as agents of their associates in Branford and Guilford, gathered with Robert Treat and other "friends from Milford" on May 21, 1666, to join in creating the new township. At that meeting, they mutually agreed to "make one township," accepted "fundamentals" to guide their life together, and pledged "to be of one heart and consent, through Gods blessing" to carry on "spiritual concernments as also civil and town affairs according to God and a Godly government." In forming this civil covenant, as solemn as the church covenant they would later affirm, their emphasis was on unity within a closed community, acting, as they put it, "of one heart" and "with one hand" in forming "one township." In the phrases that punctuate the written record of the meeting, they also made clear their intent to reach decisions and take actions through consensus: "mutually agreed upon," "mutually chose," and "mutually covenant" to their "mutual benefit."

After covenanting to form the new township, the group selected an ad hoc committee of eleven men "to order and settle" issues that would inevitably crop up in establishing the settlement. The committee immediately set to work. They decided to hold the town open to new associates until the end of June 1667, so long as they brought "due testimonials" to the committee and were approved as settlers. They also agreed that all associates, whether from Milford, Branford, Guilford, or otherwise accepted by the committee, would be allocated home lots and divisions of land on an "equally privileged" basis. Three days later, the civil covenant and related actions were put in a written document and signed by Robert Treat and Samuel Swaine on behalf of their colleagues. Treat later copied and recorded the document as the first item in the town records.[2]

A key stipulation was that prospective associates from Branford and Guilford should send word before the end of October if they agreed to the fundamentals and wished to join the new settlement. Three members of the ad hoc committee, Samuel Swaine, Thomas Blatchly, and Richard Harrison, returned to Branford in the fall to consult with their old neighbors. They reported that home lots had been surveyed and likely some trees cleared and gardens planted. No doubt they also consulted with Jasper Crane, magistrate of Branford, and Abraham Pierson, minister in Branford, about implementing godly government in the new settlement. Pierson likely took the lead in drafting two fundamental agreements, with scriptural references, to ensure there could be no confusion about the "intended design" for "our Town upon Passaick River."

Deadlines help to drive decisions, and so it was that on October 30, with one day to spare, twenty-three inhabitants of Branford and nearby towns met and subscribed to two fundamental agreements.[3] During the meeting they likely discussed each agreement at length and then voted before signing their names.[4] The key element of the first fundamental agreement was that only members of a Congregational church could be freemen of the town and have the right to vote, become a magistrate, or serve as an officer in the militia. Those who were not church members but still "admitted to Be planters" retained the right "to their proper Inheritance" and to "enjoy all other Civil Liberties and Privileges." The second agreement was short and direct: "We shall with Care and Diligence provide for the maintenance of the purity of Religion professed in the Congregational Churches." In good Puritan fashion, Pierson added four citations from the Hebrew Testament to justify godly government and the new township, presumably with his Geneva Bible at hand, including verse twenty-five from the first chapter of Deuteronomy about the twelve tribes of Israel who searched out the land that God had laid out for them: "[They] . . . brought us word again, and said, It is a good land, which the LORD our God doeth give us." By selecting this verse, the settlers affirmed their belief that God was calling them to the "good land" along the Passaic.[5]

Leaders of the Branford group sent a letter with the signed agreements to "the present Inhabitants" of the new township; those men reviewed the documents in November and "declared their consents and readiness" to sign their names, too. When the subscription period for new associates ended seven months later, an additional forty-one men added their signatures (or in four cases their marks) in Newark to "the two fundamental agreements" on June 24, 1667. With sixty-four men and their families, Newark was on its way.[6]

Godly Government

In the seventeenth century, nearly all Englishmen believed in godly rule or godly government. The debate was not whether but how God's will should be expressed in society: through the divine right of kings, the intercession of bishops and the clergy, or God's elect in separately gathered churches.[7] Newark's founders came down squarely on the side of God's elect in churches. With a millennial focus, their aim was to work toward "the Kingdom of Christ in the Congregationall way," as the Milford group explained to Peter Stuyvesant in 1661 when they first explored settling in what would become New Jersey.[8]

Godly government, in the sense Newark settlers understood it, was developed in Massachusetts Bay Colony by magistrates in consultation with Puritan ministers. John Davenport later recalled the "libertie," or blank slate, colonists had in the 1630s "to mould their civill order into that forme which they should finde to be best for themselves," given their distance from English authorities and the fact "that here the churches and commonwealth are complanted together in holy covenant and fellowship with God in Christ Jesus." In 1636, magistrates asked John Cotton to draw up a set of laws based on Old Testament precepts, which became known in time as "Moses his Judicials." While Cotton's compilation of laws was not officially adopted by Massachusetts, his work was highly influential in the development of Massachusetts and, especially, New Haven Colony, two places where the voting franchise was tied to church membership.[9] For example, in 1641, when Abraham Pierson was called as the first minister of Southampton on Long Island (within New Haven Colony), he brought a manuscript copy of Cotton's compilation with him, and it was "joyntly and unanimously Consented unto as Fundamental by the Inhabitants of this Collony of Southampton"; Pierson then copied the laws into the Southampton town records.[10]

Davenport endorsed Cotton's conclusion "that Theocracie, i.e., God's government, might be established as the best form of government wherein the people that choose civil rulers are God's people in covenant with him, that is members of churches."[11] He advocated strongly for godly government during the formation of

New Haven Colony in 1639. Then, in 1663, after the Restoration of Charles II and the failure of New Haven Colony to secure a charter, Davenport arranged for the publication of *A Discourse About Civil Government in a New Plantation Whose Design Is Religion*, a vigorous defense of godly government (see Figure 4). He wanted to reinforce arguments for godly government among inhabitants of New Haven Colony who were then considering a move to what would become New Jersey, or as the title page put it, as "published by some Undertakers of a New Plantation, for General Direction and Information."[12]

A Discourse About Civil Government provides crucial insight into the political views of Newark's founders and what they meant by "godly government." While the title page attributes authorship of the pamphlet to John Cotton, it is likely that John Davenport himself wrote it in the late 1630s to guide planning for the settlement of New Haven.[13] In the pamphlet, Davenport recommended the form of government he called theocracy, by which he meant a Christian commonwealth seeking the "glory of God" and implementing God's laws through complementary, but distinct civil and ecclesiastical polities without involvement by ministers in politics—thus, not the modern sense of theocracy in which religious leaders exercise political power. Indeed, he argued strongly against "devolving of Civil Power upon Pastors of Churches."[14] He made it clear that he intended his recommendation only for new plantations, or settlements, where the first settlers agreed upfront that they wanted to live and worship according to what they perceived as God's law—that is, communities with a premillennial focus like New Haven or Milford in 1639 and Newark in 1666. He did not expect theocracy to work where there was an already established civil order or in new settlements where the first settlers did not share a common goal of establishing a godly government.[15] Davenport asserted that church and state have separate and distinct roles, and that the two should not be confused. He defined churches as those "gathered amongst them according to Christ"—that is, Congregational churches. Public officials should not have power over spiritual matters, and church officers (ministers and deacons) should not be distracted by secular entanglements. However, church members would be better able to pass laws and regulations that followed biblical precepts than men who were not church members. Only male church members should be "free Burgesses" and have the vote, and only "free Burgesses" should serve as public officials.[16] But Davenport added an explicit caveat that those who were not church members should retain all rights in distribution and ownership of land, the administration of justice, and other civil matters. He warned that if they did not retain those rights, the church would swallow up the state, which he saw as disastrous for both parties.[17]

Newark's two fundamental agreements, as subscribed in October 1666 by twenty-three men in Branford and then in June 1667 by forty-one more men in Newark, were in full accord with the idea of godly government spelled out in *A Discourse About Civil Government*. Indeed, in preparing the first fundamental agreement, Abraham Pierson probably sought Davenport's advice. The two men were close—Davenport's son married Pierson's daughter, and Davenport likely persuaded Pierson to move to Newark since his health precluded him from

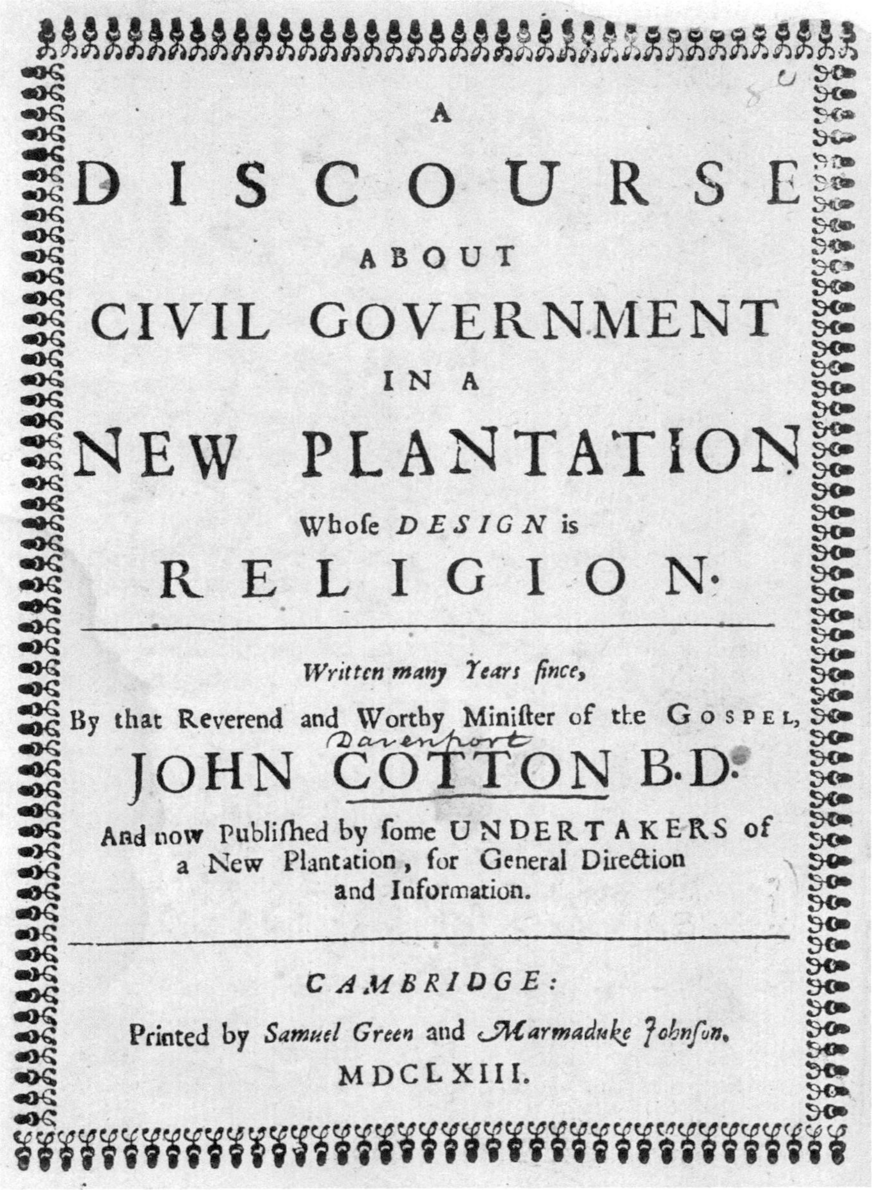
A

DISCOURSE

ABOUT

CIVIL GOVERNMENT

IN A

NEW PLANTATION

Whose *DESIGN* is

RELIGION.

Written many Years since,

By that Reverend and Worthy Minister of the GOSPEL,

Davenport

JOHN COTTON B.D.

And now Publifhed by fome UNDERTAKERS of a New Plantation, for General Direction and Information.

CAMBRIDGE:

Printed by *Samuel Green* and *Marmaduke Johnfon.*

MDCLXIII.

Figure 4. Title page of *A Discourse About Civil Government in a New Plantation Whose Design Is Religion*, 1663. Collection of the Massachusetts Historical Society.

undertaking the rigors of a new settlement. Newark's first fundamental agreement provides a succinct and clear summary of Davenport's arguments:

> That none shall be admitted freemen or free Burgesses within our Town upon Passaick River in the Province of New Jersey, but such planters as are members

> of some or other of the Congregational Churches nor shall any but such be chosen to Magistracy or to Carry on any part of Civil Judicature, or as deputies or assistants, to have power to Vote In establishing Laws, and making or Repealing them or to any Chief Military Trust or Office. Nor shall any But such Church Members have any Vote in such elections; Tho' all others admitted to Be Planters have right to their proper Inheritance, and do and shall enjoy all other Civil Liberties and Privileges, According to all Laws, Orders, Grants, which are, or hereafter shall be made for this Town.[18]

Church Covenant

The premise behind godly government was that church members were among God's elect and had been recognized as such by other church members; in this way, they were of "all men fittest, being sanctified and dedicated to God[,] to carry on all worldly and civil business to Gods ends." This could only be assured in Congregational churches, which Davenport elsewhere described as "particular visible Churches" in which "all and only such grown persons be admitted Members . . . [as] make such a publick profession of their Faith, as the Church may, in charitable discretion, conceive hath blessedness annexed to it."[19] For this reason, Newark's second fundamental agreement for "the maintenance of the purity of Religion professed in the Congregational Churches" was as essential as the first.[20]

With the civil covenant in place, the critical next step was a church covenant. The details about the development of a church covenant and the formation of Newark's church were lost when British forces ransacked the home of Rev. Alexander MacWhorter in late 1776. In his *Century Sermon* in 1801, MacWhorter attempted only a broad-brush account of the early years of the church, based largely on town records and "the relations of old people to me in former times," since he possessed "no documents or written materials."[21] Jonathan F. Stearns, who conducted wide research for his 1853 study, *First Church in Newark*, suggested Newark settlers may not have needed a church covenant since "the old Church in Branford, organized there twenty years earlier, was probably transported bodily, with all its corporate privileges and authorities."[22] His suggestion is highly unlikely to have been the case, even though such a large portion of the leaders of the Branford church left for Newark that the remaining residents in Branford felt the need to reconstitute their church with new lay leaders.[23]

Much more likely than the Branford church being transported "bodily" to Newark is that the new settlers followed the New England pattern and went through extensive consultation to discern individuals, perhaps seven in number, who might serve as pillars to covenant together and form a new church in Newark that could then admit other members and call a minister. Newark settlers formed a new community among men and women with similar world views but from different towns. They would have wanted to make sure they gathered a church of visible saints, "organized according to their own vision of religious perfection, a vision . . . very like their vision of social perfection," as historian Kenneth Lockridge described a similar process in Dedham, Massachusetts, in the 1630s. In general, New Englanders took church covenanting more seriously than civil covenanting because they were attempting to discern the grace of God. Historian Edmund Morgan described the process succinctly: "The new churches each rested on a covenant to which all members subscribed; each chose and ordained its own ministers; admitted properly qualified new members, and expelled incorrigible old ones."[24] This was certainly the pattern that had been followed in New Haven and Milford in 1639. After agreeing to a civil covenant, New Haven chose eleven men, including the Reverend John Davenport, to engage in the discernment necessary to be the "foundation stones" for forming a church. In Milford, "seven pillars," including Robert Treat's father-in-law, entered into a written church covenant that might later have served as the model for Newark's church covenant. It was not a creed or confession, but rather an expression of their sense of God's grace and the community's relationship with both God and Jesus Christ, "our only Prophet and Teacher, our only Priest and Propitiation, our only King and Lawgiver," and with each other, walking "in all brotherly love and holy watchfulness, to the mutual building up one another in Faythe and Love."[25]

If this process was followed in Newark, it likely took place in the seven months between the meeting on June 24, 1667, when the fundamental agreements were signed, and the first recorded town meeting on February 6, 1668. Discussions perhaps started during the summer, but Newarkers may have waited for Abraham Pierson to guide their discernment after he arrived at the end of September.[26] Lawrence Ward and Richard Lawrence of Branford and Micah Tompkins of Milford may have been among the pillars of the new church; Ward is noted as "deacon" in 1667 when the town created a seven-man committee to determine each inhabitant's share of the purchase price for the Newark tract. Following Ward's death, Tompkins was described as "Deacon Tompkins" for the first time in December 1670. Lawrence is noted in town records as a deacon (along with Micah Tompkins) starting in October 1674.[27] Milford's church had an elder as well as a deacon, but the office does not appear to have been filled in Newark, even though the town set aside an "elder's lot."[28]

It is likely that most of the first inhabitants of Newark were soon admitted as members of the Newark church, with the men gaining the right to vote and hold civil or military office. That had been the case in Milford, where it has been estimated that "by the end of 1644, [members of the Milford church] . . . composed 82 percent of the men receiving land . . . and 77 percent of inhabitants' wives. A full 95 percent of all families . . . had at least one spouse in communion; 63 percent had both."[29] Edward Rindler calculated a similar percentage of church members for Newark: "Fifty-seven of the sixty-nine (eighty-three percent) original settlers were elected to an office or appointed to at least one committee by 1677."[30]

Newark settlers placed a very high priority on calling a minister, because they viewed preaching as the primary means ordained by God for instructing God's people in scriptural truths. They also expected there would be times when they would need guidance on how to organize their lives together on a scriptural basis.

Newark was the only town in New Jersey (or, after 1674, East Jersey) to retain a settled minister throughout the proprietary period. Even before the first land division, it was unanimously agreed that all residents of Newark, as a "condition" of living in the town and regardless of whether they were members of the church, would be required to "pay or cause to be paid yearly in their full Proportions equally . . . for the upholding of the settled Ministry and preaching of the word in our Town." The town agreed to pay Abraham Pierson's "transport" expenses in moving to Newark. A year later, Pierson's compensation was spelled out in greater detail. The town agreed that their missed payments to Pierson be "laid out in Building his House at Moderate prises for their Labour." They also confirmed unanimously "that Mr. Parson shall have allowed Eighty Pounds by the Year, for his Carrying on the Work of the Ministry"—fully one-third of the tax they placed on themselves that year—paid in-kind in October and March "at price Current," including ("yearly") a pound of butter for every milk cow in the town. In addition, they "freely Consented by their Jointly Voteing" to cover the expense of digging his well and the rest of his transportation charges, and to relieve him of all town taxes except "the Lords Half Penny" (i.e., quitrent) and any charges "of Ways and Drainings in the Meadows."[31]

At the same town meeting where they confirmed Pierson's compensation, they voted to "build a Meeting House as soon as May be" and agreed both to provide their labor, "according to Proportions," and to tax themselves thirty pounds "for the Carrying on of the same." This emphasis on equity and proportionality, relative to the size of men's estates, extended to paying the "minister's Rate." The town gave young men just forming their own households time to build their resources: "The Men appointed to [calculate each person's share of the Town Rate] are to speak with the Young Men in our Town that are for Themselves, and to see what they will voluntarily pay to the Minister."[32] Six months later, the meetinghouse was nearly finished, and the town agreed "to provide Nails, for the closing of the Meeting House," but it took another nine months to add a wood floor "of Good ches[t] nut or Oak, of 2 inches and a Half Plank."[33] The meetinghouse was relatively small, only "26 Feet wide . . . and Thirty Six Feet Long, with 13 foot Between Joints."[34] All Newarkers would have crowded into the meetinghouse for two church services every Sunday, one in the morning and another in the afternoon. If they followed New England practice, men sat on the left and women on the right, with deacons seated beneath the pulpit, where Abraham Pierson preached and expounded on scripture. Newarkers would have returned on Wednesday evening for Pierson's weekly lecture. The meetinghouse was also used as the site for regular town meetings, which all adult men were required to attend.

Concerned about Pierson's health and observing the difficulty that Woodbridge and Elizabethtown had in attracting ministers, Newark settlers recruited Abraham Pierson Jr., who had graduated from Harvard in 1668, "to be helpful to his Father, in the exercising his Gifts in the Ministry for the space of a Year." They voted unanimously to pay him thirty pounds for the ensuing year. After a trial period, the town issued him a call in March 1672.[35] By taking this step, Newark became one of the few towns throughout New England to afford two ministers. In the 1680s, after the death of Abraham Pierson Sr., Newark remained the only town in New Jersey that consistently employed a minister who had no other occupation, such as practicing medicine or engaging in trade.[36]

A Third Fundamental Agreement

At perhaps the same gathering when the two fundamental agreements were signed in June 1667, settlers also approved "by a full Vote of the Town assembled" several resolutions regarding their life together. Every man who wished to become an inhabitant was required to "first produce and bring a certificate from the Chief of the Place from whence he comes unless the Town be upon their Knowledge satisfied in and about the Good Carriage and Behaviour of them otherwise." Similarly, every man accepted as an inhabitant had to "first subscribe his Name and declare his assent with the rest of the Town, to all and every one of our fundamental agreements." Finally, as a condition of holding land in the township, all inhabitants also had to agree to "pay or cause to be paid yearly in the full Proportions equally, to the Maintenance & allowance agreed upon for the upholding of the settled Ministry and preaching of the word in our Town."[37] The next decision recorded, addressing the possibility of dissension in the community and also called "a fundamental Agreement and Order," is set off as a separate item, so it was likely approved on a later occasion. It was agreed, perhaps following Abraham Pierson's advice, that if anyone in the town should "willingly or wilfully disturb us in our Peace and Settlements, and especially that would subvert us from the true Religion and worship of God," and would not keep their opinions to themselves despite efforts by the town or church to "reclaim" them, the town could then ask them to "quietly depart the Place Seasonably." If this happened, the town would compensate the offending person for the appraised value of his "lands or Houses," or allow him to make the best deal he could with "any Man the Town shall approve of."[38] Dissension, especially about religion, could tear the community apart, as New Haven had discovered in the first decade of its existence.[39]

Two other agreements reached in the early months of the settlement, although not described as fundamental, were also essential for implementing godly government in Newark. The first addressed the contingency where individuals might acquire land "by Gift, Sale, Exchange or otherwise" and then wish "to inhabit with us." The town decided that these individuals would not gain title or possession of the land or "be accounted Legal Inhabitants in our Town" until they subscribed to the fundamental agreements and entered "into the same engagements as his Predecessors or the rest of the Town have done." The self-contained and closed nature of the new settlement is also evident in a final three-part agreement, "solemnly consented unto and agreed by all the Planters & Inhabitants of the Town of Newark:" (1) "to be lead, ruled and governed by such Magistrates and Rulers in the Town, as shall be annually chosen by the Friends from among themselves"; (2) to apply "such orders and Law whilst they are settled here by themselves as they had in the Place from whence they came"; and (3) to impose "such Penalties as the Magistrates upon the Nature of the offence shall determine." This agreement confirmed that they would draw on scripture-endorsed laws that had been in place in New Haven Colony and would settle their disputes among themselves in their own courts. The use of the word "friends" underscores the sense of mutuality that the settlers wanted to achieve. It also recalls the very first entry in the town records, describing how "friends from Milford and other neighboring plantations" entered into a civil covenant to "make one township."

This last agreement includes the first use of "Newark" as the name for the new town, suggesting that the "solemn consent" occurred after Abraham Pierson moved to the new settlement in late 1667. In the earliest portion of the town records, the settlement is called simply "Town upon Passaick river." There is a tradition that settlers from Milford wanted to call the new settlement "Milford" but were persuaded by Abraham Pierson that it should be called "Newark."[40] The debate ever since has been whether the name "Newark" was intended to suggest "New Ark" or "New Work," since the name was variously spelled as "New Ark," "Newworke," and plain "Newark" during the early decades. But whether the intent was New Ark or New Work, the key word was "new": They believed God was calling them to do a new thing.[41]

Historian Kenneth Lockridge described Dedham, Massachusetts, in the 1630s as a "Christian Utopian Closed Corporate Community": "Christian because they saw Christian love as the force which would most completely unite their community. Utopian because theirs was a highly conscious attempt to build the most perfect possible community, as perfectly united, perfectly at peace, and perfectly ordered as man could arrange. Closed because its membership was selected while outsiders were treated with suspicion or rejected altogether. And Corporate because the commune demanded the loyalty of their members."[42]

With its emphasis on unity and good order, this description fits early Newark as well, although it leaves out the crucial land company aspect of the settlement (discussed in the next chapter). The fundamental agreements and related orders underscore the aim of Newark's first settlers to create a self-contained, inward-looking, self-governed, and exclusive Puritan community, dedicated to living with mutual concern for each other's individual spiritual growth and earthly needs within scripture-endorsed rules. This was conservative in the sense that they wished to continue what the first generation of New England colonists had attempted in Massachusetts and especially what they or their fathers had undertaken in New Haven Colony. But it was also radical in their continuing emphasis on self-determination and rejection of the idea that the Restoration of the monarchy in England in 1660 had ended the Puritan experiment with godly government. After all, Newarkers were people who had been willing to hide regicides from the king's agents just a few years earlier. As with other New Englanders, their insistence on the Congregational form of church government also had a measure of defiance, since those churches had been outlawed in England following the Restoration.

The civil and church covenants, together with the fundamental agreements, provide insights into who the first Newarkers were and why they established their new township. Nearly all the adults had been born in England, and English customs formed the backdrop for how they organized and ordered their daily lives, even though they rejected many traditional aspects of English land use, court systems, and parish organization. Jasper Crane and Lawrence Ward were from London. Abraham Pierson grew up in Yorkshire. Robert Treat was born in Somerset. Obadiah Bruen came from Cheshire. Others were from small towns in Hertfordshire and Buckinghamshire.[43] But while they were English, they were also New Englanders. They had gone through the refiner's fire of emigrating and starting new lives in what they considered a wilderness. They had tested themselves and their beliefs, often in two or three settlements, before settling in the New Haven Colony. By the time they moved to Newark, they had strong and settled views about both church and civil government that they put in place in New Jersey, even as they continued to think of themselves as New Englanders.

The first Newarkers were deeply and profoundly religious, at a time when all of society was suffused with religion. Protestant Christianity was for them as strong a framework for understanding life as market economics is for most Americans today. They were orthodox Puritans in the reformed tradition, and they professed their beliefs through Congregational church government in what had become known in the prior three decades as "the New England Way." The old world was their Egypt, and the new world was their Canaan. The Bible was at once their inspiration, the focus of their intense study, and the source of their rules for daily life. They looked to the Old Testament rather than to English law to order their daily lives and settle disputes, and to the New Testament to order their worship. With their stress on the written Word of the Bible, they put a strong emphasis on education. They insisted on a highly educated clergy, and they would have valued Abraham Pierson's training in Latin, Greek, and Hebrew at Trinity College, Cambridge, and admired his library of more than 440 books, surely the largest in the new province in the early years.[44]

Men with high status and experience were among the founders of Newark. In New England, status was gained through wealth and service to the community in civil, church, and militia roles. Among men, young, unmarried males were at the bottom; they were expected to marry, start families, and gradually earn an improvement in status by filling minor town offices. At the top were the relatively few who gained the honorific "Mr." In neighboring Elizabethtown, only John Ogden was called "Mr" among the sixty-five men who took an oath of allegiance in 1665.[45] But in early Newark, nine men were called "Mr," two more were deacons, and three others had militia titles—all indications that a remarkably high percentage of the leaders of the former New Haven Colony migrated to Newark.[46] In addition to Robert Treat, Jasper Crane, and Abraham Pierson, the high-status settlers included Obadiah Bruen, who had been a selectman in Gloucester, Massachusetts, before serving as town clerk of Pequot (later renamed New London) for fifteen years, and Matthew Camfield of Norwalk (Robert Treat's brother-in-law). Bruen and Camfield had sufficient status to be included among the twelve men named as patentees in Connecticut's 1662 royal patent.

Newark's founding settlers had close geographical or personal ties. Of the thirty-two adult male settlers from Milford, twenty-eight had emigrated from a small area near King's Walden in Hertfordshire, England. More than half of the adult male settlers had a kinship tie with another male settler, whether as sons, brothers, brothers-in-law, cousins, or nephews. For example, brothers-in-law Robert Treat and Mathew Camfield were accompanied by their sons. Josiah Ward was related to five other male settlers: He was the younger brother of John Ward, "dishturner"; cousin to Sgt. John Ward and John Catlin; nephew of deacon Lawrence Ward; and son-in-law to Samuel Swaine, whose daughter Elizabeth he married in Newark.[47]

Newark was highly patriarchal. Husbands and fathers were responsible to the community for the support of their households and for overseeing the behavior, education, and spiritual lives of all family members and any others living in their households. In New Haven, single persons were required to live in a household rather than alone, and that was likely the case in Newark as well.[48] Women could become church members, but they could not vote or otherwise take part in town affairs. The first Newarkers were also risk-takers. Many were in their forties or younger in 1666; Robert Treat was forty-four. But some were in their fifties and even sixties when they migrated to Newark, including Abraham Pierson (fifty-six), Obadiah Bruen (sixty), Robert Kitchell (sixty-two), and Jasper Crane (sixty-four). They were leaders in the towns they left behind, and they had the highest status, whether measured by wealth or by the positions they held in their church or community. Nonetheless, they were willing once again to take on the hard tasks of clearing land, building homes, raising livestock, planting and harvesting crops, and organizing their common life together. As Patrick Falconer, a later resident, wrote to a friend in Scotland in 1684, this was "not a Countrey for idle people."[49]

CHAPTER 4

For the Good of the Town

Writing in 1668 to Henry Oldenburg, secretary of the Royal Society in London, governor John Winthrop Jr. of Connecticut described the time and effort required to develop new settlements, or "plantations:" "Plantations in their beginnings have worke enough, & find difficulties sufficient to settle a comfortable way of subsistence, there being buildings, fencings, clearing and breaking up of ground, lands to be attended, orchards to be planted, highways & ridges & fortifications to be made, & all things to doe, as in the beginning of the world."[1] Winthrop could well have been describing Newark and the challenges the settlers faced in ordering their life together. Newark's settlers knew what to do because they had done it before, but that did not make the work any easier. They needed to lay out a town plat early on; once that was done, they could allocate home lots and begin to build shelters and plant gardens. Robert Vauquellin, Governor Carteret's surveyor general, began surveying in the summer of 1666, starting with a line "run in the Center or Middle Street of the Town." In early August, Carteret sent Vauquellin to London to meet with the proprietors, so Robert Treat continued surveying the town and laying out home lots. He was careful later to note in the Newark land records that he had Vauquellin's permission to continue the work: "[He] consented we should go on and lay out the lots, he being sent on business to England by the Governor, and accordingly all the home lots are laid out and reckoned by the acre, whether more or less, 6 or 8 acre lots as being laid out by a 17 foot and somewhat more rod or line through the Town."[2]

The first settlers moved to Newark not just from a commitment to godly government or out of frustration with Connecticut absorbing New Haven Colony, but also to acquire land for themselves and their children. They kept careful records of their landholdings, and they became fiercely protective of their "liberties" if their title to land was questioned or put at risk by the proprietary government. In an agrarian community like Newark, land was the source of both sustenance and potential generational wealth—from gardens, orchards, and crops they could plant, salt hay for their livestock, timber for building and heating their houses, and surplus produce and livestock for trading or taking to market. Land was also the basis of their family-based economy, in stark contrast to the indentured-servant and slave-based economy that developed in Carolina and the Chesapeake, where men of wealth were granted substantial tracts of land that they then tried to keep intact through primogeniture.

Land also undergirded patriarchal control of households. In Newark, as elsewhere in New England, sons continued to work the family land into early adulthood, before securing parental consent to marry and receiving allocations of land from their fathers or from the town in order to establish their own "competency."[3] For example, Jasper Crane had four sons who also moved to Newark: John was thirty-one and Deliverance was twenty-four when they joined their father in subscribing the fundamental agreements in Branford in October 1666; Azariah was eighteen when he added his name to the fundamental agreements in Newark the following June; Jasper Jr., just sixteen, was too young in 1667 to sign. John and Deliverance likely moved to Newark before their father to prepare for his move in early 1668; they were assigned home lots and took part in the first division of upland in February 1668 and the first division of meadow in January 1670. Azariah received his first distribution of land in 1673 at age twenty-four, a year after marrying Robert Treat's daughter Mary. Jasper Jr. apparently remained in his father's household to work his father's fields until about 1675, when he married Joanna Swaine. In August 1675, Jasper Sr. and his wife Alice transferred their remaining landholdings jointly to Azariah, then twenty-six years old, and Jasper, then twenty-four—"on Condition that my said two sons . . . shall keepe & maintaine us as long as wee both or Eyther of us shall Live[,] with all things convenient according to our Condition and Quality."[4]

Home Lots

Newark settlers tried their best to be fair to each other while advancing the development of the town. Several undated entries in the town records from 1666 and 1667 relate to land, and it is evident that the same commitment to mutuality that guided decisions about civil matters informed early determinations about the use and allocation of land. Once the center line of the town plat had been surveyed, the basic street pattern laid out, and "ranges of [home] Lotts agreed upon," "the Inhabitants then present that had full Power to order matters" consented "for the Good of the Town" that other roads, as well as "drains, Gripes, or Water Courses" could be set out "in the most convenient Places necessary . . . yea though it should fall out to be across or within any Mans Lands or Meadows what and wheresoever." At the same time and as a matter of principle, they also noted their "intent" that every landowner "should have full satisfaction" for any land used in this way.[5]

When the first settlers arrived in Newark, former neighbors clustered together in temporary shelters until home lots were allocated. They soon decided "for their better security & Neighborhood" to allow different "quarters" in the town; "the Neighbourhood of Milford and New Haven" was permitted to "take up their Home

Lotts and Quarters in that Part of the Town where they now are [i.e., to the south and west], and the Neighbours from Branford and Guilford then present, in Places where they now are [i.e., to the north and east]." Each neighborhood then decided how to allocate home lots within its quarter. In Milford, home lots had been narrow rectangles ranging in size from 2.75 to 7 acres, depending on the size of a man's estate, how much he had contributed to the purchase of the land, the size of his family, and his leadership in establishing the settlement. In Branford, no home lot was larger than 3 acres, and in Guilford, the average home lot was 3.1 acres.[6] However, in Newark, the Milford and New Haven neighbors decided, as a "whole Committee," to adopt a more egalitarian approach. They agreed on equal six-acre lots for themselves, laid out according to "the Surveyors Line," but in recognition of Robert Treat's leadership, they "freely gave way" and allowed him to survey an eight-acre lot and choose its location. They no doubt kept in mind the early New England practice of clustering homes within walking distance of the church: When John Cotton prepared his compilation of laws based on scripture three decades earlier, he included the stricture that "no man shall set his dwelling house above the distance of halfe a mile or a mile at the furthest, from the meeting of the Congregation, where the Church doth usually assemble for the worship of God." All original Newark home lots were within a mile of the church.[7]

Once the home lots had been surveyed, the Milford and New Haven neighbors met again to decide how to allocate the lots that had been arrayed along a north–south axis on today's Broad Street. After prayer, they decided to draw lots to determine the order in which they would choose. Each home lot was assigned a number, starting with the home lot next to Robert Treat. Slips of paper with the numbers were then put in a container, from which they were drawn. Thirteen home lots were allocated in this initial distribution; the first lot went to John Gregory, the second to the wife of Robert Denison, the third to Thomas Johnson, and so on. The settlers then made adjustments so no one would be short-changed. Micah Tompkins, who drew the thirteenth lot, was allowed an extra acre in a subsequent land division to make up for the "remoteness" of his home lot, and John Baldwin Jr. received an extra half acre because he was next to "the common swamp." It was also decided "that those of Brandford that were present" should make their own provisions for creating and allocating home lots. Their decisions are not recorded in the town records, but it is apparent from the land records that they also agreed to create six-acre home lots for themselves and reserve an eight-acre lot for Jasper Crane, thereby securing him equal status with Robert Treat. Other lots were reserved for an elder, a boatman, a tailor, and a mill operator.[8]

In addition to building their houses, digging wells, constructing barns, and planting gardens and orchards, settlers were required to build fences at the rear of their lots at their own cost, it being "a Common Burden with all Home Lotts, and the condition upon which those Lotts were given out." The goal was to surround the town with "sufficient Fence in the Common Line" by the end of March 1668, both as a matter of security and to create common spaces: The unusual width of the "middle highways" (eight rods or about 136 feet) suggests they provided common pasturage for sheep and other livestock once the fence was completed and before other common areas were established.[9] The tasks of maintaining and extending the common fence were often discussed at town meetings for years to come. Three gates constructed in 1667 provided access through the first fence that ringed the town: one at the northern end of today's Broad Street, another in the east at what would become today's Ferry Street through the salt meadows, and the third at the southern end of Broad Street on the way to Elizabethtown.[10]

Capital improvements markedly increased the value of the home lots, generating a significant portion of a man's estate. In 1671, the administrators of deacon Lawrence Ward's estate sold his "dwelling house, Well, Yard, Barne, Garden & Orchard," along with the fencing and several household goods, to Abraham Pierson Jr. for seventy-five pounds. Ward's household goods included "one great Winscott chair" made of white oak, which Pierson retained when he moved to Connecticut two decades later and used when he became the first rector (president) of Yale in 1701. It is still used today as the ceremonial chair for Yale presidents at their inauguration (see Figure 5).[11]

Associates

Newark was a group settlement with control over undistributed land retained by the associates who shared in the cost of the original purchase.[12] Following the mid-seventeenth-century New England model, these associates acted in effect as partners in a land company—not a land company as a speculative commercial enterprise that emerged later in the seventeenth century and became more common in the eighteenth century, but instead a communal partnership with socioreligious aims.[13] As long as common lands from the original purchase remained undivided, the associates retained a corporate existence, with interests passed on to their heirs and assigns. These interests were valuable, particularly in the early years, because land was distributed only to associates who had helped pay for the purchase of the Newark tract, regardless of church membership. As elsewhere in New England, the distinction between the associates and the "town" was not drawn sharply in early years because the men involved were mostly the same. Town meetings often acted in effect as meetings of the associates, who at times were referred to as "inhabitants" or "planters."[14] However, by the 1680s the distinctions became clearer, with "inhabitants" retaining both the collective responsibility of deciding when to make periodic divisions of land and the individual right to receive grants of land, and "planters" gaining permission to live in Newark, pay toward the original purchase, and then receive grants of land.

Although the founders of Newark were keen to attract other settlers, they imposed various conditions on top of the fundamental agreements, both to ensure potential settlers were committed to joining the community before taking up a home lot and to preserve the purity of the self-contained community. The conditions included coming with "the greatest Part of their family to Build upon the same" and then remaining for "the space of Two Years at least." If a settler received

Figure 5. The official chair of Yale College presidents, which belonged to Abraham Pierson Jr., the first rector of the Collegiate School, now known as Yale College. The chair may have been made by Lawrence Ward, an original settler of Newark, from whose estate Pierson acquired the chair in 1671. Yale University Art Gallery.

a home lot, he would not be allowed to sell his land until he stayed the full two years; if he chose to leave after completing the two-year residency, he was required to sell the property to "the Town in General," or if the town declined, to a buyer approved by the town. Any sales to nonresidents or to buyers not approved by the town would be considered void, and the land returned "into the Town's Hands" for an appraised price determined by "indifferent Men." Exceptions to this policy were transfers due to the death of the owner and the sale of a "small parcell."[15] This rule was enforced on John Gregory, who had been deputized by the New Haven Colony along with Robert Treat to negotiate with Governor Carteret early in 1666. Gregory visited Newark in the months after the purchase of the tract from the Hackensack and indicated his interest in joining the settlement. When the Milford and New Haven neighborhood drew its home lots, he received in absentia the lot next to Robert Treat, "upon Considerations that he come with his Family to build, and inhabit the same about two Years, which was the Condition of his Entertainment with us in our Town." He chose not to settle in Newark, and in late 1667 his home lot was reassigned to Abraham Pierson Sr.[16]

One settler from outside New Haven Colony who met all the conditions for admission to the town was Stephen Davis, "several years a tenant of Mr. Sam. Willis" at Hockanum, near Hartford, who moved with his family to Newark in April 1667 together with a neighbor and his family. Concerned that they were "somthing backward in tyme" and would be "late in their building and planting" if they met with "with some stop in their way at N. Yorke," Davis and his neighbor secured a letter from Connecticut Governor Winthrop asking New York Governor Nicolls to give his command "for a spedy dispatch from N. Yorke to their port, where they should settle." Winthrop assured Nicolls that the Newark settlement had his full support; Davis and his neighbor were "going about a very good publick worke in settling with others a new plantation in some place not very farr from N. Yorke on the other side of that river: to which I have beene willing to add any thing from my selfe for their incouragement."[17] Davis arrived in time to sign the fundamental agreements in June 1667. He then received a home lot along the Passaic River in the Branford and Guilford quarter of the town, and his estate was appraised to determine his proportional share of the purchase price and divisions of land. He must also have been admitted as a member of the church, because he soon took on important committee assignments, including surveying land.[18]

Newarkers kept the land company open to new associates for a few years and then, in subsequent years, occasionally admitted men as planters and allocated them a home lot if they submitted to all town orders and paid toward the original costs of the settlement, known as "paying the Purchase."[19] For example, in the spring of 1669 John Browne Jr. was "by a full vote of the Town" granted a home lot as well as a division of uplands and meadow, "according to his Estate that he does Give in . . . he paying his proportion of the Charges Laid out for it, and do Seasonably Come to possess The Same Some Time this Spring."[20] Eleazer Rogers also had his admission confirmed the same day, "provided that he do defray all the Charges and Come upon the place to Inhabit" within a three-month period "and Transport his Family Hither, as soon as he Can be prepared." In January 1670, Abraham Pierson Jr. was granted the remaining part of the home lot that had been set aside for William Leete, the Guilford magistrate and future governor of Connecticut, who put up capital for the original purchase but then decided not to move to Newark, "upon Condition that [he] pay for the Purchase Twenty four Shillings."

Similarly, several "young Men which have Home Lotts in the Town" were given the opportunity in 1673 to be included in the second division of land, "provided they pay to the Purchase as other Planters have Done."[21] A decade later, John Wilkins was admitted as a planter and given permission to buy an accommodation in the town and take up a tract of land "that other Men have not already surveyed, he paying the Purchase as others have done."[22] Some men admitted as planters apparently failed to pay the purchase; the town acted in 1681 to fine them two shillings per acre for a home lot, three pence per acre "for other Lands lying more remote," and four pence per acre for meadow—or else the home lots, upland, and meadow would revert "to the Town's Dispose." Two years later, two men were chosen to "gather up a List, as near as they can, of those that are behind in paying the Purchase for such lands as they have taken up and not paid for" along with "how many Acres such have taken up."[23]

Land Divisions

Early in 1668, Abraham Pierson wrote to his daughter and son-in-law in New Haven, letting them know that they were "to have a general court, or meeting, to settle lands, in March." The meeting took place sooner than expected, however, because on February 6, "after due preparation and Solemnization," Newark settlers drew lots for their first distribution of upland. This was a momentous step for the new settlement, and a great deal of discussion and preparation took place in advance. While settlers were keen to know which plots of arable land they would receive so they could each prepare for spring planting, they also wanted to ensure that the distribution was done fairly. It is possible they needed to work through disagreements on how best to handle the distribution before deciding, "by the General Vote and Consent of the Town," to proceed to this first division of land. During this period, Micah Tompkins admitted to "some uncomfortable differences amongst them." Those differences may have related to religious matters, but they might also have concerned this first land distribution, since it would set the pattern for subsequent divisions.[24]

Months earlier, the settlers had reached an agreement to allocate the costs related to establishing the settlement by employing the New England practice of "estates and Persons." They also agreed that this assessment, known as "contribution money," would pay not only for the "lands bought of the Natives" but for other "necessary Charges of setling the Place, and Mr. Peirson's Transport." The equal-sized home lots had been a break from the pattern of unequal home lots adopted in Milford and most other New England towns, but in employing "estates and persons" they followed the practice used in New Haven Colony and throughout much of New England.[25] This was a critically important decision because land distributions were later apportioned based on each man's contributions to the purchase. A committee of seven of the most respected and trusted leaders was charged with the responsibility "to hear, examine, and judge" the size of each man's estate, using the guideline of fifty pounds for each head of family, plus ten pounds for every child or servant in the family, plus the value of "all other kinds of Goods and Estates, Real and visible that Men intend, God willing, to transport on the Place," presumably including livestock. Married women had no legal standing and were considered one with the head of the family, so they were not assessed. One-third of each man's estate was then deducted, and the resulting amount guided what each man owed for the purchase of the land. Men paid this "contribution" over time. At his death in 1670, Lawrence Ward had a "debt to the Contribution" of £1.8s.2d, while Hugh Roberts still owed 12s.4d in "contribution money" when he died the following year.[26]

A table noting the estates for sixty-six men, before and after the one-third deduction, was inserted later in the town records, noted as "approved by the Sale Men"—the only use of "Sale Men" in the town records. This list of the associates in the land company excludes four men included in the first division who later "deserted their Lots" and includes six men, listed at the end, who were admitted as associates as late as November 1672. The one-third deductions in each man's estate reflected a communal effort to flatten differences in land allocations among men while still recognizing different levels of contribution to the purchase. Men with larger estates were affected by the deduction more than those with small estates, since men received one parcel of land for each one-hundred-pound value of their estates; for example, Robert Treat's estate was reduced by £220 (or two parcels). The resulting list of men and the size of their estates (see Table 1) guided both who would be included in land divisions and how much land they would each receive. In a joint-stock company sense, land distributions served as proportional dividends on shares in the land company. The deductions constrained the ratio between the largest and smallest allocation in a land division to about five to one, thus encouraging social cohesion. Again, this was common practice in New Haven Colony and elsewhere in New England.[27]

The town agreed that the first division would contain three-acre strips of upland suitable for planting crops, located in various fields not far from the home lots, with one parcel allocated per one-hundred-pound value of a man's estate. The town further agreed that men would draw lots to determine which parcel they would receive, except for Robert Treat, who "upon consideration of his great expenses of item & charge extraordinary for the settling the place" on top of "what he placed to accounts," was permitted to select his parcels "according to his desire."[28] The vote to draw lots was taken by a "most General Vote," while the decision to let Robert Treat choose his parcels was made unanimously. With the process settled, sixty-one men, not including Robert Treat, then drew lots for the first division of upland at the town meeting on February 6, 1668; lots were also drawn and set aside for the elder, seaman, and tailor lots, and for William Leete. In another indication of their commitment to fairness, the town subsequently permitted several men to

TABLE 1

"A SURE LIST OF EVERY MAN'S ESTATE APPROVED BY THE SALE MEN"
(BEFORE AND AFTER ONE-THIRD DEDUCTIONS)

John Browne	£308	£205	Richard Laurance	£273	£182
Mr. Matthew Camfield	500	333	John Ward	360	240
Stephen Davies	289	192	added	50	50
Nathaniel Wheeler	186	124	John Baldwin, Junr	145	97
Thomas Luddington	122	81	Hauns Albers	100	67
Thomas Richards	110	73	Samuel Camfield	174	116
Thomas Lyon	570	380	Samuel Rose	250	167
William Camp	220	134	Mr. Obadiah Bruen	200	133
Robert Denison	300	200	Mr. Morrish	385	257
Thomas Johnson	420	280	Robert Dalglesh	167	111
Martin Tichenor	169	113	Aaron Blatchly	180	120
John Catling	315	205	Stephen Freeman	440	293
John Bostick	160	120	Thomas Staples	150	100
John Ward, Jun.	250	167	Lieut. Samuel Swain	550	367
Deliverance Crane	150	100	Laurance Ward	370	247
John Curtis	197	127	Francis Linle	210	140
John Baldwin, Sen.	137	91	Mr. Jasper Crane	570	380
Joseph Walters	180	120	Mr. Abraham Pierson, Sen	644	429
Micah Tompkins	260	173	Hugh Roberts	446	297
Jonathan Tompkins	166	111	Josiah Ward	210	140
Ephraim Pennington	160	104	Thomas Peirson	200	133
John Crane	250	167	Mr. Robert Treatt	660	440
Edward Ball	160	104	Robert Limon	285	190
Ser. Richard Harrison	400	267	Samuel Plum	500	333
Edward Riggs	320	213	Thomas Huntington	350	233
Zachariah Burwell	160	104	Stephen Bond	140	94
Ephraim Burwell	150	100	Benjamin Baldwin	120	80
George Day	120	80	Alexander Munrow	100	67
John Brooks	80	53	John Browne, Junr	250	167
John Harrison	120	80	Mr. Abraham Pierson, Jun	380	250
John Rogers	350	233	Daniel Dod	150	100
Mr. Jeremiah Peck	200	134	Jonathan Sargant	150	100
Mr. Robert Kitchell Mr. Samuel Kitchell	750	500	Samuel Lyon		150

Source: *Records of the Town of Newark, New Jersey* (1864), 8.

receive adjustments to their parcels to account for roads or variations in the quality of the land.[29]

As they allocated land, Newarkers recognized that they needed a clear boundary with Elizabethtown. Representatives of the two towns met in May 1668 at the "top of Little round hill," known thereafter as "Divident Hill," and agreed on the boundary line. The town records report that the agents of Elizabethtown marked an Oak Tree with an E on their side of the boundary, and the agents of Newark marked the same tree with an N on their side of the boundary.[30]

Further divisions of land followed annually over the next three years, permitting men time to develop their holdings in sequence, without paying taxes on landholdings until they were ready to cultivate or otherwise work them. The first division of meadow—marshy land valued for its natural crop of salt hay and pasturage for livestock but not suitable for planting crops—took place in 1669. Once again, the town agreed to distribute the land by lot; this time Obadiah Bruen picked first, and Micah Tompkins drew lots for those absent. More men had been admitted as associates, so seventy-two lots were drawn.[31] To make sure the town "in General" would be satisfied that the lots had been sized appropriately, an eight-man committee was formed with the charge "to finish and perfect the first division of Meadow, in the most Just and Equal way they Can in their Best Skill and ability attain unto, as may tend to the most hopefull Satisfaction of all it may be, and to relieve and Supply any that want Meadow for their Inheritance."[32] The committee completed its work by June, at which time men could make a final claim for further amendments, given the "badness of their Meadow, or for Grass for their present supply."[33]

The second division of arable upland took place in 1670, again by lot, but this time with six acres allocated per one-hundred-pound estate. In the first break with prior practice, the town permitted men to choose in which large field their strip of land would be located, but the order in which they received their allocation was still determined by lot. For example, ten men wanted land in the field at the southern end of the town, while thirty-one men wanted their allocations, "either in Part or in whole of their divisions," in the field located in the "great neck."[34] As before, the town approved various adjustments or exchanges in the continuing effort to achieve parity in the quality of land allocated. A year later, the second division of meadow was laid out, three acres per £100 estate and again distributed by lot.[35]

For the third division of upland in 1675, the town changed its system of allocating land. Following "much debate," the town dropped its prior rule of "estates and persons" in favor of a three-tier allocation based on the size of a man's estate but no longer proportional to it. Milford made a similar change at the same time, so there may have been communication between the two towns. The town "thought it not fit to lay out an Hundred Acres to the Highest Estate" but voted instead to cap the allocation to the largest estates at forty acres, with the middle tier getting thirty acres, "and the lowest not above Twenty." All the land would "lie common, for Pasture, Timber, and Stone, till it be inclosed by Fence." The town did not vote to lay out highways to these parcels until 1681.[36]

Open-Field Farming

During at least the first decade of the settlement, Newark implemented the open-field system of farming that had been used in Milford, Branford, and New Haven, even though it was coming under increasing pressure elsewhere in New England. In this system, large fields were divided into many strips of land; the strips were privately owned, but farming was regulated communally. Over subsequent land divisions, settlers ended up with fields in varying locations.[37] What they lost in efficiency in working in widely disparate fields, they hoped to gain by receiving land of similar quality. Settlers could also share labor and equipment as needed. This cooperative approach to farming required agreement each year on which crops would be planted, how livestock would be managed, how common fields could be used, and which fields would be left fallow.[38] The town determined when the fields would be burned ("the Town hath Chosen and deputed Nath'l Wheeler and John Curtis, to Take the Care of Burning the Meadows and upland for this Year, and to take pay of the Town Treasury")[39] and when cattle should be removed from common meadow ("all Cattle whatsoever that Lye in the Neck, should be fetched out between this and the fourth Day of the next week, by the owners of them"). The town also set fines for individuals who did not cooperate appropriately. In 1672, it was ordered that "no goats at any Time of the Year shall be kept any where in the Neck, or Common fence."[40] As late as 1679, settlers still faced restrictions on what crops they could plant ("the Town consented by Vote, not to sow any Pease white or gray this Year"), with a penalty of five shillings per rod in their strip of land, "or for the smallest Quantity, as any Person or Persons shall or may sow."[41] The open-field system was phased out beginning with the third division of upland. Although settlers and their families were slow to take up third division allotments, the resulting farms were separate rectangular plots, rather than long strips in a shared field, and large enough for owners eventually to build shelters on them for weekday use, and, in due course, houses.

Newark's Land System and Quitrents

By following New England practice, the first Newark settlers put themselves at odds with Governor Carteret's efforts to collect a half-penny per acre quitrent for the proprietors from each landholder. Newark's open-field system of farming and approach to determining land allocations could hardly have been more different than the headright system contemplated by the proprietors' concessions. No allotments in any Newark land division were first surveyed by Vauquellin, the governor's surveyor general, as required by the proprietors; none carried the governor's warrant; none was registered in a timely way in the proprietary land records. Newarkers noted property boundaries and kept records that supported their land system, not the quitrent system. A man might receive more land than his three- or six-acre-per-hundred estate allotment that a town land division would suggest, due to sizing intended to make the productivity and quality of the parcels similar, but he would only pay the town rate on the three- or six-acre basis. Initially, men marked the boundaries of their upland and meadow allotments with stakes that could easily be dislodged, and only in time shifted to "sufficient stone land Marks . . . with the Two Letters of Men's Names Legally Engraven thereon, about a foot Above the Ground."[42]

Quitrents were a feature of proprietary government. They did not exist in New England, and New York relied mostly on customs duties for revenue. Elizabethtown settlers argued that they should not pay any quitrents at all on the grounds that their patent from Governor Nicolls—issued before it was known locally that the Duke of York had ceded New Jersey to the proprietors—did not require quitrents. In contrast, Newarkers understood that the proprietors would require quitrent payments starting in 1670, but they wanted to make a collective payment for just the land within the Newark tract that had been distributed, not for the entire Newark tract, and not as individuals for their separate landholdings. In 1669, James Bollen reminded Newarkers of their obligation to pay quitrents a year later; he probably demanded that they take steps well in advance to patent their lands individually. At a meeting on March 30, the town discussed "Capt. Bollens Demands in his Letter" but then almost brushed it off by deciding to refer the matter to a committee "to act and do in it as they shall see cause."[43] However, when Governor Carteret wrote to Newark early in 1670 about taking out individual patents and paying quitrents, Newarkers recognized it as a challenge to their New England township practices. After "the Governors Writing" was read at a town meeting, "the Inhabitants [i.e., the associates in the land company] or freeholders [i.e., male church members who resided in Newark but who may or may not have been associates] of the Town of New Ark" debated the issues. They voted to ask constable Thomas Johnson to present "all due Sallutations . . . to Our Worshipfull Governor" but convey their firm position that the town's purchase of the Newark tract from the Hackensack, undertaken with Carteret's support and approval, gave them legal title to the land even though they had not independently taken out patents as required by the concessions. They also asked Johnson to reference the articles they had negotiated with Carteret before settling the township. The town records capture their case: "That they do Hold and Possess their Lands and Right in the said Town, Both By Civil and Divine Right, as by their Legall purchase and Articles doth and may shew." In addition, they wanted Johnson to assure the governor that they were prepared to pay the half-penny per acre quitrent "for all our Allotted Lands, According to our Articles and Interpretations of them" (i.e., just the acreage that had been distributed for home lots and the first divisions of upland and meadow), if the governor confirmed their title to the land first ("you assuring them to us").[44] Carteret was unlikely to agree to this demand; his task was to collect quitrents from men who had received patents for their individual landholdings, and no doubt the proprietors expected quitrent revenue on the entire Newark tract, whether or not it had yet been put to productive use.

The town referred to their articles again seven weeks later when they directed Thomas Johnson and Henry Lyon to "take and receive every Mans Just

Share and Proportion of Wheat for his Land . . . [and] to Morrow to Carry to Elizabeth Town, and Make a Tender Thereof to the Gouvernor upon the account of the Lords proprietors rent for the Land we make use of, according to Articles."[45] By making this in-kind payment, Newarkers believed they were fulfilling their quitrent obligations. Carteret likely did not accept their tender because if he had, it would have set a precedent for Newark settlers paying future quitrents on their terms.

In 1671, the town again asked Thomas Johnson and Henry Lyon to go "to our Governor, in Behalf of the Town [and] make a Tender to him in Good Wheat for the Payment of their Half Penny per Acre to Him for the Lords Proprietors, in Like Manner as they did the Last Year at the Day Appointed." But this time they waited until Johnson and Lyon learned whether the governor would accept the payment on Newark's terms, before requiring "everyone to Bring his Proportion of Corn to the Constable's House" on the appointed morning. Again, the town records do not indicate whether Carteret accepted the tender. During the lead-up to the rebellion in spring 1672, Newarkers likely did not pay their annual quitrent, since there is no reference to it in the town records. After Philip Carteret returned to the province and was reinstalled as governor late in 1674, he insisted that lands be patented and quitrents paid by individuals, with arrears back to 1670, so it was no longer a town decision about making the payment.[46]

Women and Property

When the Milford and New Haven neighbors allocated their home lots in Newark, Elizabeth Riggs drew the sixth lot. The "Newark Town Book" (a record of land transactions) notes that in an extraordinary sign of respect, she was awarded an extra acre, "given for service on the place by staying the first summer." Among all the original settlers, only Robert Treat and Jasper Crane, both town magistrates, and Elizabeth Riggs were granted more than six acres for their home lots.[47] The records do not indicate what Elizabeth Riggs's "service" was during that first summer, but perhaps she provided medical care to the small group of settlers who built temporary houses, probably dug into the soil with barely a lean-to covering for their heads.

Due to coverture—the legal doctrine that, as William Blackstone put it, "By marriage, the husband and wife are one person in law: that is, the very being or legal existence of the woman is suspended during the marriage, or at least is incorporated and consolidated into that of the husband: under whose wing, protection, and *cover*, she performs every thing"—women mostly appear in early Newark records as widows administering their husband's estate.[48] Under coverture, a husband managed both his and his wife's property, but if he wanted to sell or mortgage property that his wife brought to the marriage or that had been acquired during their marriage, he had to get explicit consent from his wife to complete the transaction because of her dower claim on the property. As a result, bills of sale note the wife's consent. For example, when Samuel Rose sold a parcel of land at the rear of his home lot to John Crane in 1692, his wife Mary acknowledged her consent by signing the deed with her mark.[49]

If they survived childbirth, women tended to outlive their husbands, in part because they were usually a few years younger when they married. Widows almost always served as the executors of their husbands' estates, taking responsibility for paying debts and ensuring that legacies were settled as intended. This role reflected their partnership in managing the household economy and caring for children who had not come of age. As historian Cornelia Hughes Dayton put it, widows became "the temporary treasurer and accountant for the household, the keeper of the family document box." They prepared to handle the multiple steps involved in probate—wills, inventories, receipts, accounts of debts, and distributions from the estate—by observing women in their extended families going through the process before their turn came.[50] While widows took on their deceased husband's economic and familial role as head of household, they were still excluded from political roles. They became responsible for paying taxes on their land, but they could not vote on setting those taxes or hold an elected or appointed town office.[51]

Although early Newark was distinctly patriarchal and hierarchal, the settlers had strong egalitarian tendencies in how they allocated property to their children when drawing up wills. There are some examples of double portions for the oldest son, as in 1675 when Stephen Freeman left one-third of his estate to his wife Hannah, a double portion to his son Samuel, and equal portions of his remaining estate to his four unmarried daughters.[52] However, it was more common in the early decades for men to leave equal portions to their sons and daughters and more than the traditional third to their wives. That was the approach Hugh Roberts took when he made his will early in 1671, making his wife the executor: "I give & bequeath unto my deare & loving wife Mary Roberts, the one halfe of all my goods & Estate whatsoever: My Just debts being first paid." Roberts listed several contingencies to guide his wife in administering the estate. These contingencies reveal both the structure and concerns of seventeenth-century families, as well as the effort by a husband to exert patriarchal control even after his death. He left the other half of his estate, whether in lands, goods, or chattel property, in equal shares to his unmarried children; his sons would receive their portions when they turned twenty-one, while his daughters would receive their portions at eighteen. His wife was pregnant at the time he wrote his will, so he also made a provision for "the Child which my loving wife now goeth withall." He added that if any of his children died before they came of age, their portions would revert to his wife "for the better Enabling her to bring up my younger Children." He also left fifty shillings to his eldest daughter Priscilla, who had already married, to complete her portion of the inheritance. He directed his sons Samuel and Hugh to "abide as dutifull Sonns to Serve their dear Mother until they bee one & twenty years old at least, if shee Continueth a Widdow soe long." He considered the possibility that his wife might remarry, so he explicitly gave her the power, "with The Consent of any two of my overseers" to order her sons "to trades" if they were not willing to remain in the household after she remarried.[53]

When Samuel Swaine, captain of the town militia, became ill while in New York early in 1682, he did not have time to think through contingencies to the same degree as Hugh Roberts. Not knowing whether he was "for life or death," he left everything to his "beloved wife" Johanna Swaine "to be at her proper dispose and use according to her discretion to my children both married and unmarried, taking the advice of Christian friends for her best assistance therein." The only contingency Swaine addressed was whether his wife remarried. As it turned out, she did not remarry, but if she had, Swaine directed that two-thirds of his estate be distributed in equal shares to his children, "allowance being made out of the same to those children unmarried as near as may be to those that are married for what hath been given them already." He emphasized that his desire was "to make none difference in giving more to one than to the other."[54]

Families were expected to take care of each other—the parents taking care of their children until well established in marriages, and children looking out for their parents in old age. Life did not always work out that way, of course. Elizabeth Ward, the widow of Lawrence Ward, had no children, so after her husband died in 1670, she arranged for "comfortable maintenance during the term of her life" from her nephews John Catlin and John Ward, in return for assigning her lands to them.[55] In effect, she traded her landholdings for a life annuity. John Browne, whose wife had predeceased him, had two sons and four daughters already established in their own households, so he focused his will on his remaining son Daniel and daughter Esther. He suspected that Esther might never marry, so he left Daniel all his remaining property, with the stipulation that he "provide for & maintain his sister Esther (with what shee can do towards a lively=hood) she remaineing in a single state." If she remained single, Esther was to have equal use of the "house-hold-stuff" with Daniel while living and "at her decease shee shall have her owne bed, & beding, cloathes, & halfe of my house-hold-stuff at her dispose."[56]

Elizabeth Lyon, the widow of Thomas Lyon, managed their son Thomas's portion of the estate until he came of age, but she apparently did not trust him to respect her continuing dower rights. With the involvement of John Prudden, the minister at the time, she negotiated a detailed agreement with her son in 1704 that she would have the sole use of her dwelling house, well, and three apple trees; that her son would repair her house, reshingle the roof, and "maintain the outside fence" that enclosed her yard; that she would continue to "have part of the Barn for her use to secure her corn and Hay yearly;" that she would keep the right to cut six loads of hay in the current year, and four loads of hay each year thereafter; and that she still had "liberty . . . to pasture two cows in the two mile brook field" as well as "liberty of cutting firewood for her use." Her son also agreed "to cut and cart home to her house . . . sixteen loads of firewood . . . She finding him a cart and a yoke of oxen to perform the same." That was not all. She retained the right to all improvements on her homestead, including "house, Barn, Well, Orchard, Yard, Garden, Herbage, Fruit trees, standing and growing therein," and all the property would revert to her if her son died before she did.[57]

It was the law in Connecticut until 1723 that a husband took absolute control of any property that his wife brought to the marriage, but widows could take steps before the second marriage to reserve property for children from the first marriage.[58] That is what Newarker Sarah Davis did. When she prepared her will in March 1691, she disposed of various parcels of land left to her by her first husband to her sons from that marriage, as well as twenty acres left to her in her father's will and her "part of the shop" kept by the family. She divided all her "wearing clothes" equally between her three daughters, but she left her daughter Sarah (from her first marriage) "the bed wherein I now ly to wit feather bed, feather bolster, and pillows, with two pair of sheets, and one coverlid and the bedstead it now lies on and also all the remainder of my household stuff." She apparently expected her second husband Stephen Davis to make provisions for their children, since the only special bequest she made to their daughter Mary was her "curtains after my decease and my loving husbands."[59]

The picture that emerges from wills, estate inventories, and land transactions in the first decades of Newark's existence is of women as essential partners to their husbands in managing the household economy and raising children, but without separate legal standing while married. They had independent status only in church membership or after they were widowed. They never gained political rights to participate in town meetings or hold town office, regardless of their marriage status. A number of them could both read and write, while others presumably could read but never learned to write. Many demonstrated strong administrative skills in managing family estates after their husbands' deaths, including a clear capacity to look out for their own and their children's interests. Together, they contributed to the remarkable stability and persistence of the "family-centered, work-oriented" community that the settlers migrating from New Haven Colony achieved in Newark.[60]

CHAPTER 5

First Settlers and Slavery

Slavery is a foundational part of New Jersey's early history. It was introduced first by the Dutch and then encouraged by the proprietors after the English took control in 1664. Enslaved persons, captured by Dutch privateers from Portuguese ships, were first brought to New Amsterdam in 1627. The Dutch West India Company later imported others. Eventually, some gained freedom and created a small community across the Hudson River, including Yougham Antonius Roberts, "a Free borne Negro," who received a patent for one hundred acres along the Hackensack River in 1684. Others, more numerous, remained enslaved and worked on farms in early Dutch settlements. One such enslaved man, seeking freedom or protesting his treatment, was likely the first person charged with a capital offense after the creation of New Jersey: In 1670 Governor Carteret instructed a Bergen town court "to passe sentence of death" upon Emanuel, "a Negro belonging to the family of Captain Nicolas Verlett," if the jury found him guilty of setting fire to Varlet's barn. Anticipating a guilty verdict, Carteret encouraged the court to execute him in a manner "fitt for the terror and Example of others."[1]

In the early years after the English formed New Jersey, Governor Carteret implemented the headright system of land distribution instituted by the proprietors in their concessions. Settlers received land not just on their own account, but also additional allocations for every "able servant" and a half-portion for "every weaker servant, or slave, male or female exceeding the age of fourteen years" they brought with them to New Jersey. "Christian" indentured servants were promised a grant of land for their own use at the expiration of their contract, but no allowance was made for enslaved persons to eventually receive land. Carteret took advantage of the headright system to claim 2,700 acres on account of the eighteen indentured servants he "brought Into the Country the first Yeare." Although Carteret initially depended on labor from indentured servants, he eventually acquired at least one enslaved person, Black Jack, whom he freed in his will.[2]

No Newarkers made a headright claim on account of indentured servants or enslaved persons in their households—not because they rejected servitude, but because they rejected the headright method of distributing land. In other towns, some New Englanders made headright claims based on persons in their service, although it is not known whether they were indentured servants, except for Samuel Moore's two enslaved persons:

- Jacob Melyn, Elizabethtown: for himself and his wife, 240 acres, and for two servants, 120 acres.
- John Woodruff, Elizabethtown: for himself, his wife, three able servants, a man, and a maid, 450 acres.
- Nicholas Carter, Elizabethtown: for himself, his wife, one son, and a maid servant, 360 acres.
- William Billes, Elizabethtown: 350 acres in three parcels that he purchased, and 120 acres for "two servants brought In the Country."
- Samuel Moore, Woodbridge: 600 acres, based on ten claims of 60 acres per "head" for five daughters, three sons, and "one slave and her sonn."
- Charles Gilman, Piscataway: for himself, 60 acres, and for two able servants, 120 acres.
- John Bound, Middletown: an additional 180 acres for three servants.[3]

Enslaved persons were brought to English New Jersey in significant numbers in the late 1660s by Barbados plantation owners, squeezed out of Barbados by larger landowners but still very wealthy by the standards of early New Jersey (see Figure 6). John Berry, who served as deputy governor, received an extensive grant of land along the Hackensack River, in what became known as New Barbadoes, for himself, his wife, two daughters, one son, seven "Christians" [indentured servants], and "32 negroes." He was joined by his son-in-law Michell Smith, who brought with him "16 negroes and 3 Christian servants." William Sandford, who managed a plantation in Suriname before the Dutch reclaimed the area in the treaty ending the Second Anglo-Dutch Trade War, gained ownership of a 5,300-acre tract across from Newark between the Passaic and Hackensack Rivers. A longtime member of the Governor's Council, Sandford often presided over courts in Newark and commanded the Newark militia at various points; it is possible he was attended by his enslaved servants during his frequent visits to Newark on behalf of the proprietary government. When Sandford assigned a third of his estate to his wife Sarah Wightman in 1677, he transferred ownership of Boy Jack, Will, and Sarah, along with an option "to purchase and putt on the said Estate as many more Negroes as shall make the Number Six." And when his daughter Nidemia married Richard Berry in 1682, he gave her "one Negro man named Will and his wife" as a wedding present. John Berry's wedding present to the couple also included enslaved persons: "one Negro man by the name of Litle Sambo, one Negro woman by name Rose[,] one boy by name Tom, one Negro girl by name Fane [Fanny], one boy by name Cuffy, and one Boy by name Will."[4]

In 1680, Matthias Nicolls, a former mayor of New York, prepared a survey of East Jersey. He noted the presence of about 120 enslaved people on "out-plantations" in the province. The largest number, sixty or seventy, worked at Lewis Morris's iron

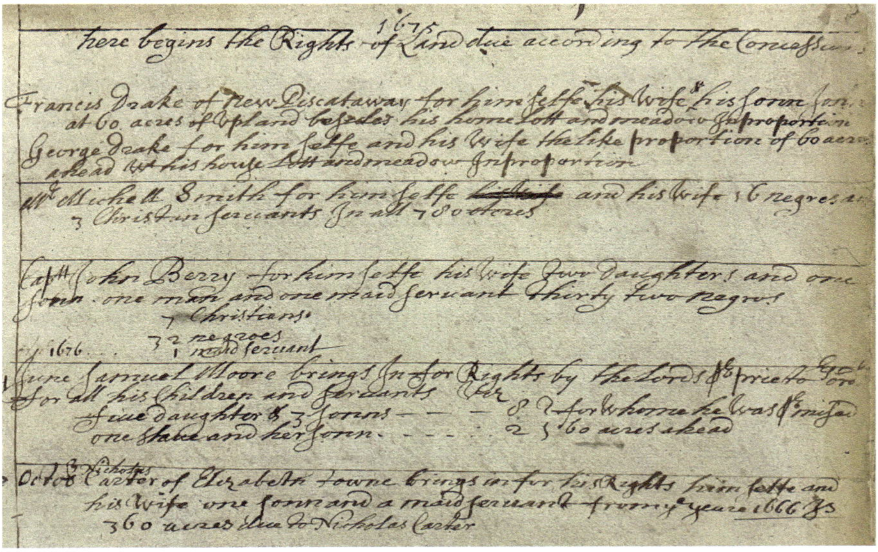
1675
here begins the Rights of Land due according to the Concessions
Francis Drake of New Piscataway for him selfe his wife & his sonn [illegible] at 60 acres of upland besides his home lott and meadow in proportion
George drake for him selfe and his wife the like proportion of 60 acres a head with his house lott and meadow in proportion
Mr Michell Smith for him selfe [illegible] and his wife 16 negres and 3 Christian servants in all [illegible]
Captt John Berry for him selfe his wife four daughters and one sonn one man and one maid servant thirty two negros
7 Christians
1676 32 negroes
1 maid servant
[illegible] Samuel Moore brings in for Rights by the Lords [illegible] for all his Children and servants [illegible]
five daughters & 3 sonns
one slave and her sonn [illegible] 60 acres a head
Octob Nicholas Carter of Elizabeth towne brings in for his Rights him selfe and his wife one sonn and a maid servant from ye yeare 1666 [illegible]
360 acres due to Nicholas Carter

Figure 6. Headright land claims, including Michell Smith for "16 negres and 3 Christian servants," John Berry for "7 Christians, 32 negroes, and 1 maid servant," and Samuel Moore for "one slave and her sonn." New Jersey State Archives.

mill or in "husbandry" on his plantation in Monmouth County, not including his unnumbered "servants and dependents." Nicolls recorded that John Berry had "20 Negros or more" on his 2,000-acre estate along the Hackensack River, while Michell Smith had "improved a good quantity" of his adjoining 1,500-to-2,000-acre plantation with the labor of "16 or more *Negros*." Mr. Baker, also from Barbados, had seven or eight enslaved people working his nearby estate. However, Nicolls did not document any small slaveholding among residents of the various towns.[5]

Under the new set of general laws enacted in 1682 after the formation of East Jersey, all slaveowners were required to provide "sufficient accommodation of victuals and cloathing." The following year merchants and major landowners asserted their dominance by pushing through "An Act against Trading with Negro Slaves," modeled on New York legislation, that aimed to prohibit small-scale trading by "negro and Indian slaves, or servants," on the basis that what they traded in return for "rum, brandy, wine or strong drink, or any other goods, wares or commodities" had presumably been stolen from their "masters."[6] A revenue act passed in 1699, but not implemented, provides insights into the value of enslaved people in East Jersey compared to other forms of "property" such as land or livestock. For the purposes of the tax, "all negroes, or other slaves, above sixteen years old" were valued at twenty-five pounds per head, enslaved persons between eight and sixteen years old at fifteen pounds per head (equal to one hundred acres of improved land) and between five and eight years old at eight pounds per head (compared, for example, to £7.10s per hundred acres of unimproved land, £3.10s for a four-year old oxen or three pounds for a three-year-old horse or mare).[7]

Newarkers and Slavery

The settlement of Newark did not depend on slavery. Communal decision-making and large families were far more important to how Newarkers organized their township and developed their farms. They were generally yeoman farmers who worked their land without enslaved labor, especially in the proprietary period. Newark's method of gradually distributing land in successive, relatively small divisions, rather than at one time in larger headright allocations, discouraged the early use of enslaved or indentured labor by allowing men and their sons to clear land over several years. However, the first settlers did not oppose slavery; it is more likely that few in the early years could afford to purchase slaves. To the extent slavery existed in Newark in early decades, it was a form of personal slavery: a single Black or Native American man or woman, a couple, or a small family.[8]

Some settlers of Newark had servants from the beginning, but how many or whether the servants were indentured or enslaved is not clear. When the Newark town meeting agreed in 1667 on a method of proportional taxation for determining "every Man's Share of the Purchase," it included an assessment of ten pounds for "every Child or Servant in the Family." Ten years later, in 1677, the town meeting voted to hire a schoolmaster "to teach the Children or servants of those as have subscribed, the reading and writing of English, and also Arithmetick if they desire it." "Servant" was an ambiguous term; it had not yet been racialized, so it could mean either an enslaved person or an indentured servant. As noted earlier, Samuel Moore of Woodbridge used "servants" to describe his "one slave and her sonn" when he put in his headright claim for land. In subsequent years, as enslavement was normalized, it became more common to apply the term "negro" as a descriptor before either "servant" or "slave."[9]

Following the example set by his peers in New Haven Colony, Abraham Pierson Sr. of Newark most likely owned an enslaved person. Pierson's "great friend and trusted ally," fellow New Haven Colony minister John Davenport, contracted for indentured servants and purchased enslaved labor. When Davenport died in 1670, the inventory of his estate included a servant valued at ten pounds. Others in New Haven Colony, including Theophilus Eaton, the first governor of the colony, whom Pierson lauded in a long funeral verse and for whom he named one of his sons, owned slaves. New Englanders took guidance about buying and possessing Native Americans and Africans, as for so many other aspects of their daily life, from scripture. They looked to Leviticus 25: 44–46 in their Geneva Bibles to sanction chattel slavery—permanent, commodified, and inheritable bondage of "heathen that are round about you" and "strangers that are sojourners among you."[10]

Pierson was one of the wealthiest men in Newark, befitting his status as minister, and had the most need for supplemental labor since he spent much of his time preparing sermons and weekly lectures. In addition to his four daughters and oldest son Abraham, who assisted him in ministry, Pierson had three other sons: Thomas, who signed Newark's fundamental agreements and received his own home lot and distributions of meadows and uplands, and Theophilus and Isaac, both still boys when Newark was settled. When Pierson prepared his will in 1671 during one of his illnesses, he did not note any enslaved persons. He focused instead on making provisions for his wife and children and for the distribution of his most prized possessions, his books. He also noted in his will that he had given horses to both Abraham and Thomas as they were setting up their own households, suggesting that Pierson continued to augment his salary as minister by breeding horses for export to Barbados, as he had done in Branford before moving to Newark.[11]

Following Pierson's death in 1678, John Ward, Micah Tompkins, and his son Thomas Pierson prepared an inventory of his possessions—including his home lot, upland and meadow acreage, and loans he had made to others—so his estate could be settled according to the terms of his will. It was a substantial estate, appraised at over £854 and several times the size of the estates of most early Newarkers. The third largest item in Pierson's estate inventory, larger even than the value of his library of 443 books, was "all the Neat Cattle and Horse kinde, with one Servant: £117.15s.0d." Since the "one Servant" was listed as chattel property on the same line with livestock, the reference is most likely to an enslaved person rather than to the remaining time on a contract for an indentured servant. It is not known whether this servant was Native American or Black, male or female, or whether the person worked with Pierson's cattle and horses or in his home. Nor is it known what value the appraisers assigned to the servant, but even if it was two or three times the ten-pound value placed on John Davenport's servant eight years earlier, it is apparent that Pierson owned dozens of cattle and horses to merit an appraisal of more than £117. The primary market for cattle and horses in this period was Barbados, which depended on New England for livestock and grains so plantation owners could focus on sugar production. Thus, even if Pierson's servant was not enslaved, his wealth stemmed not just from land and his salary but also from his engagement with the West Indies trade. As historian Wendy Warren observed, "profit and piety worked hand in hand" in these years.[12]

Merchants in New England and New Jersey followed the lead of West Indies planters in owning enslaved people, but members of the clergy, often wealthy and always with high status, were not far behind. Abraham Pierson Jr., who assisted and then succeeded his father as minister in Newark, was likely a slaveowner, although documentary evidence has not survived. His colleague, Seth Fletcher, the minister of Elizabethtown's church, owned a "nirger boy" at the time of his death in 1682. John Harriman, who was born in New Haven, graduated from Harvard the year before Abraham Pierson Jr., and served the church in Elizabethtown from 1687 until his death in 1705, was also a slaveowner. In his account book, Harriman recorded the purchase of "the Negro Toney" in 1697, perhaps to work in his cider mill, and the purchase of "an indian girle named Hagar" in 1701. Samuel Melyn, son of the merchant Jacob Melyn, was hired by the Elizabethtown church in 1704 to assist Harriman. At his death in 1711, he owned "1 Negro Woman." Theophilus Pierson, the younger brother of Abraham Pierson Jr., remained in Newark and served the community as justice of the peace and on errands to Connecticut to recruit ministers for Newark's church. He did not list enslaved people in his will, and the estate inventory following his death in 1713 is not extant, but it is noteworthy that his son David directed that his "negro boy Titus" be sold to offset his debts when he prepared his will two decades later.[13]

1726 Census

At the request of the Lords of Trade, governor William Burnet organized a census in 1726 of the inhabitants of New Jersey, distinguished by their age, gender, and color. Sheriffs in each county tallied the returns provided by local constables for the number of males and females above and under the age of sixteen, with separate counts for "whites" and "negroes." The census showed a total population in New Jersey of 32,442, with 29,861 whites (92 percent) and 2,581 Blacks (8 percent). The count for Essex County, comprising Acquackanonk, Elizabethtown, and Newark (New Barbadoes had been transferred to Bergen County in 1710), was 4,230. The number of white males and white females, regardless of age, was roughly equal in Essex County, reflecting the family settlement patterns that characterized townships settled by New Englanders. Indeed, Essex County was the only county in New Jersey in this census with more white women (1,021) than white men (992) above the age of sixteen. Blacks represented 7.3 percent of Essex County's population, less than half the percentage for Somerset (16.7 percent) and Bergen (18.4 percent) counties, but higher than the percentages for counties in West Jersey. There were more Black males above the age of sixteen (ninety-two) than Black females (seventy-eight) in Essex County, but children were evenly split (seventy boys and sixty-eight girls)—suggesting that enslavement had been in place in Essex County long enough for normal distribution by gender to occur.[14]

The substantial growth in East Jersey's enslaved population recorded in the 1726 census likely started in the 1690s, toward the end of the proprietary period. In response, the East Jersey Assembly passed "An Act concerning Slaves" in 1694, with provisions circumscribing the ability of enslaved people to visit each other or to supplement their diets with hunting and keeping swine. Enslavement spread further early in the eighteenth century as a greater number of ordinary colonists, not just prominent landowners, merchants, or clergymen, owned at least one slave. In 1713, the Newark town meeting included an assessment for "all Male White Persons at Sixteen Years old and upwards" in determining that year's town tax rate, on top of traditional assessments for each acre of land and each head of livestock. While enslaved Blacks were not included in the assessment, the fact that the town records explicitly refer to "male White Persons" suggests that the enslaved Black male population in Newark had grown to the point where town leaders thought it important to distinguish between the two groups.[15]

The 1726 census counted 308 enslaved adults and children in Essex County, but it did not provide separate counts for Acquackanonk, Elizabethtown, and Newark, the three townships that then formed Essex County. There were perhaps a larger number of enslaved people in more prosperous Elizabethtown and Dutch-settled Acquackanonk, but even after making an allowance, there were likely several dozen enslaved people in Newark early in the eighteenth century. Traces of these enslaved people are difficult to find, however. Wills from the period rarely mention enslaved people, sweeping any enslaved person or indentured servant with an unexpired term within the general rubric of "personal property." Estate inventories are the best source, since enslaved people were commodified and assigned a specific value, along with livestock, farm implements, and household goods, even if they were then grouped in a general category, as in the case of Abraham Pierson Sr.'s estate inventory, rather than listed separately. In assessing the value of an enslaved person, appraisers considered the value of the person's current and prospective labor, offset by the cost of housing, clothing, and feeding the person, as embedded in the current market price for a slave with similar characteristics. However, relatively few estate inventories from Essex County have survived—only about two dozen from before 1730 are in the New Jersey State Archives.

If surviving records are representative of the larger number of estate inventories that were never filed or later lost, Elizabethtown residents owned more enslaved people than Newarkers. Nicholas Tuttle of Elizabethtown owned three enslaved people at the time of his death in 1696, a "negro woman slave" and presumably her two children, a "negro boy" and a "negro girl," together making up more than a third of his total estate. Richard Clarke owned a "negro woman and child" in 1697, while Samuel Clarke, perhaps his son, owned "one Negro Boy" at the time of his death in 1716. William Robertson, "doctor of Physick," owned a "negro woman" in 1698 as well as 1,290 acres of land. Several Elizabethtown residents owned "one Negro Boy": Charles Allen in 1717, Cornelius Hatfield in 1718, Cornelius Bryant in 1720 (also noted in his will), and Caleb Halsted in 1722, while Samuel Scot owned "a mulatto boy" at the time of his death in 1723. John Levy's estate included "a Negro wench" when it was appraised in early 1723. Christopher Rousby was the owner of both "an old negro man" and a "young negro woman," who was considered five times more valuable. Enslaved people were rarely able to live together as a family; one exception might have been the "negro man[,] Indian Woman[,] and C[hil]d" who together were valued at fifty pounds, nearly a quarter of Joseph Plassy's Elizabethtown estate when it was appraised in 1725; however, there is no record of whether they were able to remain together after Plassy's estate was settled.[16]

With increased prosperity, slave ownership became more common in Newark in the early eighteenth century. At least three original settlers, John Curtis, Azariah Crane, and Joanna Swaine Crane, all young when Newark was founded, were slaveowners decades later. Curtis, a prominent leader of Newark toward the end of the proprietary period, left all his "moveable Estate" to his wife Hannah in 1704. His estate inventory included "one Negro man" valued at thirty pounds. Azariah Crane was the youngest settler to sign the fundamental agreements in 1667, and he may have been the last surviving original signer when he died in 1730. The son of magistrate Jasper Crane Sr., he served Newark in various roles, including deputy to the general assembly in 1694 and 1695 and church deacon for three decades. When he wrote his will in 1722, he left "my negro man James, together with my carts, plow, barrow, and other of my tools" to his youngest son John, along with various tracts of land, including part of his Newark home lot. Joanna Swaine, a teenager of fourteen or fifteen when Newark was first settled, married Jasper Crane Jr., Azariah's younger brother. The two brothers together developed land at Newark Mountain that came to be known as Cranetown, today's Montclair. After Joanna's death in late 1720 or early 1721, the inventory of her estate totaled more than £116. It is very detailed (e.g., seven glasses, 2s.; a warming pan, 7s.6d; a set of blue curtains, £1.6s; six neat cattle, £11.11s.6d; three old horses, £4.10s, etc.), but her most valuable property were three enslaved persons: "one Negro Called Andrew" (twenty-five pounds), "one Negro Woman Called Yanitie" (thirty-five pounds), and "a Negro boy Called Jemine" (fourteen pounds).[17]

Historian Wendy Warren pointed out that in this period "enslaved people did not do different work than their English counterparts," because specialized cash crops like sugar or tobacco never developed in places like Newark. She added, "Laborers were differentiated by race, even while their labor was not." In Newark's yeoman families, no one was free from household work or from the labor of clearing and planting fields and harvesting crops, or from caring for livestock, unless they were too young or too old and infirm. But racial distinctions were stark. Newarkers had large extended families, made even larger through marriage connections—so extensive that by the mid-eighteenth century the minister of the Newark Mountain church referred to them as tribes ("the tribes of Baldwin," "tribes of Harrison," etc.). In contrast, enslaved people were isolated, albeit enmeshed in the daily life of their owners, prevented from spending time with relations or other enslaved people without permission, and rarely able to sustain stable family relationships. Their owners assigned them single names, never surnames. They were completely cut off from ancestors and kin in Africa. Where settler families in Newark were patriarchal, with the distribution of inheritable estates furthering goals of family stability and perpetuity, families of enslaved people, to the extent they existed, were matrilineal since enslaved status was passed from mother to child, even if the man who fathered the child was white. Family relationships among the enslaved were also precarious; they could be broken up at any time if owners decided, for whatever reason, to sell what they considered their chattel property.[18]

Indentured servants were also commodified and had little say in the conditions of their employment. They were as enmeshed in the daily life of their owners as enslaved persons, and often as isolated and separated from kin. As noted in chapter 13, people like the Scottish Covenanter Peter Russell were banished from their native land against their will. As a prisoner, Russell endured a long, star-crossed transatlantic passage during which many died. He expected to be sold into indentured servitude when he arrived in East Jersey and thought he would never see his family again. When he had his first opportunity to write to his family in Scotland after finding himself in Newark, his five-times repeated "I know not" in the first sentence of his letter reflected strong emotions of desperation tempered with resilience that others, enslaved or indentured, no doubt felt in similar situations: "My Dear & Loving parents what shall I wryt unto you or what shall I say I know not I know not I know not I know not I know not if ye be in tyme ore in eternitie but I must wryt to you as Alive." But the loss of freedom for indentured servants was temporary, from four to seven years, even if their owners could assign their contracts to another owner in the meanwhile without their say. Unlike enslaved people, they did not face permanent slavery, and their servitude was not passed on to their children. At the end of their term, servants might gain a small landholding to farm for themselves. They had two names given by their family, not one assigned by the owner, and most spoke English as their first language. Those who could read and write could hope that letters might reach their families. Most importantly, their status was not racialized, so if they ran away, as some did, they could hope to blend more easily into a different setting.[19]

Slave owning continued in Newark throughout the eighteenth century and into the nineteenth century, while indentured servitude diminished. Clergymen like Aaron Burr Sr., Isaac Browne, and Alexander MacWhorter owned enslaved people, as did lawyer David Ogden and medical doctor William Burnet. At the time of the American Revolution, when Newarkers were split into Presbyterian and Anglican and bitterly divided between patriot and loyalist, they agreed on at least one thing: owning slaves.

PART II

Contending with Proprietary Government

CHAPTER 6

Seeds of Conflict

New Jersey's early history is chaotic and confusing, with frequent changes in proprietors and a brief period of reconquest by the Dutch. In just one thirty-month period in the decade after New Jersey was formed, the structure of government changed four times. Philip Carteret, New Jersey's first governor, was dealt a difficult hand from the beginning. His authority derived from the proprietors who appointed him to his position, not directly from royal power as in New York or by annual election as in New England. As the proprietors' influence at the royal court varied, so did Carteret's ability to impose his authority on townships and in negotiations with New York. Despite the enormous challenges he faced in developing his administration in New Jersey, Carteret did not look to share power with Newark leaders. He included leaders on his council from Elizabethtown and Woodbridge, also settled by New Englanders, but he never named Robert Treat or another Newark leader to his inner circle. He issued charters to Bergen and Woodbridge, but not to Newark, or Elizabethtown, for that matter. As a result, Newarkers were on the outside and often in opposition.

Newarkers' relationship with Carteret became increasingly fraught as they sought to protect their godly self-government and he worked to consolidate his authority. By 1669, Newarkers grew suspicious as privileges they had negotiated and recorded in their articles—distributing land within the Newark tract in the New England manner and reserving common land, holding town courts, leading and training their militia, paying quitrents as a town rather than as individuals, and apparently a promise that they could acquire land on the eastern side of the Passaic River—were chipped away or ignored by Carteret. At the same time, Carteret brushed aside the power provided to the general assembly in the proprietors' concessions "to appoint their own time of meeting and to adjourn their sessions from time to time to such times and places as thy shall think convenient." Both Newark's articles and Carteret's memorandum book for the period before 1675 are not extant, so it is now possible only to suggest how the seeds of conflict between Carteret and Newarkers were sown. But sown they were, and Newarkers proved ready to participate actively in the Rebellion of 1672.

When Governor Carteret arrived in late July 1665, he received a guarded reception from governor Richard Nicolls of New York, who had been neither consulted nor informed in advance by the Duke of York about the decision to carve the province of New Jersey out of New York and award a patent to two proprietors. Over the next year, Carteret's position grew tenuous as reports circulated that Sir George Carteret, one of the proprietors, was "out of office and in disgrace at Court" and that the proprietors' patent was broken. Carteret sent Robert Vauquellin, his surveyor general, to London in August 1666 to consult with the proprietors, since he was "all att a stand and Cannot proceed farther tell Wee . . . knowe In What Condition Wee are in here."[1]

More than a year later, Carteret finally received the confirmation he wanted, likely delivered by Vauquellin on his return. Micah Tompkins of Newark relayed the news to John Davenport Jr., who in turn informed Connecticut governor John Winthrop Jr: "[Tompkins] speaks of a ship lately come from England to Capt. Carterett, which it's said reports that he is confirmed to be their Governor and that the Duke hath sold his interest to the Lords for 10 shillings, that Straton [Staten] Island is to be under him, also that one Mr. Lovelas is expected every day to be Governor at Yorke, etc. When he comes Coll. Nichols is to return to England with his guard." This was very positive news for Carteret, and he moved confidently over the next eighteen months to consolidate his power, call the first meeting of the general assembly, and make large land grants to both his key supporters and newly arrived men from Barbados. He also developed a closer relationship with New York governor Francis Lovelace than he had before with Nicolls, although Lovelace stymied his efforts to secure Staten Island.[2]

Carteret expanded his council early in January 1668 to include his deputy secretary William Pardon, Daniel Pierce of Woodbridge, Robert Bond of Elizabethtown, and Samuel Edsall of Bergen (part of today's Jersey City). They joined Nicolas Verlett of Bergen and Robert Vauquellin; provincial secretary James Bollen was an ex officio member. A New Englander, Pierce soon fell out of favor, as John Ogden of Elizabethtown had before him, but Carteret quickly found that John Pike and Samuel Moore from Woodbridge would work with him. He showered favors on supporters, rewarding the Woodbridge men with a town charter and granting large estates to Verlett and Edsall with reduced or waived quitrent. Nobody from Newark was named, but Newarkers likely felt they could gain insights from Robert Bond, an original associate of Elizabethtown who knew Abraham Pierson from the settlement of Southampton in the early 1640s and whose son was one of the original settlers in Newark. Middletown and Shrewsbury were still claiming rights of self-government under their land grants from Richard Nicolls and did not wish to participate in provincial matters.[3]

In October 1667, Carteret sent Robert Treat a commission to serve as justice of the peace for Newark; Treat returned it, thereby voiding it. He likely declined the commission because Carteret had not followed Newark's articles and asked the town to nominate men for his consideration. He may also have been concerned that the concessions reserved responsibility for constituting courts and determining the powers of court officers to the general assembly through legislation, not by executive action of the governor. In May 1668, however, following nomination by the freeholders of Newark, Treat and Jasper Crane accepted Carteret's appointment to serve as justices of the peace. They were given "full power and Authority to Execute such Lawes as are or shall be made for the good Government of your said towne and province" as well as the task of administering oaths of allegiance to the king and fidelity to the proprietors.[4]

Newarkers put their town court system in place in January 1669, choosing Treat and Crane as the town's magistrates. The town meeting agreed there would be "two Courts in our Town Yearly, to hear and try all Causes and actions that shall be necessary and desired within our Compass and according to Our Articles," one taking place on the last Wednesday in February and the other on the second Wednesday in September. The magistrates presided over the courts, with juries of six men. Evidently, there was a temporary accommodation between Carteret and Newarkers that allowed each to consider that their authority was respected; Carteret wanted his justices of the peace to preside over courts, while Newarkers wanted their magistrates to perform that role. Since Treat and Crane were both justices of the peace and Newark magistrates, the town courts could take place—at least until the end of 1669, when the conflict between Carteret and Newarkers reached the point that Carteret recalled the commissions of both Treat and Crane.[5]

In the nineteen-month period between the appointment of Treat and Crane as justices of the peace and their recall, the relationship between Carteret and Newark leaders soured. Various factors contributed to the growing lack of trust: the deteriorating relationship between Carteret and the general assembly, Carteret's decision to grant a large tract of land to William Sandford on the other side of the Passaic River that Newarkers thought had been reserved for them, and his interventions in Woodbridge after granting the town a charter. Fresh rumors that New Jersey would be returned to New York also unsettled relations and weakened Carteret.

General Assembly

In April 1668, Carteret issued a writ of election for the first meeting of the general assembly. Each town was instructed to "make Choice and appoint two able men that are freeholders and dwellers within the said limits to be your Burgesses and Representitives for you." Newarkers selected Robert Treat and Samuel Swaine as their representatives. In summoning the general assembly, Carteret reflected on the progress that had been made in settling the province: "Whereas by the Infinite Goodnes[,] providence and blessing of the Almighty God[,] this Province of New Jersey is in a provable way of being populated[,] there being a Considerable number of families alredy settled in severall parts of the same and many more that in a short tyme are to Come and place themselves under this Government[,] for the better propagating and Incouragement thereof I have thought fit with the advice of my Councell to appoint a Generall assembly."[6]

The proprietors' concessions provided the general assembly with unusual powers, including the right to appoint their own time of meeting and adjournments and to enact all laws and acts "for the well government" of the province, with the condition that their laws allow liberty of conscience and not go against the interest of the proprietors, who would have a year to ratify or reject laws. The assembly, on paper, was also responsible for constituting courts and local militias, building forts and fortresses, and accepting strangers as "naturalized" subjects to reside in the province, although in practice Governor Carteret had already assumed these powers in a limited way before the assembly met. Finally, the assembly was responsible for laying "equal taxes and assessments" for the "publick charge of the . . . Government, and for the mutual safety, defence and security of the . . . Province."[7]

The general assembly convened in Elizabethtown on Monday, May 25, for a week-long session. Meeting separately from the governor and council, the assembly accomplished a great deal, including laws to punish any person who resisted the authority of the governor or other government officials, require all men between the ages of sixteen and sixty to furnish themselves with "good and sufficient arms" (a gun, powder, bullets, a pair of bandoliers or horn, and a sword and belt), and levy a five-pound tax on each town (for a total of thirty pounds) for the support of the government. The assembly instructed towns to deliver the levies to Jacob Melyn of Elizabethtown, who was instructed to disburse twenty pounds to James Bollen to defray the cost of Carteret's government, "and the rest as he [Melyn] shall have order to improve for our use." With this guidance, the assembly acted to retain control over both how taxes were raised and how they were spent.

Treat, Swaine, and other New Englanders who made up a majority of the assembly also put in place a body of laws based on scriptural authority. As historian Edgar McManus suggested, relying on scripture for guidance allowed New Englanders to break with English institutions and "the historical freight of the common law," and develop "a more dynamic and progressive body of American law." For example, in England, fornication, incest, and adultery had been dealt with in ecclesiastical courts, but New Englanders moved the cases to secular courts, complemented by church discipline. Burglary could be punishable by death under English law for a first offense, but New Englanders required a third offense before it could be punished as a capital crime because scripture did not call for the death penalty.[8]

The first assembly enacted eight laws for offenses where the penalty was death: murder, false witness, buggery, sodomy, kidnapping, witchcraft, seditious conspiracy, and smiting or cursing natural parents when over the age of sixteen (with limited exceptions). The assembly also provided that the death penalty could be applied for burning houses and other structures (at the discretion of the court if the perpetrator was unable to make satisfaction for the losses while held in prison without bail); burglary (on the third offense, as incorrigible, after having been branded and forced to make restitution for the first two offenses); and rape (at the discretion of the court). Adultery was not a capital offense—unlike in New England but like the Duke's Laws in New York. The first New Jersey assembly thus enacted eleven capital laws; Massachusetts had twenty-two capital laws in its code (1660), Connecticut had seventeen (1650), and New Haven Colony had had twenty-three (1656). The Duke's Laws also had only eleven capital offenses (or twelve depending on the version), although the language varies, and not all offenses are the same. The New Jersey assembly also set a high standard for imposing the death penalty: It could only be applied to "some Law established in this Province," and then only on testimony of at least "two or three" witnesses. Fifteen years later, a new "East Jersey Quaker" code was set forth during Thomas Rudyard's time as governor. This new code recognized only three capital offenses: murder, bestiality, and false witness in capital cases.[9]

Treat and Swaine were likely satisfied with the first meeting of New Jersey's general assembly. The assembly had followed the provisions of the proprietors' concessions by setting the date for their next meeting, and for annual meetings thereafter, as well as procedures for each town to elect its representatives yearly. At this point, they probably felt their relationship with Governor Carteret was on a reasonable footing.[10]

In September 1668, as the time approached for the second meeting of the general assembly, illness swept through the province. Abraham Pierson reported to John Winthrop Jr. that many in Newark "had, and sundry yet have the Ague generally with moderation." He noted that it was worse in New York, where "there is a sore disease, and mortality . . . its sayd to be the bloody flux," adding that "our governor [Carteret] is sick of it, but hopefull to recover." Carteret's illness then took a turn for the worse. Pierson wrote, "This letter lying by mee for the want of an opportunity [to post it] we heare this morning that the governour is like to dy in as much as a strong feaver comes upon him, and that he swells al over." Carteret apparently had a strong constitution, because he was fully recovered when the general assembly convened for a second time on November 3.[11]

Jasper Crane accompanied Robert Treat for this second session, replacing Samuel Swaine in representing Newark. They joined deputies from three other towns and the Delaware River settlements; deputies for Middletown and Shrewsbury were dismissed when they refused to take or subscribe to the oaths of allegiance and fidelity or to submit to the provincial laws. In this session, the assembly passed laws related to militia training, branding of horses and cattle, establishment of taverns in each town, weights and measures, and "the buying of swine or any cattle from the Indians." They also formed a four-person committee, including Robert Treat, to address issues related to "horses or cattle that may range up into the country, to the indangering the peace in respect to Indians." The chief point of contention between the assembly and the governor and council during this session was whether they should sit together as one body or separately as a lower and upper house. The governor and council advocated the latter, since that would allow them to decide whether they would assent to what the lower house enacted. Since the concessions were not clear on this point, each side claimed it was acting as the proprietors intended. By the end of the week, the assembly grew so frustrated about meeting separately and the resulting "exceeding dilatory" pace of work that they sent a message to the governor and Council and then adjourned: "Honoured Gentlemen, We finding so many and great inconveniences by our not setting together, and your apprehensions so different to ours, and your expectations that things must go according to your opinions, though we see no reason for, much less warrant from the concessions, wherefore we think it is vain to spend so much time of returning answers by writings that are so exceeding dilatory, if not fruitless and endless, and therefore we think our way rather to break up their meeting, seeing the order of the concessions cannot be attended unto." Treat and Crane no doubt shared in this frustration—a wedge was opening between them and Carteret.[12]

Barbadoes Neck

In July 1668, Governor Carteret conveyed a tract of land on the other side of the Passaic River from Newark to William Sandford of Barbados. It was a large tract, encompassing all the land between the Hackensack and Passaic Rivers, beginning at the tip in Newark Bay and extending north about seven miles, more than 15,300 acres that today comprise the towns of Harrison, East Newark, Kearny, and Lyndhurst. It was by far the largest land grant to an individual to that point, far larger than could be justified under the concessions' headright system, and the first grant to a planter from Barbados. And, momentously, it was the same tract Carteret had offered to a group of settlers from New Haven Colony two years earlier and that certain Newark settlers, apparently including Abraham Pierson, believed was still promised to them. For years, Newarkers fought an unsuccessful battle to regain the tract for their own use, eventually sustaining crippling financial losses and major political setbacks as a result.[13]

The proprietors likely instructed Carteret in late 1667 to identify a suitable tract for Sandford, the nephew of Nathaniel Kingsland, a wealthy plantation owner in Barbados known to the proprietors through West Indies correspondence and the Royal African Company's slave trade. A few years earlier, Kingsland had arranged for Sandford to manage a large plantation and its enslaved workforce in Suriname, but the Treaty of Breda returned Suriname to Dutch control in 1667, following the end of the Second Anglo-Dutch Trade War. Kingsland lost the estate (which he valued at £10,000), and Sandford was forced to leave. Setting up Sandford in New Jersey as a consolation would not have taxed either Kingsland's financial resources or his personal influence with the proprietors.[14]

Vauquellin clearly had Sandford in mind when he surveyed the land, in what was likely one of his first tasks after returning from London. He described the northern boundary as "a great spring Called by the name of Sandfords Spring," and the tract was christened "New Barbadoes" in the grant signed by Carteret and several members of his council. Sandford gained 5,308 acres of upland and another 10,000 acres of salt meadow, subject to a reduced annual twenty-pound quitrent. Carteret then helped Sandford acquire Indigenous title to the tract, "called in the

Indian Language Meghgectecock," from the Hackensack. Sandford paid compensation in wampum, goods, alcohol, and weapons and ammunition in a total value similar to but perhaps somewhat less than what Newarkers paid for their tract.[15]

Three years later, in an unusual and unprecedented transaction, Kingsland acquired title to the New Barbadoes tract directly from the proprietors for a payment of £200 and an annual rent of one Indian arrow to be paid each Christmas—even though Carteret had already granted Sandford and his associates free and common socage to the tract. As a result, the annual twenty-pound quitrent was extinguished. Two months later, Kingsland sold the southern third of the tract to Sandford for £200. Through these sharp transactions, Kingsland gained direct title to the land and was relieved of the quitrent with a net outlay of only the cost of his legal fees in London and Barbados. A question remains about what favors or loans he may have provided to the proprietors to merit such favorable terms. Governor Carteret and his council were not parties to these transactions. Secretary James Bollen appears to have first learned about them in May 1673, when he entered them in the province's deed book, and he took care to confirm the second transaction between Kingsland and Sandford with two men who had witnessed the deed in Barbados.[16]

John Berry, another Barbados planter, soon followed Sandford to New Jersey, acquiring large tracts of land to the north of New Barbadoes in June 1669. Berry was immensely wealthy compared to other settlers in New Jersey, but not by the standards of the hugely profitable, but savagely brutal sugar economy in Barbados. Smaller landowners had been squeezed out by larger, more profitable planters in Barbados, where a big planter owned at least sixty slaves, while a "great planter" (presumably including Nicholas Kingsland) possessed, on average, 115 slaves; Berry owned thirty-two slaves.[17] Carteret appointed both William Sandford and John Berry to his council in August 1669; neither man had any experience with or indeed sympathy for the New England township form of government, but they would both play significant oversight roles in Newark over the next several years, no doubt to the frustration of Newarkers. They were likely also well positioned to join Philip Carteret in the middle of the profitable trade that New Jersey and New York developed with Barbados: beef, pork, peas, flour, butter, and horses to Barbados with strong liquors, sugar, cotton, molasses, and ginger in return.[18]

In this same period, Carteret had to deal with fresh reports that raised new questions about the durability and legitimacy of the proprietors' hold on New Jersey—and thus his authority as governor. In February 1669 Samuel Maverick, one of the royal commissioners for New England, relayed to John Winthrop Jr. a summary of guidance sent to Governor Lovelace of New York: "Staten Iland is adiudged to belong to N: Yorke. The L. Barkley is under a cloud, and out of all his offices, and offers to surrender up the Patent for N. Jarsey. Sir. G: Carterett, his partner, is in Ireland, but it is thought he will likewise surrender, and then N. Yorke will be inlarged." In June, Maverick passed along news to Winthrop that Sir George Carteret had informed Governor Philip Carteret that "New Jarsey is returned to his Royall Highnes [the Duke of York], by exchange for Delawar." In broad outline, the plan was for New York to absorb what later became East Jersey, while the proprietors would retain what later became West Jersey, plus some land on the far side of Delaware Bay taken from Lord Baltimore's propriety. More specifically, as made clear in the draft agreement sent to Philip Carteret, New York would gain "all the lands on the West side of Hudsons River . . . till It Comes Within 40 miles of Delaware Bay River . . . With all the Townes now settled and planted namely the Corporation of Bergen New Barbados Newark Elizabethtowne Woodbridge, Shrewsbury, Midleton, and New Piscataway." Philip Carteret was directed to stay in New Jersey longer "to put the affairs in order."[19]

Woodbridge

In response to the prospect of changing boundaries for New Jersey, Philip Carteret rushed to reward members of his council with more favors. He made new land grants of 2,000 acres each to James Bollen and Robert Vauquellin, and a smaller grant to William Pardon during the summer (each with reduced quitrent payments), along with a large grant to himself.[20] He also issued a charter to the town of Woodbridge confirming their "immunities and privileges," to ensure their acquiescence with his authority. Settlers in Woodbridge were New Englanders from Newbury, Massachusetts, but they were less cohesive and more moderate in their view of royal authority than most others in early Massachusetts.[21] They proved unwilling to follow the lead of Daniel Pierce, the founder of Woodbridge, whom Carteret dismissed from his council and later worked to isolate from his fellow townsmen. They also rapidly distributed land in a process starkly different than Newark's methodical and sequential divisions of land carried out over years.[22]

In 1669, Woodbridge residents decided to seek immediate allocations of large parcels of upland and meadow "by the Concessions"—that is, the headright system set up by the proprietors. On August 20, four days after they "thankfully" accepted "the Charter Now obtained" from Governor Carteret, the town voted "that the Rule for the Inhabitants to take up their proportions of Land Should Be Exactly According to the Rule of the Concessions." A land grab was soon underway. The town permitted inhabitants "to Look out . . . parcels of Land that may Be Most Suteable for their accomodations . . . and when By them pitch't upon to Inform the Town . . . for their consideration and approbation." In this way, men in Woodbridge gained larger landholdings more quickly than they would have under a normal New England township model—on average, about sixty acres more per man than Newark residents.[23]

Carteret took advantage of this hunger for land to impose his authority. The Woodbridge town charter required every man to hold "his Land by pattent from the Lords proprietors," record his holdings in both the provincial and town books, and pay the halfpenny per acre quitrent each year beginning in 1670. Once the charter was confirmed, Woodbridge land grants were recorded as made "by virtue of the Governors Warrant," not as a grant by the town. Over the next year, Carteret took a hard line against "nonconformists" (his term) like Daniel Pierce, who were slow to patent tracts, threatening forfeiture of their lands. In April 1670, he wrote Vauquellin, who lived in Woodbridge and laid out the town, that if Daniel Pierce "will Not patten that land that is aloted for him, you may ley it amongst the Rest to those that will." And when Carteret learned that "some particular persons" not only refused "to hold their Lands Surveyed and patented According to the Articles made and the Charter granted" but instead obstructed Vauquellin in laying out meadow lots for others, he instructed Vauquellin to consider them as "non Inhabitants" and deprive them of "any Right or title to any Meadow or Land" in Woodbridge—in effect, stripping the nonconformists of any benefit from their investment in the purchase of the Woodbridge tract. He also refused to provide a receipt to nonconformists for paying their quitrents, although he held on to their payments. Finally, in October 1670, outraged that several men who refused to patent their lands continued "to have their Voices in the Towne Meetings," Carteret declared that "from this Day forward" they were stripped of their rights as freeholders "and by Consiquence are Not to have any office whatsoever: Nor to have any Vote or Voice in your Towne Meetings upon any publick Business whatsoever." He authorized the town to seize their landholdings and dispose of them "to any other persons that will Be obedient and Submit themselves to the Laws and Government of the province."[24]

Carteret's threats and warnings had their intended effect on the people of Woodbridge. By the end of 1670, forty-five men had patented their lands, while no resident of Newark or Elizabethtown had taken out patents. But Carteret's assertion of his authority to bypass the town meeting in determining who would enjoy both property (inhabitant) and political (freeholder) rights within the town boundaries no doubt caused alarm among Newarkers, who considered those essential responsibilities for any township organized on the New England model. They likely received regular firsthand reports of developments in Woodbridge from Samuel Treat, Robert Treat's son and a recent Harvard graduate, who was hired by Woodbridge to preach and serve as their minister for several months during this period.[25]

Newark Follows a Different Path

With reports circulating in 1669 about the proprietors' possible loss of New Jersey, Woodbridge residents chose to work with Carteret to lock in land distributions before any change took place. Newarkers opted instead to retain close contact with Connecticut and New York. In February 1669, Abraham Pierson wrote to governor John Winthrop Jr., alerting him that "Captaine Treat is now going to York, and so intends for Milford, and Hartford, who will be ready to inform what he can." Five months later, Newarkers instructed Jasper Crane and Robert Treat "to advise with Col Lovelace [governor of New York] Concerning our Standing, Whether we are designed to be Part of the Duke's Colony, or Not." Notably, Crane and Treat were also instructed to discuss "the Neck [i.e., the New Barbadoes tract granted to William Sandford], and Liberty of purchasing Lands up the River, that the Town Wou'd Petition for." Lovelace probably referred them to his secretary Matthias

Nicolls. In December, Newarkers voted that a letter about New Barbadoes Neck and acquiring other lands "up the River" should be sent to Nicolls "in the Town's Behalf—and signed by Mr. Treat in the Name of the Town." When Governor Carteret learned about this letter, which he no doubt considered disloyal if not seditious, he recalled Treat's and Crane's commissions to serve as justices of the peace, forbidding them "to Act or doe any thing more by vertu of the said Commissions or by any other Authority but what shall be derived from me." To drive the point home, Carteret ordered Thomas Johnson, constable of Newark, to post the notice dismissing Treat and Crane "in some publiq place of your meeting[,] hereof you may not faile."[26]

Undaunted by Carteret's action, Newarkers held their annual town elections two weeks later, on January 1. They chose Treat and Crane once again as magistrates and added Matthew Camfield as a third magistrate. They also selected Treat and Crane as deputies for the general assembly "if there be any"—an indication that the assembly likely did not meet during 1669 when the status of the province was so uncertain. Newarkers gathered again later in January for a "general Meeting" to address important land issues. Once again, the town proceeded in accordance with their articles, which they considered both a foundational document and their primary defense against encroachments by Governor Carteret. To that purpose, they agreed that "the Articles should be copied out, at a Town Charge," no doubt expecting they would soon need to refer to them.[27]

As conditions in New Jersey remained confused and uncertain, Newarkers emphasized what they knew best: township self-government under the leadership and guidance of magistrates. Thus, at the New Year's town meeting in 1671, the town not only elected officers as usual, but they also renewed their "solemn Agreement to submit to Law and Authority among our Selves, Till it Be settled in the Province." In noting this agreement in the town records, the recorder added a reference to the action the town took in 1667 to "submit to law amongst ourselves." This assertion of independence was probably also a response to Carteret's order the prior October extending the jurisdiction of courts in Bergen and Woodbridge to hear cases from all townships, including Newark. At their next town meeting in February, Newarkers voted to empower Henry Lyon and Thomas Johnson, two Newarkers who maintained an open line of communication with the governor, to make a formal request that Carteret once again confirm Treat and Crane as "magistrates or Justices of the Peace," having been nominated by the town. In a modest concession, Carteret recommissioned the two men as justices of the peace on February 24, noting it was at the request of "the Inhabitants of Newark upon Pisawak River."[28]

In the end, the Duke of York did not compel the proprietors to exchange New Jersey for lands along the Delaware River, but Newarkers had made clear their preference for exploring closer ties to the stable government of New York rather than remaining under a tenuous proprietary government unfriendly to townships. For now, they were in opposition; rebellion would come later. They continued to build relationships with New Yorkers. When Abraham Pierson and his wife made a visit to New York toward the end of 1671, Governor Lovelace invited him to preach, likely to the Dutch Reformed congregation whose minister Johannes Megapolensis had died the prior year. While there, Pierson and his wife were entertained "with syngular and bountifull respects" by Cornelis Van Ruyven, receiver-general of customs, and his wife. Pierson, who suffered a return bout of kidney stones, appreciated their "liberality" while he was detained for three weeks. He likely felt that outside of the New England towns of Newark and Elizabethtown he was respected more in New York than in New Jersey.[29]

CHAPTER 7

Rebellion

On January 22, 1672, the Newark Town meeting authorized Robert Treat and Samuel Swaine to consult with John Ogden of Elizabethtown, or with anyone else they saw cause, about "what may be the Safest and Best Course to be taken for the Town, about our Lands and Settlements here." This urgent vote, which took place just three weeks after the long, customary town meeting on the first day of January, was the result of several years of disagreement and conflict with governor Philip Carteret. It would culminate a few short months later in the rebellion of 1672.[1]

Carteret's decision to prosecute William Meeker and seven other Elizabethtown residents for pulling down Richard Michell's fence was the proximate cause for Treat and Swaine's consultation with Ogden. Michell was one of Carteret's indentured servants who accompanied him to New Jersey in 1665. When his term of service came to an end, Carteret assigned him a house lot in Elizabethtown without consulting with the town, in direct contravention of the New England township method of allocating land and admitting new residents. Michell planted his garden and leased a fenced portion of his home lot to George Pack, who intended to plant tobacco. In a similar transaction a year earlier, Carteret had sold a home lot to another former indentured servant, Claude Valot. The residents of Elizabethtown had not made an issue of that transaction because Carteret had transferred title in his own land that he had acquired from others a few months earlier. Michell's situation was different because Carteret gave him a lot within the town boundaries that he did not personally own, without first consulting with the town.

The leaders of Elizabethtown did not let Carteret's challenge pass. The issue was discussed at a town meeting in June 1671, and the majority voted "that Richard Michell should not injoy his lott given him by the Governor." It was further agreed that some men should "pull up Richard Michells fence."[2] William Meeker and seven others, including Luke Watson, one of the founders of Elizabethtown, and John Ogden Jr., son of another founder, carried out the task the following morning. A few months later, thinking the issue of Michell's lot had been addressed properly and in good time, Elizabethtown residents nominated Meeker as their constable. At that point, Carteret had not yet decided to escalate the episode into a confrontation, and in October he confirmed Meeker's commission as constable.[3]

Carteret's subsequent decision to bring charges against Meeker went to the heart of the conflict between provincial and township control over the distribution of land. By prosecuting Meeker and others, Carteret aimed to impose his oversight over the allocation of land throughout the province, just as he had in Woodbridge—and in this way challenge the independence of township governments in Newark and Elizabethtown. Edmund Andros would undertake similar challenges to township government in Massachusetts a decade later, but Carteret tried first. The fact that he later briefed the proprietors on the episode and directed that the trial transcript be copied into the council minutes underscores the fundamental importance of this case.

To lay the groundwork for bringing charges against Meeker, Carteret secured general assembly approval in December 1671, likely over the opposition of representatives from Newark and Elizabethtown, to convene a special court of oyer and terminer and establish the new proprietary office of provost marshal. He soon named Samuel Moore of Woodbridge to serve as provost marshal, with power to execute any warrant from any court in the province. Moore would go on to play a prominent role in devising and executing the legal strategy that Carteret employed for the next several years.[4] After the court of oyer and terminer was commissioned in February 1672, Moore prepared arrest warrants for William Meeker and seven other Elizabethtown residents. News of the pending indictment must have leaked, triggering the emergency Newark town meeting when Robert Treat and Samuel Swaine were authorized to consult with John Ogden about "our Lands and Settlements here." For Newarkers, the prospect of this trial, with its threat to their New England–style town government, raised existential issues they could neither ignore nor accommodate. They no doubt agreed that Elizabethtown leaders were entirely within their rights in voiding the transfer of land to Michell. They also knew Meeker from his prior residence in New Haven, and they were prepared to support him to the end.

The special court convened for the first time in late February in Elizabethtown. Carteret stacked the seven judges with members of his council and men whose positions depended on his continuing favor. However, he also included Robert Treat among the judges, perhaps hoping to drive a wedge between Elizabethtown and Newark. If so, it did not work; Treat absented himself when the trial took place on March 8. A twelve-man jury, drawn mostly from Woodbridge and Bergen and including two members of Carteret's council, was sworn in. In silent protest, the eight defendants left the courtroom without entering pleas after the indictment charging riotous assembly was read. The trial proceeded without them. Samuel Moore called witnesses to build the case that since "three or more" acted together "without any due process in law . . . to do an unlawful thing in an unlawful manner," their destruction of Richard Michell's fence constituted a "riot" in breach of the king's peace. The number of participants was a key element of his argument. Robert Morse and Stephen Crane, also leaders of Elizabethtown, had torn "down the

Figure 7. Meeker House in Newark, built in 1676, was photographed before it was torn down in 1909. The Newark Public Library.

Claboards of Richard Michells house, and pluck[ed] up the pallasades of the garden," but were not charged with riotous assembly since they were only two in number.[5]

Moore introduced evidence from the Elizabethtown town meeting the prior June, when the majority agreed that Michell should not keep the home lot given him by the governor, but as he intended the court did not accept the town vote as exculpatory for Meeker or the other defendants—in effect nullifying the role of township government in land allocation. The jury retired but soon returned a guilty verdict against Meeker and the others. The court summoned the men to appear and then imposed a fine of five pounds on William Meeker and three pounds on each of the seven other defendants.[6]

Meeker long resisted paying the fine. William Pardon, a member of Carteret's council who had both testified against Meeker and served as one of the judges, claimed he suffered "indignities, Losses and Injuries" when he tried to collect the fine. Six years later, the proprietors awarded six parcels of Meeker's property in Elizabethtown to Pardon as compensation for his injuries. Newarkers rallied to support Meeker. Even though he was persona non grata with both the proprietors and Carteret, Newarkers agreed in November 1676 to make a joint "contribution" for his support. Meeker built a house in Newark that remained in his family for more than two centuries (see Figure 7).[7]

The verdict against Meeker and the others led to an extraordinarily unsettled time in the history of early New Jersey. Newarkers viewed the trial and verdict as an attack on township government. Governor Carteret had made it clear that he would no longer recognize the township method of allocating land and approving new residents that he had accepted six years earlier when he agreed to articles establishing Newark and other towns settled by New Englanders. Surprisingly, Robert Treat chose this moment to depart Newark and return to Milford. Records are silent about why he left at this time of peril for the town he had founded and led for six years. All that is known is that the Newark town meeting chose John Browne Jr. two weeks after the Meeker verdict to replace Treat as recorder and custodian of "all the Town's Writings." Treat's son John and daughter Mary remained in Newark. Perhaps family or business matters required Treat's presence in Connecticut, but it is more likely that he was so vocal in his criticism of the Meeker verdict and Governor Carteret's leadership that he found it wise to absent himself. He may have returned briefly at the end of the year, but from this point on he was no longer actively engaged in Newark's affairs.[8]

On March 26, three weeks after the verdict, the general assembly convened in Elizabethtown without a writ from Governor Carteret. The proprietors would later pinpoint the start of "the great disorders" to this date. John Ogden of Elizabethtown likely took the lead at the assembly meeting, supported by Newark deputies Jasper Crane and Samuel Swaine. They no doubt justified meeting without the governor's summons by referring to the proprietors' concessions, which gave the assembly power "to appoint their own time of meeting." The assembly passed various laws, now lost because William Pardon, the provincial deputy secretary, refused to enter them into the provincial records or even return the original copy to the assembly. Carteret considered the assembly meeting illegal, and he responded by commissioning another special court of oyer and terminer on April 3 to bring new charges.[9]

In mid-May the assembly convened a second time without a writ from the governor. Two representatives each attended from Elizabethtown, Newark, Woodbridge, and Piscataway, joined by one from Bergen. Again, the deputies relied on the concessions, which granted the assembly the power "to appoint themselves a president" if the governor and his deputy "wilfully refuse[d]" to be present. They elected James Carteret, son of Sir George Carteret, to serve as "president for the Country" and issued a proclamation justifying their actions. By choosing James Carteret, they attempted to demonstrate their nominal loyalty to the proprietors, while blaming Philip Carteret for abrogating their rights and privileges.[10]

James Carteret, the second but oldest surviving son of Sir George Carteret, was an ambitious and arrogant man, who claimed his father "had given him his part of the province." When Philip Carteret's council and Governor Lovelace of New York asked him "to shew any Grant or Commission or legal power" from his father, "hee Scorneth to Shew his Power to such fellowes as wee, neither need hee soe doe being on his own Land." Despite his blustering, he proved a weak reed. A onetime vice admiral of the British Fleet (through his father's influence), he later abandoned his family and slipped into a dissolute and drunken life, essentially disowned by his father.[11] That Newarkers and other New Englanders chose such a man as their vehicle to displace Philip Carteret as governor is a sign of their desperation and limited options.[12]

Philip Carteret blamed James Carteret for the challenges he faced. In a letter dated May 8, 1672—less than a week before James was elected president by the assembly—Philip complained to his brother Peter Carteret, governor of Albemarle in the Carolina province, that "since the arrivall of Capt: James Carterett [in the fall of 1671], hee hath created so much trouble with a company of Factious New England people that I dare not leave the Countrey till I receive further orders from his Father and my Lord Berkely." Calling James "a person of such troublesome spirit that I beleeve his Father sent him here to be rid of him," Philip went on to describe how in his view James had stirred up dissension: "Ever since his comeing here [he] hath made it his endeavor to make a party to himselfe & his first essay was upon the Councell but seeing hee could not work them to his Will nor anie other of the honest party hee then stuck to the discont[ent]ed New England people whom he supports with high & mighty promises when hee comest to sitt in the chaire of Proprietie."[13]

After being named president, James Carteret issued warrants in the king's name as head of the provincial government, requiring Philip Carteret's provincial officers "to cease acting in their Offices untill they receive orders from himselfe." In response, Philip Carteret and his council undertook measures to isolate James Carteret and those involved in what they called "illegal Actings." On May 28, they issued a protest against the assembly's "muteny and Rebellion" but offered to bury the "illegal proceedings" in "oblivion" if members of the assembly renounced their actions and submitted to their authority within ten days. At the same time, they granted various long-requested privileges to Middletown and Shrewsbury, both to keep them from joining the rebellion and to further isolate Newark, Elizabethtown, and Piscataway. They also wrote to New York Governor Lovelace to convey their version of the "irruption at New Jersey." Lovelace sought to navigate between the two Carterets, proposing mediation to "heale those Wounds which (perhaps) the Enemyes to his Majestie & Lord Proprietors would bee gladd to see fester into a Gangreen, & soe become incurable."[14]

James Carteret countered that he had found New Jersey "inhabitants . . . in a raw & undisciplined Condition" because Philip Carteret had forbidden them "to Exercise themselves in Military Affayres or Discipline." He also spread stories that Philip Carteret had a "considerable quantity of Armes & Ammunition" as well as "a Considerable Stock of monneys or Merchandize," finally forcing him to issue a denial on July 1. Meanwhile, James Carteret resisted showing any evidence that he had his father's charge to represent him. In this standoff, Governor Lovelace decided not "to interpose in the Affayre any further," and the council determined that their best recourse was to send Philip Carteret to London to consult with the proprietors; he sailed for England at the end of July.[15]

Confident in the rightness of their actions, Newark, Elizabethtown, and Piscataway sent a long petition to the proprietors, listing grievances and complaints, and signed (at least) by their deputies in the assembly. They could not afford to send someone to London to lobby for their position in person, but they thought their arguments, presumably with reference to the concessions, would be sufficient. While waiting for the response from the proprietors, Newarkers reconstituted their godly government at a town meeting in June. They chose magistrates for the year—which normally took place at a town meeting on January 1—and reinstated their own quarterly town court, with Jasper Crane presiding. On August 10, within two weeks of Philip Carteret's departure, men attending the Newark town meeting took a vote "concerning the Government." The wording of the motion is not known, but it was incendiary enough that in February 1676, after the tide had turned decisively against Newark, the town ordered the text "obliterated" from the town records.[16]

The province remained in a tense standoff through the fall of 1672 and spring of 1673, waiting for fresh news to arrive from London. Governor Lovelace cut off contact with James Carteret in mid-October but relented when Thomas Delavall, a wealthy merchant and mayor of New York, suggested a path toward "accommodation" until the proprietors resolved the conflict.[17] James Carteret retained sufficient status that Delavall blessed the marriage of his second daughter Frances to him in April 1673. Israel Chauncy of Stamford reported news of the marriage to Governor Winthrop, referring to him as "Mr Cartwright that is Governor of N: Jerrsy." Alexander Bryan, writing from Milford, added gossip that James Carteret would inherit a large estate providing an awe-inspiring £20,000 per year: "Capt. DeLavall knowes it is good striking while the Iron is hott, the Young Gentleman is now his fathers Eldest Sonne and heire to a great estate by an unckle soe that it is reported of twenty thousand a yeare att least to belong to him." Relaying other news, Bryan added, "Wee heare of noe vessell come to N Yorke this yeare allthough severall of their owne vessells . . . went out 10 or 12 months since." That would soon change.[18]

Response to the Rebellion

On May 1, 1673, Alexander Bryan wrote again to Governor Winthrop, this time with the first report of James Bollen's return from London—even before news about his return reached New York or New Jersey. A ketch out of Milford happened to meet Bollen's vessel off Long Island near Southampton: "The Company being Strangers our master was helpfull to bring them as far as our Harbour and they stayd not but went towards new Yorke." The ship had left England in December, sailing via Faial Island in the Azores, where they "tooke in some wine." The voyage ending up lasting more than four months. Bollen relayed news that Philip Carteret had been confirmed as governor and would follow in a later vessel. He also reported that "Capt James Cartwright that turnd out Philip is For present out of his Fathers Favour and not to medell with any buissnes" there. In addition, Sir George was "much insenced," not just with James Carteret but also "with those that sided with Capt James in that buissnes." In the days ahead, Newarkers learned just what the proprietor's anger meant for them.[19]

Bollen soon made his way to New Jersey, bringing with him a letter from King Charles II, another letter from James, Duke of York, and a declaration and other orders from the proprietors. Philip Carteret's council, meeting for the first time in nine months, ordered the letters "published In the severall townes," starting with Bergen on May 5 and then Newark on May 7, so that "the turbulent spirits" may be "inform'd of their mistakes, and how they have been misled."[20] There was much to publish, and none of it was good news for Newarkers. Driven to action by reports from Philip Carteret, Samuel Moore, and James Bollen in London, the proprietors attempted to bring the full weight of royal and imperial authority against Newarkers and other supporters of the rebellion.[21]

The proprietors spelled out "the true intent and meaning" of their concessions in a declaration dated December 6, 1672. No doubt incorporating recommendations from Philip Carteret, they made several changes to the powers of the general assembly and sharply curtailed the authority of town meetings. Going forward, the governor and council were responsible for appointing "the times and places of meeting of the General Assembly," and they could constitute courts without the involvement of the general assembly. The proprietors also made it explicit that the general assembly would meet as a bicameral body, with deputies or representatives in a lower house voting on acts and the governor and council as an upper house reviewing them, with acts to become law when confirmed by the proprietors. The role of townships, carefully negotiated in articles years earlier, changed dramatically. The governor would now have the power to admit "planters and free men," and only freeholders who held their lands by patent from the proprietors could vote or hold any "office of trust." Even more troubling to Newarkers, the proprietors declared that only the governor and council could allocate lands to individuals. All civil and military officers would be appointed directly by the governor and council, bypassing nominations by towns. The governor and council could also raise a militia "in case of foreign invasion or *intestine mutiny or rebellion*" (emphasis added). Finally, new town charters (e.g., for Newark) would be confirmed only by special order of the proprietors.[22]

Responding to the "great disorders" in the province, the proprietors issued a second declaration, also dated December 6, 1672, directed "to all Adventurers, Planters, Inhabitants, and all other Persons," confirming all land patents recorded by July 28, 1672, disavowing the Nicolls grants to Elizabethtown and Navesink, and declaring null and void all land titles not patented and recorded in the provincial records (including all Newark land titles). They required payment of all quitrents, but for the first time explicitly allowed in-kind payment. They also commanded that "the chief actors in attempting the making an alteration on our government" be proceeded against in law, "except they shall immediately upon publication hereof make their addresses to our Governor and Council for remission of their offenses." At the same time, they allowed reparations to anyone who sustained losses or damages after March 26, 1672 from the rebellion.[23]

To reinforce their declarations, the proprietors secured a letter from King Charles II to John Berry, deputy governor during the absence of Philip Carteret, in which the king referred to those who had refused to submit to the proprietary government, including Newarkers, as "turbulent and disaffected persons" and ordered that those who did not "forthwith . . . yield obedience" to the laws and government of New Jersey should "upon pain of incurring our high displeasure . . . [be] proceeded against with due severity according to law."[24] Finally, the proprietors sent a letter directly "to the pretended Representatives of Elizabeth-town, Newark, and Piscataway," acknowledging the "long petition from you" with "pretended grievances and complaints." Noting that they had discussed the particulars of the petition with Philip Carteret and James Bollen, then in London, they offered to hear all parties while Philip Carteret remained there, "if you will send over any person to make good your allegations in your petition." The proprietors added that they expected "for the future you will yield due obedience to our Government and laws within . . . New Jersey."[25] While this document had a velvet-glove tone, an iron fist was evident as news spread that the vessel on which Bollen sailed had brought a "store of amonition For the Supley of Yorke as allsoe For the province bee yound Yorke [i.e., New Jersey]."[26]

Deputy Governor Berry took systematic measures before Philip Carteret's expected return to impose new control over the towns. Notably, he started with Newark. He presided over a court in Newark on May 22, replacing Jasper Crane as presiding officer. The same day, with reference to the proprietors' declaration of December 6, he issued an order "to all the Inhabitants of Newark" to have their landholdings surveyed by the surveyor general and patented within three weeks. If they followed through, they would be able "to Chuse theire representatives that the affaires of the province may be the sooner and better settled." If they failed to patent their lands "within the tyme limitted," they would "forfeit such land as they are settled uppon."[27] Berry's final order, also issued on May 22 in Newark, set a date when those who attempted "an alteration in their Government" could "crave remission" from the council. Berry pointed out that he and the council "did reasonably Expect that [requests for remission] would have bene (by way of petition) presented this session [i.e., during the court held at Newark that day]." Even though those individuals were "slack and remiss therein," the council would allow them until the assembly convened in Bergen in June to make their submission, but "after that tyme" they could "expect no favor but what the Law affords."[28]

Newarkers were in a dire situation, but they did not seek remission or take out patents. They no doubt felt the asserted weight of royal and imperial power, but they apparently continued to think they had been misunderstood and were in the right. They believed they had adhered to the conditions negotiated with Philip Carteret in the articles establishing Newark six years earlier and, unlike Carteret, had respected the provisions of the proprietors' concessions. They had been willing to pay quitrents, collectively if not individually, but Carteret had rejected their payments. They thought it was Carteret who had changed the rules, not them. They believed they were not turbulent and disaffected people—just focused on implementing godly government within their community. They decided they needed someone with authority to stand up for them.

Winthrop's Intervention

On May 14, one week after the letters and declarations from London were published in Newark, Jasper Crane and Abraham Pierson wrote urgently to governor John Winthrop Jr. of Connecticut, asking him to send his "testimony, as farr as saifly and freely you can," to the proprietors on their behalf (see Figure 8). They contemplated sending someone to London to appeal to the proprietors, and they thought a letter from Winthrop, perhaps the best known and most respected individual in the colonies, would help their cause. Crane and Pierson noted that "some ill-affected towards our people" had reported to the proprietors that Newarkers were "of unquiet and troublesome behaviour," tending to "our disparagement, and dammage." They added that the proprietors had given "a fair hint" they would listen to petitions from Newarkers "if we see cause to stand upon it." If Winthrop could send a letter and if Samuel Wyllys, a senior and influential magistrate in Connecticut, could also sign it, "he having bin sometimes with Sir George Carteret," then the proprietors might give "credit to what we shall truely and honestly say touching our estate." Crane and Pierson were both well-known to Governor Winthrop and respected by him, but they took care to remind him about other leaders of the Newark community: "Now honored Sir, you have known ourselves, Mr [Obadiah] Bruen, Mr [Robert] Bond, leftenant [Samuel] Swaine and we suppose brother [Micah] Tompchins, brother [Richard] Harrison, Serjeant [John] Ward, and brother [Richard] Larance of Branford, and it may be others of our people; if you please that you having knowne our conversation and behaviour in the place whence we came, we desire your testimony."[29] Winthrop endorsed the letter, "Mr Jasper Crane & Mr Pierson at New Ark in New Jersy, received May: 21," and, cautious as ever, he responded by asking for more information about Newark inhabitants.

Crane and Pierson wrote again to Governor Winthrop on June 16—a long letter in Pierson's hurried handwriting—repeating their "former desire for a testimoniall." But this time, they also asked Winthrop to let the proprietors know his views on how best to settle a province like New Jersey: "whether in townships where accommodations ly conveniently for such purposes or els in farmes which tend to the spoyleing of cohabitation, civill society, safety, learning & religion. Capt: Philip Catteret did much lean that way." Crane and Pierson then turned to answering Winthrop's request to "name the men at our Town." They acknowledged that Winthrop might not know some of them, but they assured him, "They are honest and peaceable men." They added as well that "sundry other good men are with us." They listed nineteen men, including Crane's son-in-law Thomas Huntington, Pierson's son Abraham, and Robert Bond, formerly a member of Carteret's council but now joined with the Newarkers:

> We suppose you know Mr [Obadiah] Brewen, his son John Brewen is also an honest and wel disposed man, Leitenant [Samuel] Swayne[,] Richard Harrison[,] Serjeant John Ward[,] Samuell Plumb[,] Stephen Freeman formerly of Milford[,] Michael Tomkins Jonathan Tompkins both very honest men, Brother Joseph Waters Cowper from the aforesayd Town[,] Samuel Kitchell[,] Thomas Hunting-

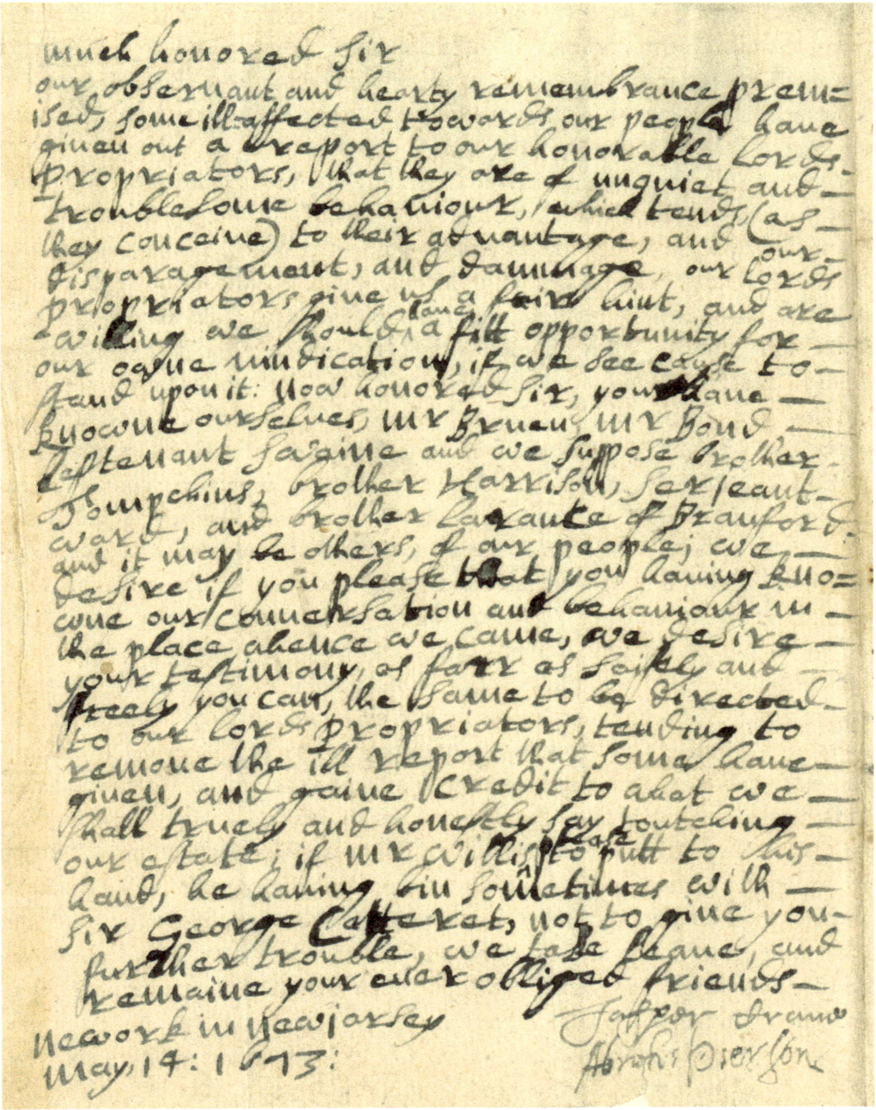
much honored Sir
our observant and hearty remembrance premised, some ill affected towards our people have given out a report to our honorable Lords Proprietors, that they are of unquiet and troublesome behaviour, which tends (as they conceive) to their advantage, and our disparagement, and dammage, our Lords Proprietors give us a faire hint, and are willing we should have a fitt opportunity for our owne vindication, if we see cause to stand upon it: Now honored Sir, you have knowne ourselves, Mr Brewen, Mr Bond, Leftenant Swaine and we suppose brother Tompkins, brother Harrison, Serjeant Ward, and brother Laurance of Branford, and it may be others of our people; we desire if you please that you having knowne our conversation and behaviour in the place whence we came, we desire your testimony, as farr as safely and freely you can, the same to be directed to our Lords Proprietors, tending to remove the ill report that some have given, and gaine credit to what we shall truely and honestly say touching our estate; if Mr Willis please to putt to his hand, he having bin sometimes with Sir George Carteret, not to give you further trouble, we take leave, and remaine your ever obliged friends

Newark in New Jersey
May 14: 1673:

Jasper Crane
Abra: Pierson

Figure 8. Letter to Governor John Winthrop Jr., signed by Jasper Crane and Abraham Pierson, requesting his "testimony" to the proprietors "to remove the ill report that some have given" about Newarkers' "unquiet and troublesome behaviour," May 14, 1673. Collection of the Massachusetts Historical Society.

ton who married Mr Craines daughter[,] Mr Robert Bond sometime of East Hampton[,] Br: John Brown sometime Miller at Melford[,] John Baldwin son to John Baldwin who is of somewhat imperfect speech of Milford[,] Br: Stephen Davis sometime of Hockanum[,] Br John Ward the dishturner sometim of Branford is here and My son who is Teacher of our Church[,] Richard Laurance who lived in the lane next to my house at Branford who is one of our deacons.

Crane and Pierson closed their letter with mention of their neighbors in Elizabethtown, letting Winthrop know that "if our people send for England" it was likely Samuel Hopkins "wilbe one to go, if not Mr [John] Ogden also." Both men were of "commendable conversation," so they suggested that if Winthrop knew them, "to give a good character of them wilbe commodious."[30]

On July 2, the same day he received Crane and Pierson's second letter, Winthrop sent the requested testimonial to Sir George Carteret, drafted by Samuel Wyllys but signed by both Winthrop and Wyllys, expressing strong support for Newarkers and their neighbor John Ogden in Elizabethtown. Winthrop and Wyllys noted that "divers persons of good Repute and approved intigritie who were formerly . . . in publique offices in this Collonie [Connecticut], viz: Mr Jasper Crane, Mr John Ogden, Mr Robert Bond, Mr Abraham Pierson, Mr Obadiah Bruen with many of our Loving nighbours and freinds, well disposed men, of sober and peaceable conversation Did transplant them selves and families into your Honours Province." Winthrop and Wyllys explained that these men, "well known to us but strangers to your Honour," asked us "to give you our Carrectere of them so they might not be misrepresented." Winthrop and Wyllys added that while their "former aboad in this Collonie was both acceptable and usefull and their Returne to us would be very gratefull," in sending their letter they wanted instead to promote the hard work of achieving "progress and prosperity" in New Jersey. Ignoring the long presence of Native Americans, they wrote:, "[T]hat good work of subdueing the earth and replenishing of it, which in this remote desert part of the Worlde never formerly inhabited, or Cultivated is a very dificulte work and Requires much hard Labour to Subdue so Ruffe, and woody a wildernes in this Cold Clymate and where Cloathing is very deare being far distant from the market so that the people will need to more encouragement which we doubt not Upon all occasion will be affoarded them." Following Crane and Pierson's suggestion, they ended the letter with an endorsement of townships: "We would further make bold to suggest unto your honours Wisdom and Prudence as very expedient that your Collonie be branched out into Convenient Townships, which we find best conduceing to safety and the advancing of Civill Societyes."[31]

Copies of the letter soon circulated in New Jersey, buoying the spirits of Newarkers but irritating Deputy Governor Berry, who wrote to Winthrop complaining "of some blacknes endevoured to bee throwne on the person at present in the Government of our Province." Berry added that "some mens [were] boasting of greate things you have donne for them, as well in writing into england, in theer commendation, and also incouraging them with strong invitations to remove from hence into your government." Responding to Berry's letter, Winthrop adeptly deflected his criticism by focusing just on the question of the settlers returning to Connecticut. Enclosing a transcript of the letter to Sir George Carteret, he insisted that "it hath beene very farr from acting or intentions, to incourage, or invite any one to a removall thence." Winthrop also ignored Berry's report, included in his letter, about Samuel Treat's "reproach of the government and dishonor of our Lords [Proprietors]." Samuel Treat was then a preacher in Woodbridge, but his views about the government were likely shared by his brother John and other residents of Newark. Through Winthrop, Berry wanted Robert Treat to know that his son Samuel had not acted like a gentleman. At the same time, his account of the incident reveals how the assertion of royal and imperial power had failed to calm resistance in New Jersey and, as well, how little practical enforcement power the proprietary government had:

> [S]ome caraidge of Mr Sam: Treate . . . tends to the reproach of the government and dishonor of our Lords, for which being called before my self and Counsell was required to stay a few houers, that his words (which he disowned) might bee proved, who unlike a gent: slighted our order and unkowne to us departed, for which Contempt and for his words wee shall call him in question if our officer Canne meete with him. I give you a hint of this, for that if he be called to an account for it, his Father (whome I must respect) may neither wonder, nor Condemne us of rashnes, and if we meete not with him, to lett you know hee is departed hence under a Cloud, and not like a gent: who dares answer his action, which is noe character of an honest man specially one . . . who undertakes to bee a teacher of others.[32]

However, any tension between John Berry and John Winthrop or concern about Samuel Treat's criticism of the provincial government was soon moot. The Dutch captured New York a few days later, and everything changed again.

CHAPTER 8

Reprieve

Newark's plans to send an agent to England came together quickly. At a town meeting on July 1, 1673, "it was Voted, and agreed by the General and universal Consent and Vote of all our People, that there should be an Address by way of Petition, sent to the Lords Proprietors of this Province." The town agreed to defray the cost by imposing a tax proportional "to the number of those who join in the said Petition." Within days, the town formed a committee to negotiate with Thomas Delavall of New York "about Money to send a Messenger to England." Together with Elizabethtown and perhaps Piscataway, Newark chose Samuel Hopkins as their agent to deliver the petition and meet with the proprietors in London, with the aim of "removing of the Grievances incumbent, and obtaining of what may be necessary for the Good of the Province, and of this Plantation." Delavall apparently agreed to advance the necessary funds to finance Hopkins's voyage and his expenses in London, since his daughter Frances and her husband James Carteret joined Hopkins for the initial leg from New York to the Chesapeake.[1]

Hopkins grew up in Milford, so Newarkers would have known him from his youth. After moving to Elizabethtown in 1670 with his young family, he rapidly gained status, in large part from his service as provincial secretary to James Carteret in 1672 and 1673; Abraham Pierson and Jasper Crane granted him the honorific "Mr" when they informed Governor Winthrop that they would likely select him as their agent. Hopkins introduced a strongly Puritan tone to some of James Carteret's correspondence, such as his letter to Governor Lovelace in June 1672 that included references to "Jehu, & Ishmaelite Spirits" and citations from Proverbs. Hopkins also encouraged James Carteret to dispute New York's ownership of Staten Island, to Lovelace's great irritation because he owned extensive farms there. Lovelace refused even to open a letter from James Carteret in September 1672 when he found "the Superscription to bee Mr Hopkins his Hand, with whom I never had any Correspondence (neither desire I any)."[2]

Hopkins collected the latest news in New York before sailing to the Chesapeake in mid-July on the first leg of his voyage to London, taking special note of Lovelace's plan to travel to Hartford toward the end of July to consult for several days with Governor Winthrop. However, news had not yet reached New York that a squadron of Dutch warships had arrived off the Chesapeake on July 11, 1673. The Dutch were fresh from seizing prizes in the West Indies and intent on capturing merchant ships laden with tobacco from Maryland and Virginia—spoils of war during the Third Anglo-Dutch Trade War that had broken out more than a year earlier. The Dutch fleet, under the command of admiral Cornelis Evertsen the Youngest and admiral Jacob Benckes, engaged the English fleet in the Hampton Roads over several days in what has become known as the Second Battle of the James River. The Virginia tobacco fleet mostly escaped up the James River, and all but one of the Maryland tobacco ships slipped by the Dutch. Evertsen and Benckes kept their distance for five days, burning four ships that had run aground and two others they had captured. But other ships sailed unsuspecting into their reach, including the ketch with James Carteret and Samuel Hopkins on board.[3] While detained by the Dutch, James Carteret facilitated their negotiation with governor William Berkeley of Virginia for an exchange of prisoners. He and his wife were set ashore in Virginia on July 21, but Hopkins continued to be detained by the Dutch.[4]

When news of this naval battle reached Boston on July 29, it was immediately suspected that New York would be the next target, with collateral impact on New Jersey. John Davenport Jr. passed along an early report to Governor Winthrop, adding, "It is thought (at least) they have a design upon N:Y."[5] Needing to take on fresh water, the Dutch fleet sailed on July 24 toward the Delaware River, but when they reached Delaware Bay two days later, they resolved to continue on to Staten Island and New York Bay, where it was easier to take on clean water. The fleet anchored off Sandy Hook, New Jersey, on July 29.

At this point Admiral Evertsen summoned Samuel Davis, captain of the ketch on which James Carteret and Samuel Hopkins had sailed, to question him about New York's fortifications. He promised Davis he would "give him his sloope and Cargo againe" if would he "deale Faithfully with him." Aiming to divert the Dutch from New York, Davis insisted that "in the space of three hours the Governor Lovelace could raise five thousand men & one hundred & fifty peice of Ordinance fit for service upon the wall" of Fort James at the tip of Manhattan. He also asserted that New York had recently "received a good supply of armes & ammunition." The latter may have been true, but the rest of Davis's report was pure fabrication. Evertsen then turned to Hopkins, whom he had also summoned, to confirm Davis's intelligence. Hopkins, who had little respect for Governor Lovelace and no love for proprietary government in New Jersey, told the truth: "[T]here might bee betweene Sixty and Eighty men in the Fort, and in three or foure dayes time it was possible they might raise three or foure hundred men, & that there was thirty or thirty six peice of ordinance uppon the wall that a shot or two would shake them out of their Carriages."

William Hayes, a London merchant who was also present at the meeting, provided an account of Hopkins's exchange with Everton to one of Governor Winthrop's correspondents. In a later affidavit, Hayes added that Hopkins also informed the Dutch that Lovelace was absent visiting Winthrop in Hartford, and "encouraged the Dutch to proceed to the takeing of Arthur Cull [i.e., Achter Col, the Dutch name for the portion of New Jersey settled by New Englanders], having discovered to them allso the weakenes of that place."[6]

Hopkins has been tarred by some as a "traitor" for exposing how vulnerable New York and New Jersey were, but what he did is not different in kind from the intelligence that English seamen, deserting from their impressments, provided the Dutch during the Second Battle of the James River, or the navigational help two English pilots provided Dutch ships at the mouth of the Chesapeake—or indeed Bishop Gilbert Burnet's role fifteen years later when William III invaded England at Torquay with a vast armada and some forty thousand soldiers and mariners at the start of the Glorious Revolution. William Hayes, the source of the report about Hopkins, changed his account over time, perhaps trying to divert attention away from his own role in the meeting with Admiral Evertsen. In the first rush after the surrender of New York, Hayes said the Dutch had questioned Hopkins; by the time he made his affidavit in December 1673, his story had evolved: Hopkins "did voluntarily declare to the Dutch that what [Samuel] Davis had informed was alltogether false."[7]

More on point were questions about how New York had been caught so off guard more than a year after leaders learned that war had again been declared between England and the Netherlands. As Israel Chauncy noted within a week of the city's surrender, New York's lack of "preparation to encounter with an enemy" was "much wondered at." The Dutch arrival was the mirror image of what had happened nine years earlier when the English first took New York, except this time the Dutch fleet was larger, with nine frigates among their twenty-one-ship fleet, and if anything, the English were less prepared than Governor Stuyvesant had been in 1664. During the two days after the Dutch ships were spotted off Sandy Hook, Captain Manning, who had been left in charge while Governor Lovelace was away, could only muster about seventy-five men to defend Fort James. Long Island town militias did not provide the assistance that Manning requested, and the small force at Fort James was ill-prepared to resist Dutch shelling due to "the ill condition of the Fort by the badnes of the carrages and platformes." Late in the afternoon of July 30, under great duress, New York surrendered to captain Anthony Colve and a large contingent of Dutch soldiers.[8]

Achter Col

To inhabitants at the time, the capture of New York likely felt more like a restoration than an interruption. The Dutch had governed New Amsterdam for four decades, followed by nine years of English rule with the name changed to New York; now the city was restored to the Dutch and called New Orange. Similarly, the Dutch had controlled New Netherland for decades; now the English settlements of New Jersey, after less than a decade of proprietary government, were again Dutch territory, generally called Achter Col. With the prospect of regaining a large measure of godly self-government, Newarkers embraced the change. They immediately joined with Elizabethtown, Piscataway, and Woodbridge to petition the Dutch Council of War for permission to send delegates to "surrender . . . their towns under the obedience of their High Mightinesses, the Lords States of the United Netherlands, and his Serene Highness, the Prince of Orange" and to receive an audience with the Council of War before they granted any request from "their late Governor, Capt. John Berry." At their first meeting as a Council of War on August 2/12,[9] Admirals Evertsen and Benckes, joining with captain Anthony Colve and two other captains, accepted the petition from the four towns and set the following Tuesday for the audience. The Council of War then issued separate orders to Bergen and to Middletown and Shrewsbury to also show up on the same day, prepared to surrender.[10]

At a town meeting on Monday, August 4/14, the night before the meeting with the Dutch Council of War and just five days after the surrender of New York, Newarkers voted to approach "the Generals at N. Orange" with a proposal for "a priviledged County between the Two Rivers Passaick and Araritine [Raritan], or with as many as will join with us." With this proposal, Newarkers wanted to carve out the towns settled by Puritan New Englanders as a separate governmental entity, excluding both the Dutch in Bergen and the Baptists and Quakers in Middletown and Shrewsbury. They likely thought Elizabethtown and Piscataway would join them in the proposal but recognized that Woodbridge would hesitate. The town meeting also agreed that "if none will join with us upon that account," their representatives should request "what may be necessary for us in our Town" at their meeting in New Orange. In the end, the Dutch authorities in effect met Newark halfway: They treated Bergen like other Dutch settlements near New Orange, but they included Middletown and Shrewsbury in their administration of Achter Col.[11]

On August 8/18, the Council of War delivered its response to a new petition from "Elizabetts Towne, Neworke and piscattaway" (Woodbridge had decided not to join the petition), granting the inhabitants of the three towns "the same Privileges and Freedoms" accorded to Dutch towns. These privileges included possessing their "paid for lands" unmolested; not being impressed into service against their own nation "in time of war with his Majesty of England," although their ships and boats could be seized for that purpose; disposing of their property by will under Dutch laws of inheritance and allowed to "depart from this government with their property" within six months if they obtained a passport from the governor; and "freedom of conscience as the same is permitted in the Netherlands." Deputies from Woodbridge, Middletown, and Shrewsbury then appeared before the Council of War and were, at their request, granted the same privileges. Finally, John Berry, William Sandford, Samuel Edsall, and Laurens Andriessen—all members of Philip Carteret's council—appeared and requested that their land holdings be confirmed and that they be granted the same privileges "as all other inhabitants of Achter Coll, lately called New Yarsey."[12]

The Council of War was remarkably efficient in putting a new government in place for Achter Col. In just three weeks, they received the surrender of the towns, ordered the towns to nominate magistrates, and then named and swore in magistrates for each town. On August 9/19, the Council of War sent orders to each of the English towns in Achter Col to nominate six men as magistrates (a double number, following Dutch practice), from whom the council would select three to serve in each town, as well as two men to meet with deputies from the other towns to nominate three men to serve as schout (or sheriff) and three to serve as secretary for Achter Col. The Newark town meeting took place as requested, and Newarkers submitted their nominations.[13] The Dutch chose Jasper Crane, Robert Bond, and John Ward as Newark magistrates and selected John Ogden as schout and Samuel Hopkins as secretary for Achter Col. With the departure of Robert Treat to Connecticut a year earlier, Ogden was the most senior and experienced leader in the province, and Hopkins returned to the same position he held under James Carteret. Ogden and Hopkins were granted "full power, Strength & Authority" to administer "the forme of government late in practice here . . . which is Customary in our Native Country" and "governe as well their Inhabitants as Strangers."[14]

The Dutch sent military officers to each town to administer an oath of allegiance, noting which men took the oath and how many were absent. They found that Newark, with eighty-six men, was the largest town, closely followed by Elizabethtown, with eighty. Together, the two towns most committed to New England practices and most opposed to proprietary government made up more than two-fifths of the 391 men living in Achter Col. Assuming an average of five people per household, the population of Newark was about 430 in this period; the other towns in Achter Coll added about another 1,500.[15]

The Newark militia, with officers newly selected by the Dutch, soon scheduled a training day due to perceived danger from Native Americans following a recent robbery, and "fear of what may further ensue," even though the sachems and chiefs of the Hackensack, accompanied by about twenty of their people, had already met and ceremoniously exchanged gifts with Evertsen, Benckes, and Colve in New Orange to confirm their intent to live in peace with the Dutch. In Newark, each man under sixty and above sixteen years of age was ordered to "meet together with their arms well fixed" at eight in the morning on October 1/11, bringing with him "half a Pound of Powder, and Twelve Bullets fit for his gun, or Two Pounds of Pistol Bullets."[16]

Nearly all the Dutch decisions for Achter Col favored those who had challenged Philip Carteret's government. John Ogden and Samuel Hopkins faced down resistance to their new authority when dealing with individuals who had been leaders in the former proprietary government. When they carried out the Council of War's order to seize Philip Carteret's estate and property, Robert Vauquellin (Carteret's surveyor general) refused to hand over various items he had removed from Carteret's house. The Council of War provided Ogden with "some soldiers" to arrest Vauquellin and deliver him to New Orange for examination. Vauquellin remained defiant, claiming that "the Duke of York had still an interest in Fort James, and that there would be another change [in government] within half a year." The council banished him, as an example to others.[17]

Barbadoes Neck

Several weeks after the Dutch takeover, the Newark town meeting approved the acquisition of Nathaniel Kingsland's 10,000-acre estate across the Passaic River from their town. This decision, so promising at the beginning, would backfire spectacularly and burden Newarkers financially for almost the next decade. Newarkers had had their eyes on the tract of land for years, going back to Philip Carteret's tentative offer of the tract to a group from New Haven in 1666. Called simply "the Neck" by Newarkers, it was also known as Barbadoes Neck because Kingsland was a resident of Christ Church parish in Barbados. It stretched north on the eastern side of the Passaic River and further east to the Hackensack River (see Figure 9). As noted in chapter 6, William Sandford first acquired the property in 1668 as a trustee for Kingsland. In 1671, the proprietors granted the tract directly to Kingsland, bypassing Governor Carteret, who oversaw all other land grants. Kingsland then sold 5,000 acres to Sandford. In the same year, Newarkers offered, without success, to acquire either Sandford's portion or Kingsland's remaining estate, or possibly the entire tract. Their plan was to create a new land association "to enter on Treaty of Sale, and to Buy the Neck of Capt. Wm. Sandford, or his uncle [Nathaniel Kingsland], or Both if they Could Agree for it." No inhabitant of Newark would be compelled to take part, but "none shall be exempted from the liberty of Purchasing, that doe Now Desire It." The voluntary expressions of interest were sufficient for the Newark promoters to offer as much as £800 paid in-kind over four years in "cattle and Provision . . . with some Pipe Staves." Abraham Pierson Sr. led this initiative, although as investor, not as minister. The town asked Pierson "to draw up the Letter, with the Names and Shares . . . and to keep a Copy of Mens Names and Shares Adventuring." In the event, however, the offer by the Newarkers in 1671 fell through or was not accepted.[18]

Since Kingsland was an absentee landowner, the Dutch confiscated his property as part of their seizure of houses, lands, and personal property belonging to the Duke of York, Governor Lovelace, Governor Carteret, and other absentee landowners. Newarkers prepared to pounce. On September 6/16, 1673, the town agreed that a petition should be sent "to the Generals at Orange, that . . . We might have the Neck." Ten days later the town instructed their magistrates to meet with the Dutch Council "about terms for the neck and if they can to buy it." Anthony Colve, newly named to serve as governor-general while Evertsen and Benckes prepared to depart, was sympathetic to the request from Newarkers. He was also someone Newarkers thought they could trust, since their Calvinist beliefs gave them a shared outlook on the world. Colve ordered the forfeiture of Kingsland's estate and directed that written notice be given for a public sale in New Orange at the end of October. He also authorized the town of Newark to drive cattle and hogs off the confiscated land and sell them by public auction.[19]

John Catlin and John Ward were chosen by the town on October 13/23 to negotiate the purchase of Kingsland's property "as Cheap as they can." The negotiation was successful, and they agreed to the terms with the Dutch two days later, thereby

Figure 9. The Barbadoes Neck tract was opposite Newark, situated between the Passaic and Hackensack Rivers. Map no. II in Elizabethtown Bill in Chancery, 1747 [Detail]. From the Collections of the New Jersey Historical Society.

avoiding a public auction. The same evening, the Newark town meeting unanimously agreed to four next steps: taxing every "individual Man or Planter" in Newark proportionately to the size of their estate to pay for the purchase; deputizing Jasper Crane, Jacob Melyn, and Samuel Hopkins to "see after Confirmation" of the terms of purchase and to seek "further Easment" of the payment schedule; selecting John Ogden, Jasper Crane, Jacob Melyn, Samuel Hopkins, John Ward, Abraham Pierson Sr., and Stephen Freeman to "take the Patent" in their names on the town's behalf and to give security for payment of the purchase; and delegating responsibility to Stephen Freeman, Thomas Johnson, Stephen Davis, John Ward, and John Catlin "to Order every Thing to the best Advantage they can" for taking possession of the tract. Three weeks later, the town meeting directed Samuel Swaine and Jasper Crane to seek further "easment in Respect of Payment for the Neck;" revised terms were accepted on November 15/25.[20]

The deed of sale, signed on November 19/29 by Anthony Colve, records Jacob Melyn of Elizabethtown as the purchaser, "who hath afterwards assigned and conveyed his right to the inhabitants of the town of New Work." Further, as agreed by the town, the deed of sale names John Ogden, Jasper Crane, Jacob Melyn, Samuel Hopkins, John Ward, Abraham Pierson Sr., and Stephen Freeman as patent holders (or elsewhere, "trustees") on behalf of themselves and for the rest of the inhabitants of the town of Newark. In addition to providing security for payment, these men, four from Newark and three from Elizabethtown, were likely also the largest investors in the new land association.[21]

The initial satisfaction about acquiring the Kingsland tract may have given way to buyer's remorse among some as the first purchase payment came due at the end of February 1674. For that or some other reason, the town accepted a proposal from John Catlin and Edward Ball to purchase part of the Neck from the town. At the end of January, five men were chosen to complete "this Business about the Neck" with Catlin and Ball, and three other men were chosen to accompany them "to see the Neck, and bring Information about the same." By the end of February, the town was ready to enter into a detailed agreement with Catlin and Ball, now joined by Nathaniel Wheeler and John Baldwin Sr., to acquire part of the Neck in return for paying £310 over three years to the "vendue Master at York," thereby relieving the town of that portion of the purchase price. This subdivision would remain part of Newark, and the four men would be "liable to bear their Part of the rates to the Ministry and Country according to Proportion, together with the rest of the Town." They could sell parcels of their land to others to defray their costs and earn a return on their investment, but Newark retained the right to approve and admit any new inhabitants. The agreement also spelled out a requirement for free access to town lands and the creation of a "highway" eight rods wide, "with Room convenient for the Town's Cattle."[22]

Ball, Catlin, Wheeler, and Baldwin were confident enough in their venture to borrow the full amount of their first-year payment from two Dutch merchants: sixty pounds from Gabriel Minvielle and £43.6s.8d from Pieter Jacobse Marius, payable in three years "in good clean winter wheat and pork and peas all recovered at current prices here within the City of New Orange . . . together with the interest of ten per cent per annum," and secured by a mortgage on the Neck tract. But they were also smart enough to include a key provision in their agreement with the town, that if their part of the Neck "shall be lost by any Claim of Kingsland or any in his Right, within the space of Two Years, the Town shall be liable to return them so much of the Money as shall by that Time be paid by them." When this provision kicked in, it led to years of dispute and financial burden for Newarkers.[23]

Return of the English

On April 16, 1674, John Davenport Jr. wrote from Boston to Governor Winthrop with "newse of peace betweene England & Holland," adding, "N:Y. by Articles is to be returned to the English." It took two more months for confirmation to reach New Orange, at which point Colve began to prepare for the inevitable transition. When he finally received official notice from Holland on June 21/July 1, he promptly proclaimed the Treaty of Westminster, ending the Third Anglo-Dutch Trade War. The treaty included a provision that its terms, including the return of New York to the English, would be observed after October 24/November 3 on the far side of the Atlantic. When negotiating the treaty, the Dutch preferred the profitable sugar colony of Suriname over retaining control of New Orange, while the English were keen to reclaim it. Indeed, a few months earlier, the English Council on Trade and Plantations had studied what would be required to retake New York. Philip Carteret was among those who provided advice to the council. He recommended sending six warships, one fire ship, and six hired ships with five hundred soldiers, along with sufficient arms and ammunition for both soldiers on the ships and one thousand volunteers from Long Island, New Jersey, and "places adjacent." He thought the recapture would take no more than two or three weeks, and then the hired ships could turn to loading tobacco in Virginia for their return voyage. In November 1673, the Council of Trade (including Sir George Carteret) determined that New York was crucial to English imperial aims of maintaining trade with Barbados along the Atlantic coast and endorsed plans for retaking New York. However, it proved unnecessary to launch the expedition, since the Treaty of Westminster achieved the same end more quickly and with less cost.[24]

News of the return of the English caused great consternation among supporters of the Dutch government in New Orange and Achter Col. Newarkers and other New Englanders feared for the future of their township government and title to their lands. On June 29/July 9, 1674, soon after the Treaty of Westminster had been proclaimed, the three towns of Newark, Elizabethtown, and Piscataway petitioned Colve for confirmation of their "possessions and Purchased bounds in After = Coll, in the tenure of freeholders." The Newark town meeting chose Jasper Crane and Abraham Pierson Jr. to carry the petition to the governor. Sensing urgency to act, the town followed up four days later and chose John Browne Jr. "to present this Petition to the Court again at New Orange." As news filtered in about the imminent return of Philip Carteret and the appointment of Edmund Andros as governor of New York, the town also rushed to negotiate with Hackensack leaders for "that Tract of Land as lieth above our Town, by the River"—that is, Acquackanonk, hoping to extend their landholdings even more while Colve remained governor, but they did not succeed in closing the transaction.[25]

As late as October, some Newarkers continued to hold out hope, naively, that the Dutch would retain control. Visiting his friend Israel Chauncy in Connecticut, Abraham Pierson Jr. spoke "much for [Colve's] justification in his former and more late proceedings; and . . . was in great hopes that the Dutch would still hold the rule there." Hope soon turned to desperation. Edmund Andros arrived on October 22/November 1 and anchored near Staten Island for eight days while Colve completed preparations for the handover. Abraham Pierson Sr. made a last-ditch plea to Colve to confirm Newark's purchase of the Kingsland estate. As Alexander Bryan reported to Governor Winthrop, "Mr Peirson spake with the Dutch governor about the Land that there people had bought at After = Cull, & had payd a Considerable sum to the Governor for." Colve advised Pierson not to trouble himself about it, because he expected Andros to "subscribe to the Articles wherein there should be an Act of Confirming what he had Done." Colve followed through on his promise, and Andros agreed that any sale or contract made "either before the Dutch came into these Parts, in July 1673 or during their Government here, the same is to bee and remaine of full force and Power, . . . Notwithstanding the late alteration of government."[26] However, matters played out differently in New Jersey when Philip Carteret, having crossed the Atlantic on the same ship with Andros, restored the proprietary government. After consulting his council, Carteret issued a proclamation on December 11 encouraging lawsuits to reverse land acquisitions that took advantage "of the late distractions and Changes in Government." Acting on this proclamation, attorneys for Nathaniel Kingsland sued to reclaim his New Barbadoes estate.[27]

James Carteret also returned from England in the same fleet as Andros and Philip Carteret, although on a different ship. Shunned by his father and no longer with pretense to authority, he was reduced to taking up residence with his wife Frances on his father-in-law's property in Harlem. Eighteen months later, Philip Carteret wrote to his brother, "Capt. James is here, drinking as much as ever. He trades on my friendship as much as he can; all the same I desire to have as little intercourse with him as possible. His wife has given birth to a daughter." By the end of the decade, James was dissolute, and his wife left him to return to her father's household.[28]

With the departure of the Dutch, Newark's reprieve was over. For more than a year after welcoming the Dutch, Newarkers confidently faced the future as Achter Col's largest town, with bold plans for further expansion. They developed a constructive relationship with the Dutch authorities in New Orange and consulted closely with John Ogden and others in nearby Elizabethtown. Town leaders used this period to carry out key elements of godly government through frequent town meetings, with little apparent discord. But now, with the fourth change in New Jersey government in thirty months, Newark was on the outside again. Once more, their world was turned upside down.

CHAPTER 9

Hard Times

Newarkers faced sudden changes after Philip Carteret's return to New Jersey at the end of 1674. Considered "seditious Spirritts" who had covered their guilt from rebelling one year "with the Mantle of Treason . . . by inviteing an Enemy to protect them" the next year, they were immediately targeted by the restored proprietary government. At the same time, they confronted ruinous debts from the collapse of their investment in the Kingsland tract. By February 1675, just three months after Philip Carteret's return, Newarkers wrote to friends about their "sad state," claiming "that unlesse things alter, there will be no abiding . . . there long." After a heady period of influence and confident expansion, Newarkers now faced hard times.[1]

The Dutch conquest had voided the claims of the Duke of York and the proprietors to New Jersey, but in February 1674 King Charles II regained title to the land by right of conquest, once the Dutch agreed to the Treaty of Westminster. The next month, Lord Berkeley sold his half interest in the province to a group of investors led by Edward Byllynge; this half interest led in due course to the formation of West Jersey. In June, Charles II confirmed Sir George Carteret as proprietor of the remaining half of New Jersey, soon known as East New Jersey, charging him to "use your utmost Endeavours, to prevent all Troubles and Disorders there for the future." He also signed a letter to inhabitants, warning them to "yield Obedience to the Laws and Government . . . there established," or else be prosecuted "upon Pain of incurring our high Displeasure." Two weeks later, the king granted the territory of New Jersey to his brother the Duke of York, who then regranted the eastern half to Sir George Carteret as sole proprietor.[2]

At the end of October 1674, just before Philip Carteret returned from England after twenty-seven months away, Newarkers prepared for the transition by naming a nine-man committee, drawn from both town and church leaders, "to consider of such Things as may tend for the Good of the Town." In an unusual move that recognized their need to be flexible and responsive in the face of uncertainty, the committee was given "liberty" to debate issues and meet with others without calling a town meeting.[3] The committee soon learned what they would be up against. The restored proprietary council summoned deputies from each of the towns to Bergen on November 6 to hear the new orders and declarations brought by Carteret from England, including the letter of King Charles II and directions from Sir George Carteret. All towns except Shrewsbury sent representatives.

Sir George Carteret's detailed "directions, Instructions and Orders," read to the town deputies on November 6, acknowledged "the great disorders in our Province, occasioned by several persons" and confirmed the original concessions as augmented two years earlier following the rebellion. All landholdings should be patented and arrears of quitrents paid; no man could hold civil or militia office unless his lands had been patented. Governor Philip Carteret was granted an additional 2,000 acres, and the assembly at its first sitting was charged with levying a tax to pay his arrears and provide for his maintenance and support. Middletown and Shrewsbury were given the right to be incorporated as a reward for their "faithfulness" following the rebellion. In an explicit warning to dissenters and disturbers of the peace, Sir George Carteret promised to build a prison and to "send over guns and ammunition as a magazine," paid for by quitrent revenue. In addition, new provisions discouraged appeals to England: Any person or party making an appeal would first have to pay all costs and fines assessed by the court in East New Jersey and then provide a security of one hundred pounds and a further twelve pounds as "a fine to the Judges" for the appeal.[4]

Before Philip Carteret crossed the Atlantic on the *Diamond* with fellow passenger Edmund Andros, Sir George Carteret sent a brief letter to the council in which he expressed his expectation that they would receive him as governor "with great satisfaction" after "so many broyles and troubles." The council replied to his letter on November 7, noting that they hoped, in a short time, with the help of the governor, to bring "to a right Understanding" all those who had "stood in Opposition." They added that they were very sensible of "the Disorders and Troubles" caused by "old, turbulent People" more willing to submit to the Dutch "than to their lawful King and Lord." Despite warning in their letter that "much cannot be expected to be done till the Spring, the Winters being here very hard, and difficult for each of us to come together in one Place," the council met with Governor Carteret in Elizabethtown on December 11 and issued several orders to impose royal and proprietary authority over those who had welcomed the arrival of Dutch forces, "by which Means the whole Frame of our Government hath been disjointed." The governor and council started with Newark, just as they did after the rebellion. They ordered the surveyor general to spend March there, "running out and further surveying Land," so that each holding could then be patented. Their plan was that Elizabethtown would follow in April until mid-May, then Piscataway from mid-May until mid-June, and the Navesinks until mid-August. Inhabitants were warned that if they prevented surveys from being carried out or did not then immediately seek patents, their landholdings would be seized.[5]

The governor and council issued several other decrees on December 11. These included orders to provost marshal Samuel Moore to collect the fines that had been imposed on William Meeker and other residents of Elizabethtown for tearing down Robert Michell's fence in 1671, and those fined by a court of oyer and terminer in June 1673 for "several Riotous misdemeanours." There is no record of who was convicted at the 1673 court session, but a report circulated in this period about Newarkers suffering from "great fines." Perhaps Jasper Crane, one of Newark's deputies to the assembly in May 1672 that named James Cartwright as president, was among those fined. Lying low or perhaps ill, Crane did not take part in any negotiations with Governor Carteret in this period, even though he had been nominated by the town as a magistrate a few months earlier. The council also consolidated judicial authority by establishing a special court to convene in Elizabethtown on March 9, at which the council, "as the present Magistracy of the province," would present warrants and articles "to suppress every disturbance & to preserve the peace of the Collony." Newark's town courts would not convene again until 1676, after the general assembly reestablished them.[6]

The Newark town meeting, aware of the December meeting of the governor and council, commissioned eight men to go to Elizabethtown "to treat with the Governor upon the particulars written." They directed the delegation to try first to reach an agreement without showing Carteret the written proposals, "but in Case he will not hear them," the document was to be left with him. There is no record of what proposals the Newarkers made, but they likely concerned patenting the Newark tract and paying the required quitrents collectively as a town, in a way that would enable the town to continue to control land transfers and admission of new residents. Carteret would have been in no mood to make concessions, but he may have been open to further discussion.

Abraham Pierson Sr. soon turned again to Governor Winthrop for support—this time without success because his letter went astray. William Jones, magistrate of New Haven, reported to Winthrop in early February that "old Mr Peirson . . . sent a letter Directed to your honor" asking "your favor to Improve your intent som way for them." The letter was sent via John Ball of New Haven, who had visited his brother Edward in Newark, but "unhappily [Ball] lost it on his Journey" back home. Jones could only guess at the contents, but he knew its loss would be of "great concernment to the poore people of N. Wark," suffering "by reason of great Fines and hard termes Imposed on them." Separately, Newarkers also kept Samuel Wyllys informed about their "afflicted state & Condition," but there is no record that either Winthrop or Wyllys intervened again on Newark's behalf.[7]

Land Patents

Toward the end of February 1675, the Newark town meeting instructed Thomas Johnson and Thomas Richards to meet with the governor again and "declare the Minds of the Town about pattenting." They were to inform Carteret that the town did not "for the present" accept his proposed terms. If Johnson and Richards succeeded in meeting with Carteret, they did not make progress. Two weeks later, on March 8, the Newark town meeting was still prepared to debate with Carteret about issues related to patenting. "Both Mr. Pierson's"—father and son—and Samuel Kitchell were asked to prepare a document outlining the town's position for others to present to the governor and "debate with him about that Matter." However, there is no evidence that Carteret relaxed his insistence that all Newarkers have their landholdings surveyed, take out separate patents, and then pay current and past due quitrents individually.[8]

Surveyor General Vauquellin presumably began surveying Newark landholdings at the beginning of March, as instructed. The task took much longer to complete than planned, and he did not finish surveying Newark lands until the end of the summer. With the surveys completed, the first group of Newark leaders and office holders, led by Jasper Crane, capitulated in late August and patented their lands. Abraham Pierson followed seven months later, in March 1676. By the end of 1679, fifty-six Newark landowners (about 70 percent) had taken out patents, fewer in number than in Bergen, Woodbridge, and Shrewsbury, and the same count as in Elizabethtown. Proprietary officials were simply not able to compel full compliance with their orders, especially if the individual did not hold civic and militia offices. However, the Newark town meeting took the initiative in 1677 to ensure the town's "bill of Sale from the Indians" and boundaries of the Newark tract had been entered in the provincial records; they had not, but three weeks later provincial officials duly recorded them. Newarkers did not want any lingering questions about the legitimacy and boundaries of the Newark tract.[9]

Barbadoes Neck Fallout

Following the withdrawal of Jasper Crane from public office in late 1674, Thomas Johnson emerged as the most important leader of Newark. He was a member of nearly every Newark delegation sent to meet with Carteret in this period and was apparently respected by both sides. A former resident of New Haven and original settler of Newark, now in his forties, he was sworn in as constable of Newark on December 12, 1674, having agreed to publish all orders and proclamations, execute all warrants and commissions, and prevent "all UnLawfull assemblies."[10] One of his early tasks as constable was likely delivering a warrant to John Catlin and Edward Ball to appear at a special court in March to answer a suit on behalf of Nathaniel Kingsland to retrieve that part of his former estate over which they claimed ownership. Kingsland's attorneys apparently also sued the town itself because their portion of the estate was also forfeited. In his December 11 proclamation, Carteret reversed land transfers during the Dutch period where the landholder could not show a lawful title either from the first owner (e.g., the acquisition by Catlin, Ball, Wheeler, and Baldwin) or where there had not been a "lawfull confiscation, tryall, condemnation and sale" made by the Dutch.[11] Newark's purchase of Kingsland's Barbadoes Neck estate would appear to pass the second test, but Kingsland's attorneys must have made a persuasive case that the confiscation of his estate by the Dutch and its subsequent sale had not been carried out legally. The result was that Newarkers lost the Kingsland tract but still owed the money they had borrowed to acquire it.

Efforts to deal with this financial calamity continued for years. On one track, Newarkers tried to recover the payments they had made to the Dutch authorities for the estate, and on another track, they worked to make John Catlin and Edward Ball whole after they triggered the clause in their agreement with the town that provided for reimbursement if Kingsland challenged the sale within two years. At the same time, Catlin and Ball appealed their court-imposed fines for damages suffered by Kingsland. John Catlin was involved in all aspects, as attorney for Newark and for himself, and as a defendant with Edward Ball. At the end of February 1675, the Newark town meeting chose Catlin and two other men to go to New York and "upon good Advice to lay an Arrest upon [the] Person and Estate of Nicholas Bayard," receiver-general and vendue master of New Orange under Anthony Colve, to recover their payment for the Kingsland estate. They argued that if the confiscation and sale were reversed, then Newark should recover the funds they put up to acquire the estate. Three weeks later, the town gave its consent to seek a summons for Bayard and deputized two men to "carry some writings upon that account" to New York. The case was brought before the Mayor's Court in New York on April 21, 1675, recorded as *Abraham Pierson cum Associates, Plaintiffs, v. Nicolaus Bayard, Defendant.* The court ruled that Bayard had not been given sufficient notice when summoned and ordered the plaintiffs to take out a new summons. There is no record of further action in the case until the town meeting decided on February 7, 1676, "by Vote," to sue Bayard to recover "the Money which was paid upon Account of the Neck." Thomas Johnson was chosen to go to Woodbridge to ask Samuel Moore to represent Newark in the suit. Again, there is no further record of this suit in either the Newark town records or New York court records; perhaps Samuel Moore advised against proceeding. In a final, fruitless attempt to recover the funds, the town sent two letters to Holland in May 1678, one to Anthony Colve and the other to the Court of Admiralty, seeking "reparation for our Expence about the Neck."[12]

In the meanwhile, John Catlin and Edward Ball prepared their own defense against the suit brought by Kingsland's attorneys. A special court heard Kingsland's suit in March 1676 and awarded him damages of £97.10s. Catlin and his associates filed a writ of error with the council in June, and the case was carried over to the next meeting in August, when the council sat as a court of chancery. The court confirmed the damages to Kingsland but reduced them to £61.5s plus £3.10s court costs. Catlin and the others were given fourteen days to pay the damages and court costs, which they were both unable and disinclined to do. In October, Governor Carteret issued an order to "levy the goods and Chattels" of Catlin and his associates to the value of £64.15s, but the record is silent about whether Catlin and the others ever paid the fine.[13]

Newarkers suffered crippling financial losses from the reversal of the Kingsland sale. To the degree they used their own resources for the purchase, it was a total loss because they could not recover any amount from the Dutch. To the extent they borrowed funds for their contribution to the purchase, they still had to make payments to their lenders. For years, the town worked to pay down the debt, with new committees assigned to track down men behind in paying their share of "the Neck Money" and determine what should be raised in another levy. The financial ordeal was not finally settled until 1682.[14]

Loss of Self-Government

While Newarkers wrestled with issues related to Neck money, Carteret systematically limited the scope of Newark's self-government and introduced levers of control to prevent future dissent. Carteret's most important lever was the requirement to patent lands, under threat of having property seized if the landholder did not secure a patent. Another effective lever was restricting town or militia offices only to men who patented their lands. Later, Carteret and the council tightened the screw further. In October 1678, citing Sir George Carteret's directions in July 1674, they ordered that no one could vote in any town meeting until they patented their lands—and the town would be fined if they admitted an unqualified person to vote.[15] Newark had always restricted town offices and voting at town meetings to church members; in this and other ways, the new orders overruled Newark's fundamental agreements. The challenge to town government was so great that while Newarkers chose deputies to the general assembly, a town clerk, town treasurer, and various officers at their meeting on January 1, 1676, they no longer elected magistrates. Instead, justices of the peace, nominated by the towns but commissioned by Carteret, were now responsible for calling town meetings and setting the "major part" of the agenda for each meeting. Justices of the peace performed similar functions as magistrates, but they acted in the name of the king, not as representatives of the town, and were answerable to the governor. In addition, Carteret made it clear that no town would receive a charter unless patents were taken out and quitrents paid, both current and in arrears. He cited this requirement when Newark petitioned for a charter in 1678 "with as good Privileges as our Neighbors at Woodbridge have." Fewer than twenty-five Newarkers had patented their lands by that point, so the governor quickly declined their request: Only "when they have Completed their pattents for the Land they have already within the purchase made from the Indians" would he consider granting the town a charter "reasonable and Convenient for Us to Give and for them to Enjoy."[16]

Carteret also took control of town militias and put them "in a postur of defense" as news of King Philip's War reached East New Jersey. He appointed "military Officers" in each of the towns, including William Sandford, a member of his council, as captain of the Newark foot company. Carteret charged Sandford with making an account of every man between the ages of sixteen and sixty and mustering them for training at least four times each year.[17] In a coordinated effort to extend control in the province, the council required that oaths of allegiance to the king and fidelity to the proprietor be administered to every male aged sixteen and older "that are freeholders and Inhabitants." Just as the Dutch authorities had done two years earlier, the council also directed justices of the peace for each town to record the names of individuals taking the oaths and forward them to secretary James Bollen, along with the names of everyone who refused.[18]

Having consolidated judicial and military oversight, Carteret and his council still faced the challenge of raising funds to cover the cost of government. They were determined to prevent men from holding office if they had not patented their lands, but the surveyor general's slow progress in completing surveys tied their hands. In August 1675, the council debated their conundrum. They were unable to raise a levy "without the Consent of the Inhabitants in General," but a general assembly could not be called "at present," since inhabitants were "not yett capacitated thereunto by patenting their lands" due to the surveyor general's backlog. The council settled on a hopeful compromise: They would raise funds for the maintenance of the governor, as ordered by the proprietor, through a "free & Voluntary good Will and free gift of the Inhabitants." William Sandford and Thomas Johnson were appointed to take up the subscription in Newark, with half due in December and the rest within the next year. Newarkers likely responded to this request with considerable reluctance; they knew that under the concessions only the general assembly had authority to levy taxes, and besides, they had significant other debts to deal with. They apparently chose discussion and delay rather than rejecting the request outright. The town meeting sent a delegation to Elizabethtown a couple of weeks later in response to "the Writing now come from the Governor" to learn more and perhaps buy time.[19]

In late 1675, Governor Carteret was finally compelled to call a general assembly to raise funds for his maintenance ("paying of publicq debts") and to address threats from King Philip's War in neighboring colonies, "not knowing how soone theire Rage may be Extended to this Province." Newark elected John Ward and Thomas Johnson as their deputies to this assembly, which convened on November 4 in Elizabethtown and met for eight days before adjourning for a fortnight and then resuming deliberations. The assembly strongly supported putting the province in a posture of defense and prohibiting the sale or repair of arms and ammunition to Indians. They also set up county courts, including one for Elizabethtown and Newark, that would meet twice a year, and clawed back the prerogative of towns to hold monthly courts for "small matters." The assembly passed twenty-eight acts and another thirty-seven provisions related to capital laws, in effect putting in place a fresh provincial law code following the Dutch conquest. Perhaps most important for Newarkers, the assembly passed an act of oblivion abolishing all fines and charges for actions between 1670 and June 1, 1673, "for making an alteration in the Government here settled by the Lords." The act also extended a pardon for all offenses, including "revilling speeches, practices, or intents tending to . . . disturbance" during the same period.[20]

Newarkers were significantly more responsive to orders of the general assembly where their deputies had a vote than they were to peremptory orders of the governor and council. At its New Year's Day meeting in 1676, the Newark town meeting selected townsmen to serve on the monthly court, "it being ordered by the General Assembly."[21] The assembly, meeting in April, noted that "there are many which have not subscribed any thing" for the governor's arrears, so it ordered every town to choose three men to take up the subscriptions. The Newark town meeting soon complied. The assembly also established town officers for packer of meat, sealer of leather, and sealer of measures at its April session; the town meeting quickly filled those posts as well.[22]

Six more sessions of the general assembly followed in quick succession over the next three years. With the assembly meeting on a regular basis, the Neck account finally settled, and the decision in 1679 by another thirty Newarkers to take out patents, Newark settled into a brief period of relative calm. It lasted until governor Edmund Andros of New York challenged Philip Carteret's right to govern and imposed his authority on East Jersey.[23]

CHAPTER 10

Transitions

The death of Abraham Pierson Sr. in August 1678, at about age sixty-seven, marked the end of an era. Pierson personified the first generation's fierce commitment to godly government. After emigrating to New England in 1639, he had taken in John Cotton's sermons in Boston. He then brought a manuscript copy of Cotton's "Moses His Judicials" with him as the founding minister in Southampton, Long Island, copying passages from it into the town records. Later he spent twenty years as minister in Branford, where he was a close associate of John Davenport, perhaps the most determined advocate in New England for godly government. It gave him special pleasure that his "choice and precious daughter" Abigail married John Davenport Jr. in 1662. In addition to being Newark's spiritual leader for eleven years, he provided timely aid to the town by reaching out to Governor Winthrop during the crackdown after the rebellion of 1672. As Cotton Mather remarked about Pierson, "where-ever he came, he shone." After Pierson's death, Obadiah Bruen, one of Newark's most respected residents, marked the transition in Newark's church: "It hath pleased God . . . to imbitter our comforts by taking to himself our reverend pastor, Aug. the 9, 1678." Bruen added that the Newark church had called "Mr. Abraham Pierson, who follows in the steps of his ancient father in godliness—praise to our God." He thought the younger Pierson was "well rooted and grounded in the faith, one with whom we can comfortably walk in the doctrines of the faith."[1]

During the months following Pierson's death, the new generation of leaders, notably Thomas Johnson, John Curtis, and John Ward, led the town through a process of renewing control over key aspects of their life together, based on the founding covenants. That these steps were considered necessary may reflect some backsliding among townsmen, but it was more likely an effort to affirm first principles during a time of transition. In an initial measure, they sought confirmation for taxing each other to compensate their new minister. At a town meeting on September 30, 1678, "it being fully and unanimously consented to, and agreed upon by every Planter now present, all being called by name," Newarkers agreed to pay eighty pounds annually and provide firewood for the younger Pierson's maintenance. That was followed early in February with a vote limiting what townsmen could plant: "The Town consented by Vote, not to sow any Pease white or gray this Year." The next day, the town confirmed its control over both admitting planters (i.e., landowning residents) to live in Newark and allocating plots of land within the Newark tract—two of the key attributes of Newark's commitment to the New England township model. Samuel Dod and Anthony Oliff confessed to the town meeting that they had taken up land before being admitted as planters, "contrary to a Town Agreement." Once they recognized the town's authority in these matters, they were admitted and had their landholdings confirmed. Oliff's situation made the town's position clear: His land had been "laid out to him by the Surveyor" at the foot of First Mountain, but the town insisted he first needed their permission to reside among them before he could patent his land with the provincial government. Five other men also appeared before the town meeting to confess that they had each taken up land "contrary to a Town agreement," and in each case they were granted the land, having acknowledged town control.[2]

The death of Sir George Carteret in January 1680 led to a different transition, characterized by disruptive claims and counterclaims between Philip Carteret and New York governor Edmund Andros about jurisdiction over the province. Newarkers were mostly bystanders, but they made their views known, especially when the assembly met. There had long been friction between Philip Carteret and successive governors of New York over whether New York could impose customs duties on all merchandise intended for New Jersey (or later East Jersey) and whether New Jersey could establish its own port and collect its own duties. In 1676, Philip Carteret renewed his complaints to Sir George Carteret about the "unneighbourly dealing" of Governor Andros in imposing customs duties on "whatsoever vessel come bound to New Jersey & passing by New Yorke," even if the goods were consigned to and off-loaded in New Jersey—unlike, he asserted, in Governor Lovelace's day when goods bound for other colonies could pass by unquestioned. He urged Sir George to use his influence to persuade the Duke of York to issue an order to "stop this dayly Injury."[3] The Duke of York deferred ruling in New York's favor so long as he needed allies at court and Sir George Carteret retained influence. As a result, the issue festered and remained unresolved.

Andros claimed authority to govern both East and West Jersey on behalf of the Duke of York, asserting that the proprietors controlled only the distribution of land and quitrent revenue, not the government itself, but he held off making his move until a propitious time. He got the opening he wanted after Sir George Carteret resigned, in declining health, from both the Privy Council and Admiralty Commission in 1679, and then died early in 1680.[4] In March, Andros extended the Duke of York's jurisdiction over East Jersey, brusquely telling Philip Carteret in a forceful letter that he had no "legal authority" to govern East Jersey and dispatching an associated proclamation to the seven towns in East Jersey, including Newark. Carteret rejected Andros's argument, pointing to the king's "express Commands to yield Obedience to the Government, established by Sir George Carteret." Carteret's council stood with him in this dispute, as did Newarkers early on, likely fearing that any new disruption would place their land titles at risk. Newark leader Thomas Johnson joined council member William Sandford in delivering Carteret's response to Andros in New York, along with various supporting documents. After reviewing the materials, Andros sought to discuss the matter with Sandford and Johnson, but they demurred, claiming they did not know the contents of the letter and "did not have authority to speak any thing conserning it."[5] Determined to proceed with the takeover, Andros summoned an assembly to meet in Woodbridge and ordered each town to send deputies. Newark resisted the order. The town instead stood with Carteret's government, at least for the present, informing Andros "that they have taken the Oath of Allegiance to the King and Fidelity to the present Government, and untill they have sufficient Order from his Majesty we will stand by the same." When taking these votes, Newarkers were likely aware that Governor Carteret had countermanded Andros's writ earlier the same day and informed Andros that his "emissaries" would be prosecuted as "spies or Disturbers of the Publick Peace" unless they came with a particular message for him as governor. Carteret added that he would appeal to the king to settle the question of jurisdiction: "It was by his Majesty's Command that this Government was established, and without the same Command can never be resigned but with our Lives and Fortunes, the People resolving to live and dye with the Name of true Subjects and not Traytors."[6]

A forceful man of action, Andros was not easily put off. With a small delegation, he came uninvited to Carteret's residence in Elizabethtown on April 7. Each man made his case for exercising the functions of government based on his patents from the king but remained unpersuaded by the other's arguments. Carteret again proposed that the dispute should be appealed to the king and his advisors, but Andros dismissed the idea. Three weeks later, Andros took more direct action, dispatching soldiers to Elizabethtown with a warrant to arrest Carteret. Arriving unannounced in the middle of the night, they broke down his doors, rousted him from bed "most barbarously and inhumanly and violently," and took him by force to New York, where he was imprisoned. Newarkers saw an opportunity to leverage their current support for the proprietary government to request both more land and a town charter. On May 3, the town meeting voted to petition deputy governor John Berry (who took over after Carteret was imprisoned by Andros) and the council for a grant of the "land and Meadow called Poquanuck" as consolation for having been "hindred and deprived of the [Barbadoes] Neck, and Hockquekanung [Acquackanonk]," along with a town charter "for the whole" (that is, the original Newark tract and the requested new grant of land). However, Newark's gambit was unsuccessful.[7]

After four weeks in prison, Carteret was brought before a special court of assizes in New York at the end of May, on the charge that he "presumed to exercise Jurisdiction and Government over his Majesty's Subjects." Andros viewed the proceedings from a raised platform constructed for the occasion. Carteret first thought to deny the authority of the court and not enter a plea, but he then decided to lay out his case before the jury. Letters from Andros in prior years addressed to him as governor were perhaps his most telling exhibit. The jury deliberated and returned a not guilty verdict. Enraged, Andros sent them out twice more to reconsider. Each time, the jury returned the same not guilty verdict. Finally, the court accepted the verdict but required that if Carteret returned to "New-Jersey, he should give Security or Engagement not to assume any Authority or Jurisdiction there, Civil or Military." Thus, Andros got what he wanted, even if he lost the trial. Two weeks later, "attended by his whole retinue of ladies and gentlemen," Andros made a magnanimous show of escorting Carteret to his home in Elizabethtown, having meanwhile taken full charge of the East Jersey government.[8]

Even before Carteret's trial in New York, Andros issued a new order requiring each East Jersey town to choose deputies to a general assembly. This time Newarkers cooperated, electing Thomas Johnson and John Ward on May 24 to represent them when the assembly met in Elizabethtown nine days later. Andros expected a brisk session at which the assembly would accept the king's patent as the basis of government and replace their laws with the laws of New York. Instead, echoing the Exclusion Parliaments in England in this same period, the assembly insisted on Magna Carta instead of the king's patent as "the only Rule priviledge and Joint Safety of every free borne English man." The assembly also asserted that "the Lawes formerly made in this Province to bee the most fitting," as opposed to New York's laws. In addition, they demanded that "ther be a generall assemblie Called once a yeare" in October, as promised in the proprietors' original concessions and as a "right belonging to every free born Englishman." Andros rejected these demands and, finding the assembly's proceedings "dilatory and tedious," left Elizabethtown for several days. Newark's deputies were in full accord with the assembly's stance, and they joined the speaker in a final round of negotiations with Andros's council on June 11. Neither side budged. Andros dissolved the assembly on June 12, but members of the assembly had discovered newfound unity around their demand for privileges listed in the original concessions as the bulwark against arbitrary decisions by Andros and his council.[9]

John Curtis, who had represented Newark in the assembly the year before, likely declined election to the assembly called by Andros since he would have had to take an oath of allegiance to the new government. He made his opposition to Andros publicly known at a tavern in Elizabethtown on June 4 while the assembly was meeting. A witness heard Curtis make "railing Speeches" against Andros, saying "what a pox had Sir Edmund or any belonging to yorke to try Governor Carterett." According to the witness, Curtis called Andros "a pitifull fellow to take him away soe Cowardly" and argued that "the Collony were fooles if they did not make him know itt." Four days later, Curtis again made his views known at the tavern. This time he was joined by one Dr. William Taylor, who also spoke against Andros, calling him "a Rogue and a traitor." Newarker John Ward "bid him hold his tongue," but Taylor persisted. After learning about the exchange, Andros issued arrest warrants for both Curtis and Taylor. Curtis was quickly arrested in Newark, while Taylor was spotted in Newark but left before he could be taken. After Andros and his secretary Matthias Nicolls examined Curtis in Newark on June 10, he was transferred to the custody of the sheriff of New York, charged with "publickly uttering approbrius and scandalous words against the Governor and Government." He was later released on bail but then failed to show up for a court date. A new warrant for his arrest was issued on August 4 and sent to different towns, including Woodbridge and Elizabethtown, but there is no further record of the case. The charges may have been dropped, as Taylor's were, after giving security for future good behavior.[10]

More changes were soon at hand, and they led to the restoration of Philip Carteret's government—although once again the news was slow to cross the Atlantic. In the fall of 1680, the Duke of York granted an indenture for East Jersey to Sir George Carteret's grandson and heir, a boy named Sir George Carteret of Hawnes, covering both the land of East Jersey and "all necessary Government there." The Duke of York's secretary, Sir John Werden, wrote to Andros on November 6 "to prevent . . . any doubt of the validity" of the new grant. However, Andros did not receive the news before being recalled to England. He departed in January 1681, leaving Anthony Brockholls in charge as deputy governor with jurisdiction for New York and East Jersey. Weeks later, Philip Carteret received notice from Lady Elizabeth Carteret, Sir George Carteret's widow and sole executor of his estate, about the Duke of York's clear assignment of the powers of government to the young Sir George Carteret. As guardian to the boy proprietor, she "wholly disown[ed] and declare[d] that Sir Edmund Andros had never any such Order or Authority" over the government of East Jersey. Philip Carteret issued a proclamation on March 2, 1681, canceling scheduled court sessions and indicating that he would soon call an assembly. Brockholls and Carteret continued to spar over jurisdictional issues until Brockholls finally received Werden's letter to Andros in mid-May.[11]

Revolution of 1681

Newarkers elected Thomas Johnson and John Curtis as their deputies to the general assembly summoned by Carteret in late July. The only law passed was a restriction on selling or serving Native Americans "any sort of strong drink, viz. rum, brandy, wine, cyder, strong beer, or any other intoxicating liquor," but Carteret reported to Lady Elizabeth Carteret that the council and deputies unanimously declared that Andros's takeover of East Jersey's government had been illegal. After four days, the session was adjourned until October. The deputies used the intervening months to prepare for a much more contentious session, which historian Richard P. McCormick called the "Revolution of 1681." Again, Newarkers played a prominent role: Thomas Johnson and John Curtis were specifically identified by Carteret's council as among the "cheife Contrivers" of the protest.[12]

Members of the assembly turned to the promises spelled out in the proprietors' original concessions, especially those related to the powers of the assembly, as their constitutional protection against arbitrary government. They had experienced extraordinary instability and changes in New Jersey's government over the sixteen years since Philip Carteret first arrived in 1665: the rebellion of 1672; confirmation of proprietary authority with revised concessions followed by the recapture of New Netherland by the Dutch in 1673; the restoration of proprietary government, sale of West Jersey and creation of East Jersey in 1674; Andros's takeover in 1680; and now Philip Carteret's return as governor with Lady Elizabeth Carteret as "proprietrix" and guardian for a boy proprietor. Men had taken oaths of loyalty to two proprietors, the Dutch, a single proprietor, Andros's government, and now a proprietor again. Assembly leaders were still stung by Andros's rejection of their petition the year before for annual meetings, as a right they claimed was due all Englishmen based on the Magna Carta. Thus, it is not surprising that deputies chose to resist new assertions of power and authority by Philip Carteret and his council. When the assembly convened in Elizabethtown on October 19, the deputies immediately sent a note to the governor and council, asking "to bee informed whether wee are to look upon the late Grant from the Duke to the Proprietors as the Foundation of our Government." Carteret and his council suspected the deputies were referring to the arguments that Andros had made: "Wee well hoped that none of the seed sowne by Sir Edmond Andros had taken so deep a roote." But the deputies had a different issue in mind: They wanted to make the proprietors' original concessions, dated February 10, 1665, the basis of East Jersey's government, "taken according to the Letter without any Interpretation whatsoever." This would not only restore the assembly's right to appoint their own time of meeting, enact laws as long as they did not limit liberty of conscience or go against the interest of the proprietor, and take responsibility for constituting courts and local militias, but it would also reopen the question of whether the deputies constituted a unicameral general assembly (as the deputies wanted since they would hold the majority) or whether the governor and council made up an upper body and the assembly a lower house in a bicameral general assembly. To make this claim, however, the deputies had to argue that the proprietors' revisions to the concessions, spelled out in their "Declaration of the True Intent and Meaning . . . of their Concessions" in December 1672 after the rebellion, were somehow void.[13]

The governor and council requested that delegations from both the council and assembly meet "to debate and remove these Scruples." The assembly appointed a four-member committee comprised of speaker John Bowne, a Baptist from Middletown, Thomas Johnson of Newark, Edward Slater of Piscataway, and John Ilsley of Woodbridge. No progress was made, and the assembly resolved on October 21 that the proprietors' 1672 declaration was "a Breach of the Concessions under the Pretence of which certain persons have presumed to Act to the greate prejudice of the Inhabitants here settled." Carteret and his council could not accept this interpretation, of course, and they grew increasingly exasperated with the deputies. Nonetheless, they agreed to another meeting. For this fresh debate, the deputies chose a new four-man committee, again led by John Bowne, Thomas Johnson, and Edward Slater, but this time replacing John Ilsley with John Curtis of Newark—thus Newark's deputies made up half of the committee. Again, neither side budged. The assembly then declared the proprietors' 1672 declaration was "prejudiciall to the Power and Priviledges of the general assembly and people" and urged that it be "made voyd and of none effect." The gauntlet had been thrown. The council and assembly exchanged increasingly pointed messages over the next several days, with neither side shifting its position. The assembly insulted Carteret personally by referring to the proprietors' 1672 declaration as "a bratt begotten in New Jersey and sent for England to be borne and Retransported to New Jersey to be fed with the groanes and Oppressions of the People." The council insisted that the assembly pass a bill raising revenue to cover the expenses of the government, required under the concessions, but the assembly responded by insisting that several acts, already passed by the assembly, should first be "passed and returned back to this house." Faced with a stalemate, the governor and council dissolved the assembly on November 1. The next day the assembly protested the dissolution, declaring it "contrary to the Concessions and an Innovation of the Government."[14]

The governor and council wanted the last word. They prepared their interpretation of the events and distributed it widely. They noted that several deputies, "fickle unconstant and unstable men"—explicitly including Thomas Johnson and John Curtis of Newark—had also served in the 1679 assembly session when they had recognized the validity of the proprietors' 1672 declaration amending the concessions. They argued further that "the wicked designes of unfaithfull unconstant & evill dispossed men strickes at Government and Reaches as deepe as hell." Newarkers were unmoved by these arguments. At the beginning of January, they again selected both Thomas Johnson and John Curtis as their deputies "for the Year ensuing."[15]

The assembly did not meet again while Philip Carteret was governor. Sir George Carteret's will had directed the trustees of his estate to sell various properties, including East Jersey, to settle his debts. The trustees made several efforts to sell the province privately for at least £5,000, but without success. Finally, they put it up for auction, at which a group of twelve Quakers led by William Penn acquired the province, along with quitrents in arrears and the right of government, for £3,400. The lease and release deeds were signed on February 1 and 2, 1682. A few months later the twelve new proprietors agreed to expand their consortium by each selling a half share. All but three of the second group were also Quakers. The Duke of York issued a new patent to the "Twenty-Four Proprietors," as they came to be known, and soon Thomas Rudyard took office as deputy governor. A month later, in December 1682, Philip Carteret died in Elizabethtown at age 43. His widow sent the "moste unwellcom and sad tydings" to his mother, noting that the "barborrouse and unhewman Actions of Sir Edmund Andros and his Mercyless Souldiers" had left him with bodily infirmities that "made his Life . . . at his Latter end most uncomfortable."

The new government of the Twenty-Four Proprietors, combined with Philip Carteret's death, marked another abrupt transition for the inhabitants of the province.[16]

CHAPTER 11

Compromise

The Twenty-Four Proprietors acted essentially as an investment corporation to make and receive distributions of land, collect quitrent revenue, and (they hoped) earn a profit from the subsequent sale of land. They accepted responsibility for the government to provide a stable and attractive environment for land investments by merchants seeking large estates and individual farmers, tradesmen, and servants wanting a new start. They also planned a new capital city at Perth Amboy that could become a center of commerce and government, but Elizabethtown remained the capital in the meanwhile.[1]

Scottish investors among the Twenty-Four Proprietors took the initiative in attracting new settlers, as the English investors soon emphasized Pennsylvania and West Jersey over East Jersey as a refuge for Quakers. To learn about their new acquisition, the proprietors turned to Matthias Nicolls's description of the seven towns and major estates of East Jersey that he had prepared in 1680 when Edmund Andros sought to incorporate the province within New York. Robert Barclay, a Scottish Quaker chosen by the Twenty-Four Proprietors as governor of the province, kept a copy of Nicolls's account in his papers, and George Scot printed it in his *The Model of the Government of the Province of East-New-Jersey in America*, published in Edinburgh in 1685 to promote settlement of East Jersey among Scottish merchants and tradesmen (see Figure 10). Nicolls estimated that Newark had one hundred families in 1680, or a population of roughly five hundred, smaller than Elizabethtown (150 families) and Woodbridge (120 families), but the same size as Middletown and larger than Piscataway (eighty families), Shrewsbury (eighty families), and Bergen (seventy families). He added that Newark was the "most compact Town in the Province."[2]

Deputy governor Thomas Rudyard and his successor Gawen Lawrie sent detailed reports to the London-based proprietors hungry for additional information about East Jersey. They noted that Newark was distinctive among towns in the province for having a settled minister: "The People being mostly *New England* men, doe mostly incline to their way, and in every Town there is a meeting house where they

THE
MODEL
OF THE
GOVERNMENT
Of the
PROVINCE
OF
EAST=NEW=JERSEY
IN
AMERICA;

And Encouragements for ſuch as Deſigns
to be concerned there.

Publiſhed for Information of ſuch as are deſirous to be Intereſted in that place.

EDINBURGH,
Printed by *John Reid*, And Sold be
Alexander Ogſton Stationer in the
Parliament Cloſs. Anno
DOM, 1685.

Figure 10. Title page of George Scot's *The Model of the Government of East=New=Jersey in America*, 1685, published to attract new settlers to East Jersey. From the Collections of the New Jersey Historical Society. All rights reserved.

worship publickly every Week. . . . We know none that hath a settled Preacher that follows no other Imployment, save one Town *Newark*." Peter Watson, a new settler, provided more information in a letter to his brother: "There are here very good Religious People, they go under the name of Independants [i.e., Congregationalists] but are most like to the Presbyterians, only they will not receive every one to their Society." Watson noted that there were then (1684) no ministers "within all the Province of East Jersey, except one who is Preacher in Newark [Abraham Pierson Jr.]: there were one or two Preachers more in the Province, but they are dead [Seth Fletcher in Elizabethtown and John Allyn in Woodbridge], and now the people they meet together every Sabbath day, and Read and pray, and sing Psalms in their Meeting-houses."[3]

Newark was also considered distinctive for its cider. Soon after he arrived to take up his position as deputy governor, Rudyard reported, "At a town called Newark . . . is made great quantities of Syder, exceeding any we can have from New England or Rhod Island or Long Island." Gawen Lawrie later noted, "Sider [is] good and plenty, for 1d per Quart." In a different report he added, "They make abundance of good Cyder, especially at one Town called Newark which is esteemed at New York, and other places where it is sold, beyond any that comes from New England." John Reid, former gardener to the Lord Advocate in Edinburgh, wrote to a friend in 1684, "Fruit trees also prosper here. Newark made about a thousand barrells of Sider last year." Newark settlers had planted orchards when they settled the town, no doubt bringing scions with them from Connecticut, and they quickly found that Newark's soil and microclimate were especially suited to growing apple trees and producing cider. Over the next century and more, Newark cider would gain a reputation as the best in America, earning praise from Thomas Jefferson, among others.[4]

Seeking a Land Settlement

Newarkers prioritized confirming title to their town lands each time there was a change in government, and the transition to the Twenty-Four Proprietors was no exception. Because Newarkers insisted on retaining town control over allocating land parcels within the boundaries of the Newark tract, reaching a resolution with the new proprietors was not straightforward. It took a decade of negotiation, with numerous proposals and counterproposals, to achieve a compromise acceptable to both sides. In 1683, deputy governor Thomas Rudyard and his council received many petitions from individuals, including several from Elizabethtown, for new land grants and patents covering existing holdings. No one from Newark petitioned individually for a grant. True to their New England township model, they voted at a town meeting on March 22 to form a committee "to endeavor in the Town's Behalf the obtaining a legal Settlement" for their holdings and "a Charter for the whole Town's Bounds." A petition to this effect "from the Inhabitants of Newark" was presented to Rudyard and the council the next day, and Rudyard indicated he was willing "to see those Town bounds the next month the wether being seasonable."[5]

Nothing appears to have come of this petition, perhaps because Samuel Groome, the new receiver-general, calculated what Newarkers owed on quitrents. He determined that forty Newarkers had patents covering 5,844 acres, or about 60 percent of the Newark tract. The yearly quitrent for Newark was somewhat more than eleven pounds, with total arrears of almost £140. This amount paled compared to the more than £1,150 due from Barbados planters on their large estates and was significantly less than Shrewsbury's arrears, but it was more than Woodbridge's and Piscataway's. Groome wrote to the East Jersey proprietors in August 1683 that he planned "shortly to write to, and demand in all places of the Quit rents, and Arrears. They generally say they will pay." However, Newarkers no doubt wanted confirmation of their town lands before paying arrears.[6]

In May 1684, within three months of Gawen Lawrie presenting his commission as deputy governor in place of Thomas Rudyard, the Newark town meeting formed another committee "to consider and draw up something as may be in Readiness, if Occasion be, to manifest our Right and Title to the Land we bought." They tried again in December 1684, this time forming a twelve-member committee "to treat with the Governor." Four members of that committee arranged to meet with Lawrie in Elizabethtown the following month "about their quit rents, and their town bounds," as Lawrie later recalled. He wanted a written proposal, which the Newarkers refused to provide, instead reading "a long paper about their Indian right" and requesting a general patent for all their unpatented town lands in return for "a small acknowledgement" or annual payment. Lawrie countered with a proposal that "after the Proprietors sevenths were sett out" they could have a patent for unsettled lands at about a farthing per acre—provided current patentholders paid their arrears of quitrents, and those who had not yet taken patents did so and paid their arrears. The Newark delegation left to consult with the other committee members. When they returned four days later, they basically repeated their request. Lawrie again insisted on payment of arrears first, saying he would then "treat with them on easie terms." No agreement was reached, which Lawrie blamed on their waiting to see whether major landowners, including John Berry, the former deputy governor, paid their quitrent arrears.[7]

The newly created Board of Proprietors of the Eastern Division of New Jersey, charged with making land grants and otherwise looking out for property interests of proprietors—separate from their right of government—met for the first time on April 9, 1685. This distinct structure allowed the board to continue to meet even after the proprietors relinquished their right of government in 1688, when East Jersey was consolidated into the Dominion of New England, and again after New Jersey became a royal colony in 1702. In advance of the inaugural meeting of the board, Samuel Groome completed a fresh analysis of quitrents. This time he noted fifty-six men from Newark holding patents for 5,637 acres and owing almost £179, with less than twenty pounds having been paid. While less than what Shrewsbury, Elizabethtown, and Middletown owed, it was significantly more than Piscataway. In contrast, Woodbridge and Bergen landowners were essentially current with their quitrents. Groome's analysis made it difficult for Newark to negotiate for a charter confirming their town boundaries and privileges. The Board of Proprietors also presumed individual patents, as did residents of other towns in East Jersey, while Newark tried to stay the course with its township approach to land distribution.[8]

Collective control of town lands had been an essential element of Newark's township government since its first settlement. In 1674, when Newarkers replaced the office of magistrate with seven townsmen, elected annually and charged with dealing with all town business "according to the best of their Judgement for the good of the Town," the inhabitants reserved three essential powers to themselves: allocating land, admitting inhabitants, and determining the method of levying rates or taxes. When the town meeting confirmed this change in the structure of town government in 1682, and again the following year, it included the key proviso that "it infringe not on any of the three things prohibited in the Town Book." These votes emphatically underscored the importance Newarkers placed on retaining town control over town lands—and explain why Newark remained at odds with the proprietors.[9]

Thomas Johnson, John Ward, and several other inhabitants of Newark petitioned the Board of Proprietors in April 1685 for "a patent for a township and corporation of Newark town bounds," promising to pay an annual quitrent of fifty pounds, well above the amount calculated by Samuel Groome. The board received the petition respectfully but determined that it was not "safe" for the governor to respond to the petition, "inasmuch as there are many particular patents for lands made by the former governor to several of the petitioners and others in Newark, which patents are all in force." The board advised the governor to consider Newark's petition only after all the patents were surrendered "for the use of the Lords proprietors." This proposal to surrender the individual patents granted by Philip Carteret was unacceptable to Newarkers, so the issue remained unsettled.[10] The Newark town meeting addressed the issue twice more during the summer months: in June, confirming the committee formed the prior December "to treat with the Proprietors, about our Settlement," and in August, selecting five men to assist those summoned by the Board of Proprietors in defending "our just Rights and Titles to our Land." When a Newark delegation led by Thomas Johnson and John Ward met with the board again in October 1685, they requested a patent for their town and "confirmation of their just right to their purchased bounds, as the same is expressed in their Indian Deed of Sale." They dropped their prior request for a charter and offered to pay ten pounds annually in rent for their unallocated town land. The board did not bite, informing the Newark delegation that they would only deal with the new petition once all arrears in quitrent had been paid for lands already patented. They added pressure by bringing suits in the Court of Common Right against several Newarkers who had not patented their land, including Abraham Pierson Jr.[11]

At this point, some Newarkers may have wondered whether it was worth retaining their New England township structure, given the ongoing disputes with the Board of Proprietors. If so, they did not carry the day. Instead, the majority of inhabitants at a town meeting in November 1685 voted that two men should "go from House to House" of those who had not subscribed to the town's "fundamental Covenant" and "return their answer to the Town." And in April 1686, the town charged a three-man committee to study the third division of land that had taken place years earlier, "to see how much each one hath exceeded what he should have taken up, or come short of what they might have taken up," so the town could make necessary adjustments to the allocations. In January 1687, the town meeting returned to the issue of "our Settlement for the Town Bounds," forming still another committee to negotiate with the Board of Proprietors. A year later, to buttress their case, Newarkers secured a deposition from Robert Treat, then governor of Connecticut, about his negotiations in 1666 with Philip Carteret and the Hackensack for the Newark tract. Treat's account was important because it helped Newarkers make the case that their "Indian title" had been sanctioned at the time by Governor Carteret. A similar deposition by Samuel Edsall, also in March 1688, confirmed Carteret's role: "By order of Governour Phillip Carteret and upon the request of the inhabitants of Newark, I did for them purchase of the Hackingsack Indians a parcel of land." When Azariah Crane and Edward Ball applied to the board in April on behalf of the town for a warrant to run the town boundary line, likely informing them about the depositions, there was some movement in the standoff. This time the board suggested if the inhabitants settled with the proprietors for their quitrents, "then their bounds [would] be made good to them." Newarkers responded by forming still another committee "to endeavour a legall Settlement with the Proprietors."[12]

After ten years of negotiations, Newarkers finally reached an agreement with the Board of Proprietors in 1693, when governor Andrew Hamilton made a new proposal with incentives for the "old settlers and first adventurers" of Newark—that is, those men with shares in the original land association that acquired the town lands. Early that year, the town meeting chose a new committee "to treat with the Governor and Proprietors about our Settlement." Four men traveled to Perth Amboy at the end of February and discussed "an amicable and friendly accommodation" with the board in which their title to the lands would be confirmed in return "for a yearly acknowledgement." As before, the board insisted that all, not just some, Newarkers should first take out patents on the lands they already possessed "and pay their arrears of quit rent for the time past and the time coming." At this point, governor Andrew Hamilton introduced a new element to the negotiations to break the stalemate. With support from his colleagues on the board, Hamilton proposed that if patents were taken out for all lands, and if all past and "coming" quitrents were paid, "old settlers" could each receive an additional one hundred acres of land within the bounds of the Newark tract at a much-reduced annual quitrent of six pence. In effect, Hamilton's proposal acknowledged the shareholder rights of men who invested in the original purchase of Newark but transferred control over allocating the remaining unappropriated land from the Newark town meeting to the Board of Proprietors. It was a creative compromise that gave each side something they wanted. Most Newarkers gained additional land, while the board secured some revenue (about fifteen pounds plus payment of arrears) and acknowledgement that it controlled confirmation of land titles and allocation of unappropriated land within the township.[13]

Newarkers tested the compromise to see whether it would hold. In August 1693, the board heard a petition from John Curtis, the recognized leader of Newark at the time, for confirmation of his patent from Governor Carteret and a new grant of "100 acres of land as an old settler at 6 pence per annum, all within the bounds of Newark." The board approved these requests with the stipulation that he pay past and future quitrents. Then, in December 1693, John Gardner petitioned for four hundred acres in the right of Abraham Pierson Jr., whose land he had purchased the year before, plus one hundred acres at six pence per annum in Pierson's right as an old settler. The board granted him 180 acres at the standard half-pence per acre quitrent if he paid the arrears going back to 1670 (thus showing Pierson had not paid quitrents), plus the promised one hundred acres within Newark bounds as an old settler. At the same meeting, Azariah Crane and Jasper Crane Jr. jointly petitioned for one hundred acres within Newark bounds "in the right of their father [Jasper Crane] who was an old settler," and Azariah Crane joined with his brother-in-law John Treat in making a similar claim for one hundred acres in Robert Treat's right as an old settler; both petitions were granted.[14]

The "old settler" grants led more than two dozen other Newarkers to petition for similar one-hundred-acre grants at the Board of Proprietors meeting the following April. This flood of requests gave the board pause. However, after "a full debate and deliberate consideration," the board approved a detailed motion confirming the compromise first proposed a year earlier by Governor Hamilton: "[W]hether it be for the interest of the proprietors or not that the inhabitants of Newark, who are old settlers of the said town, shall have 100 acres of land to each of them granted, at 6 pence per 100 per annum quit rent within the bounds of the said Town of Newark upon their amicable agreement with the proprietors and taking out their patents and paying all their by past arrears of quit rent and in time to come."[15]

Six members of the board voted in the affirmative, "especially considering the badness of the land," while one member dissented, arguing that it was not in the proprietors' interest. The board then proceeded to approve the one-hundred-acre grants. A year later, John Browne Jr. petitioned for his old settler grant, plaintively explaining to the board that he had been absent in New England when his neighbors received their grants and that "his friends, whom he trusted in his absence," failed to petition on his behalf. Still other Newarkers made old settler claims in April 1696, in apparently the last round of such claims. All petitions were granted so long as those who had old patents resigned them and took out new ones.[16]

The old settlers who received an unexpected grant of one hundred acres benefited greatly from having their land titles and the town bounds recognized. Several Newarkers more than doubled their landholdings, including John Baldwin Sr. (seventy-eight acres before receiving the new one-hundred-acre grant), John Baldwin Jr. (forty-four acres), Samuel Freeman (ninety-two acres), Theophilus Pierson (eighty-eight acres), Robert Dalglish (forty-two acres), Jonathan Sears (sixty acres), and Samuel Rose (sixty acres). Other Newarkers gained by selling their newly granted land to Dutch settlers; for example, Hans Albers sold his one hundred acres, and John Curtis sixty of his one hundred acres to Thomas Jurianse.[17]

However, Newarkers may not have been recognized at the beginning all the ramifications of the compromise. In January 1694, the town meeting voted, as they had many times in previous years for other individuals, to allocate sixty acres of land to Robert Young, "he paying the Purchase as others have done," but it was the last time such a vote occurred. Similarly, in March 1694, the town admitted eleven new "planters" as inhabitants, again as they had many times in prior years, but this, too, proved the final time the town meeting held such a vote. When Zophar Beach acquired a two-acre home lot in Newark in 1696, he secured his title from the proprietors, not the town.[18]

The designation of "old settlers" in the compromise with the Board of Proprietors marked a clear distinction for the first time between shareholders in the land association that acquired the original Newark tract and current residents who made up the Newark town meeting. Until this point, the two groups had been essentially the same, as demonstrated by the several town votes in prior years establishing committees to negotiate with the proprietors for a "settlement," but now there were enough residents of Newark who had not purchased or inherited shares in the land association that it was no longer appropriate for the town meeting to take up issues related to land in the original Newark tract. Thus, the town meeting was not involved when John Curtis and Robert Young petitioned the Board of Proprietors in April 1696 "in behalf of the rest of the Freeholders" for a patent for streets and commons in Newark and for two hundred acres to support the town minister. At the end of the year, the board approved their request and issued a patent with an annual quitrent of six pence "sterling monie of England" to John Curtis, John Treat, Theophilus Pierson, and Robert Young on behalf of "the Old Settlers of the Towne of Newark." The four men—not the town—became trustees for a home lot and two hundred acres of upland and meadow in five tracts, "for the Parsonage"; a burying place; a market place (today's Harriet Tubman Square, formerly Washington Park); a training place (today's Military Park); a watering place for cattle; and "the Streetes of the sayd Towne of Newark as they are now Layd out."[19]

The town meeting still retained control over several items—setting tax rates, electing town's men and deputies to the assembly, hiring and paying ministers, implementing acts of the assembly, and setting the dates when livestock would be permitted to graze in the commons—but the nearly three-decade experiment in creating and sustaining a New England township with control over allocating land, admitting inhabitants, and administering justice had been reduced to a pale shadow of the one intended by the founders in the town's original fundamental agreements.

CHAPTER 12

Turbulent Times

When deputy governor Thomas Rudyard formed his council and convened the first general assembly under the Twenty-Four Proprietors early in 1683, he made a determined effort to allay concerns of East Jersey residents, believing "it hath been very unhappy heretofore under an ill managed Government." Thomas Johnson and John Curtis participated in the assembly as Newark's deputies. They carried instructions from a committee established by the Newark town meeting "to consider of some things as they think may be for the Town's Good, in order that our Deputies should promote the same at the general assembly." The first assembly session in March was constructive and much less contentious than the last one held under Philip Carteret. Rudyard's patience, however, was likely tested in the May session, when the deputies reverted to form, contesting proposed legislation and requesting near-daily conferences with the council, with the Newark deputies again taking prominent roles.

The assembly passed eighteen acts in March, four more in May, and then another twenty-one in November and December, which together established the legal structure for the province under the Twenty-Four Proprietors. Some acts directly affected Newarkers, such as those regarding swine, horses, and fences—regulations that earlier in Newark's existence would have been set by the town meeting. Members of Rudyard's council also advanced concerns of high priority to themselves, but of less relevance to Newarkers, including restrictions on the entertainment of "negro Servants" by Native groups (John Berry, an enslaver, was instructed to carry a message to the sachems), trading with "negro and Indian slaves, or servants . . . [who] frequently steal from their masters and others," and purchasing land from "Indian Sachems and Indian natives" without advance approval from the proprietors.[1]

The detailed provisions of the legislation about horses drew opposition from Newarkers, who likely raised horses for trade to Barbados, as Abraham Pierson Sr. had done. The act, passed late in 1683, established the new position of chief ranger in each county with responsibility for "taking up and receiving all strays," and prohibited anyone else from ranging the woods "upon pretence of getting up of wild horses or strays" without advance license, subject to a stiff five-pound penalty. In February, the Newark town meeting instructed town leaders to suggest changes to the act and then present them to Thomas Johnson and John Curtis, Newark's deputies for the year, "that we may not be hindred to take up our Horses out of the Woods."[2]

Newark continued to elect deputies each year at its New Year's meeting, but the general assembly did not assemble again until April 1686, when, for the first time, the assembly met in Perth Amboy; all prior sessions going back to 1668 had taken place in Elizabethtown. The resident proprietors considered Perth Amboy "more conveniently situated, and near the center of the province, and the most encouraging place for trade and traffick by sea and land." For Newarkers, however, Perth Amboy was much less convenient than Elizabethtown. Although John Curtis and Thomas Richards were elected deputies in 1686, only Curtis attended the assembly session in Perth Amboy. That was the case for assembly sessions in 1687 and 1688, too. Newarkers likely thought it sufficient to pay per diem costs for just one deputy who could keep a wary eye on but not fully engage in the government of the Twenty-Four Proprietors.[3]

Newarkers were perhaps wise to keep their distance from provincial matters, but they would soon be drawn into more pressing regional issues. The Twenty-Four Proprietors maintained only a tenuous hold on their right of government even as they tightened control over land distribution in East Jersey. Soon after the Duke of York succeeded to the throne as James II in February 1685, following the death of his brother Charles II, he ordered his attorney general to consider quo warranto proceedings against the proprietors of East Jersey, West Jersey, and Delaware, challenging the legal basis of their right of government. New York Governor Dongan sent frequent reports to London in this period, complaining about East Jersey's encroachments on New York's privilege of collecting customs duties. East Jersey's proprietors managed to have Perth Amboy designated a port of entry in 1687, but their success would have mattered little to Newarkers, since they conducted their trade through New York. Later that same year Dongan managed to secure an order from James II directing East Jersey to assist New York's defense against a possible invasion by the French from the north. At its session in May 1688, East Jersey's assembly complied with the royal command by approving a tax of "one penny on the pound" on all estates.[4] However, still another major disruption in East Jersey's government took place before the tax could be collected. In April 1688, James II expanded the Dominion of New England to include East Jersey, West Jersey, and New York. As always, it took weeks for the news to cross the Atlantic, and the East Jersey government continued to function in the meanwhile. The assembly held a session in May, and the council met on June 19, but once word about the expansion of the Dominion reached East Jersey, the council did not meet again until September 1692, a gap of four years.

Sir Edmund Andros, governor of the Dominion of New England since James II formed it in 1686, toured the Jerseys late in the summer. His commission was proclaimed in Elizabethtown on August 15, 1688, and in Burlington four days later. Andros thought he settled East and West Jersey "to their great satisfaction" by confirming current officeholders in their positions. However, it is unlikely Newarkers welcomed the expansion of the Dominion, having no doubt heard a litany of complaints from contacts in Boston about how Andros had centralized royal authority by ending the representative assembly in Massachusetts, forcing landowners to take out new patents, and banning town meetings except for the sole purpose of electing civil officers.

A week after proclaiming the Dominion in East Jersey, Andros received news "by expresse from Boston" about the birth of a son to King James II. He staged a large public celebration in New York on August 27, with plentiful food and drink, gun salutes, and a great bonfire outside the fort. He also ordered a day of public thanksgiving the following Sunday throughout the Dominion. Whatever Newarkers thought of the proprietary government or the Dominion, they would not have welcomed the birth of a male heir to James II, which threatened to establish a Roman Catholic succession to the throne of England. It was reported that Anglican, French, and Anabaptist congregations in Boston published the thanksgiving proclamation "with all demonstrations of Joy," but the three Congregational churches did not read the proclamation or "take any notice of that day." Newark's Congregationalists likely also ignored both the proclamation and the day of thanksgiving.[5]

The Dominion of New England was representative of James II's effort to assert his absolute sovereignty and create a bureaucratic, centralized government modeled on Louis XIV's government in France. James II expected total loyalty when he appointed officials and military leaders, many of them Roman Catholic, to their positions.[6] Governing on the king's behalf from Boston, Andros implemented an authoritarian, centralized structure, even moving New York's public records there. To manage the Dominion of New England effectively, Andros depended on frequent communication not only within the colonies but more importantly with London. However, during the epochal crisis of William of Orange's invasion of England in 1688, Andros was frozen in place for months without guidance or fresh instructions. He likely thought James II, with his standing army of some forty thousand troops, would deal with this new invasion with the same dispatch as he had Monmouth's Rebellion in England and Argyle's Rising in Scotland a few years earlier, but he could not be sure. News of James II's warning in October of a sudden invasion from Holland reached the colonies two months later and was proclaimed by Andros in January, but it was March before Andros received confirmation that William of Orange's invasion had indeed taken place early in November. William's declaration in late November calling on his followers to disarm and secure all papists finally reached Boston early in April. Two weeks later, a public uprising in Boston overthrew the Dominion government, and Andros and several of his council members were jailed. The Glorious Revolution had crossed the Atlantic, and it would soon spread to New York and at least part of the Jerseys.[7]

Newarkers likely tapped into merchant networks for news during this turbulent period, rather than waiting for official pronouncements by colonial officials. Merchants nurtured information sources among reliable trading partners to guide their business decisions and manage trading relationships. Newarkers had access to several of these networks. Henry Lyon, resident of Elizabethtown and landowner in Newark, was a small-scale merchant but no doubt had his sources, and Jacob Melyn, their former colleague in the New Barbadoes transaction, had shifted his operations to Boston. William Jones, a New Haven magistrate and merchant whose daughter married a Newarker, presumably also kept them informed. In addition, John Treat may have sought advice and news from his father Robert Treat, who had been removed as governor of Connecticut by Andros but remained at the center of Connecticut politics. Through these and other contacts, Newark leaders were participants in a larger Calvinist alliance of New Englanders, Dutch and German merchants, and French Huguenot settlers, all with deep religious convictions. They formed what historian David Voorhees called "a resistance movement" focused on "the reestablishment and preservation of the true protestant religion." It is noteworthy that when Jacob Leisler, a prominent merchant and New York militia captain, emerged as the leader of New York's Glorious Revolution in June 1689, he counted both Melyn and Jones among his correspondents.[8]

The New York City militia, fearing a French invasion and distressed by the disrepair of Fort James at the tip of Manhattan, seized the fort in early June. Lieutenant Governor Nicholson fled to England a few days later. On June 8, a ten-member Committee of Safety, modeled on the one created weeks earlier in Boston, was formed to govern in place of Nicholson and a mostly absent city council. On June 22, Jacob Leisler and other militia leaders proclaimed William and Mary, first at the fort and then in the city. At the end of the chaotic month, the Committee of Safety—essentially a Calvinist alliance as interim government—was reconstituted on a regional basis, with five of the original ten members joined by several new members, including John Curtis of Newark and Henry Lyon of Elizabethtown. This was Newark's first direct engagement in what came to be known as Leisler's Rebellion.[9]

Thirteen members were present when the regional Committee of Safety met for the first time in New York on June 27. Along with Curtis and Lyon, East Jersey was represented by William Lawrence of Hackensack. Other men represented the city and county of New York, Westchester County, Kings County, Queens County, Tappan, and Staten Island. Suffolk and Ulster Counties and "most of New Yarsay" did not send representatives, but Connecticut sent two observers to provide advice and support. Over the next three days, the new Committee of Safety took shape, addressing critical issues of defense, security, and revenue. But first they asserted their legitimacy by requiring members to show written "power and authorizations . . . from their Respective places." Henry Lyon was one of three who "came with verball order," but he quickly agreed to bring proof of his "power to apeare." John Curtis produced his authorization, although the Newark town records do not record a vote; perhaps he secured the support of the seven townsmen instead.[10]

In their first meeting, the Committee of Safety agreed "by all votes" to accept recommendations from both Connecticut and Jacob Leisler to raise a company of fifty soldiers for securing the fort and to contribute toward the repair and improvement of its fortifications "for the preservation & Safety of the people, till order from their majesties" reached New York. Curtis and Lyon agreed that Newark and Elizabethtown would together provide for two soldiers, paying them thirty shillings per month plus provisions; Bergen County was allocated four men. Connecticut pledged to pay the wages of an additional ten soldiers once the committee succeeded in procuring fifty soldiers.[11] The next day the committee discussed reports that "some Ill minded and disloyall Impudent persons" were sowing ethnic divisions by claiming that securing the fort was an "ill designe against the English" by the Dutch. In response, the committee declared unanimously that taking the fort was "Singely & Soley for their majesties Service" until orders and directions arrived from London. No person, they asserted, had any reason to leave the city or "slack their hands In their usuall trafficke and trade." They also urged all persons in both the city and country to aid and assist Jacob Leisler in his efforts "to suppress any foreign or Intestine enemy."[12]

Good Calvinists, the committee also recommended a day of solemn thanksgiving on July 17. With support from Curtis and Lyon, the committee encouraged "the ministers & towns In the collony & new Jarsey" to praise God for making William "the glorious Instrument of delivering his people from popery and slavery."[13] Newarkers no doubt endorsed these sentiments and happily joined in the day of thanksgiving. In the next century, Newarkers' continuing association of the Protestant cause with William, both as Prince of Orange and as King William, would be reflected in Aaron Burr Sr.'s decision to give the name Nassau Hall to the first building constructed in Princeton when the College of New Jersey moved there from Newark in 1756, and in a nearby area taking the name "Orange" in 1780.

So long as there was a chance that James II might recover his throne with support from the French, most East Jersey residents did not openly show allegiance to William and Mary. Newark, much of Elizabethtown, and some parts of Bergen County were in William and Mary's camp, perhaps joined by New Englanders in Woodbridge and Piscataway, but Anglicans and Quakers throughout East Jersey were openly opposed or at best cautious. When Jacob Leisler sent troops into East Jersey in July to urge residents to join with them for the country's good, John Johnstone, a Perth Amboy resident and future mayor of New York, "sett at Liberty" arms and horses that the troops had seized "upon suspicion." Johnstone subsequently came into New York and was seen by someone who "had a Mind to Revenge him selfe for Severall affronts"; he was brought into the fort where Leisler or his associates engaged him in debate "for the satisfaction of the people." At length, Johnstone agreed to surrender his sword to Leisler and was "reconciled" to the "reality of the whole matter." Leisler then asked him to take the lead in proclaiming William and Mary in East Jersey, offering to furnish him with a dozen soldiers and the printed proclamation. Johnstone refused, suggesting instead "other Justices there in New Jarsey" who might do it. Like many other large landowners, he perceived greater risk in ending up on the wrong side of James II than benefit in being among the first to proclaim William and Mary.[14]

On this occasion, Leisler allowed Johnstone to leave the fort "freely without molestation of the people." Months later, as he grew increasingly frustrated with East Jersey's role in harboring his opponents, he might not have been so accommodating. He wrote to Gilbert Burnet, Bishop of Salisbury, in January 1690 that Quakers in East Jersey and Pennsylvania "encourage if not outdo the Roman Catholics" in supporting James II. Richard Townley of Elizabethtown, an Anglican who had married Elizabeth Carteret, Philip Carteret's widow, drew his special disdain. He charged Townley, with others, "of committing riot upon our Justices bordering next to them" (presumably justices of the peace in Newark and Elizabethtown) and of "owning none save King James [and] openly drinking his health." Leisler ordered Townley's arrest in February, but Townley evaded capture. Leisler wrote again to Burnet in March, once more naming Townley as a chief adversary, along with James Emott, secretary to the East Jersey Board of Proprietors: "The raging spirit of malice obstructs us much in the neighbouring Colony of East Jersey whither our Chief adversarys fly for sanctuary and are embraced—Coll. Townley[,] one Mr Emott an Attorney and some more of their principall members asserting that the Throne of England is not vacant, for that whilst King James was in France he remained in his owne dominions being annexed to the Crowne."[15] John Curtis and Henry Lyon were likely Leisler's source about Townley's views and activities. Lyon and Townley both lived in Elizabethtown, and many townsmen would have been willing to pass along news to Lyon, even if he was unable to arrange for Townley's arrest.

Records from this period are scarce, so it is not clear whether Curtis and Lyon continued to serve on the Committee of Safety after the summer of 1689. Newarkers no doubt supported efforts in East Jersey to secure the Protestant succession, even if major landowners and former provincial officials held back. The threat of invasion by France, whether by sea or overland from Canada, took on new urgency in February 1690, when a company of more than one hundred French soldiers, accompanied by Native American allies, attacked the unguarded New York village of Schenectady, leaving sixty men, women, and children dead and all but one of the houses burned; twenty-seven residents were taken as prisoners to Canada. In response, Leisler organized an ultimately unsuccessful expedition to invade Canada. Newark did its part, sending three soldiers and paying their expenses "for the time they were out, according to our Agreement." Piscataway also provided men for the expedition, and Henry Lyon helped by supplying the expedition with 300 pounds of cheese.[16]

In March, towns in East Jersey perceived that French and Indian forces were threatening their area. The Newark town meeting voted on March 25 to form a committee "to order all affairs in as prudent a way as they can, for the Safety and Preservation of ourselves, Wives, Children and Estates" and to join "with those in military Capacity" in taking defensive measures. In the absence of any provincial government, Henry Lyon reached out to the Woodbridge town meeting with the request to join Elizabethtown and send "one able Man to Range the Woods Above the Towne in Company with them and Others of our Neighbouring towns, in order to prevent a Danger (before it comes to our homes) threatened By the french & Indians." When they met on April 5, the Woodbridge town meeting agreed "by Vote" to choose a "fit person" and pay him twenty shillings each week out of town funds. In this way, towns in East Jersey, including Newark, continued to govern themselves and jointly face emergencies during the four-year period after East Jersey was merged into the Dominion of New England, when neither the council nor the assembly met. Years later, in a petition to King William, residents of East Jersey cited the failure of the Twenty-Four Proprietors "in time of Actual War," from June 1689 until August 1692, to provide "any Military officers to Command or Give Directions, in Order to Our Defence, or Magistrates to put the Laws in Execution" as one of the reasons to replace them.[17]

Henry Sloughter, sent by William and Mary to serve as governor of New York, arrived in March 1691. Within days, Leisler handed over the fort, but only after trying to negotiate terms. Sloughter had Leisler arrested once he left the fort and then prosecuted him for treason before judges drawn from his fiercest opponents. Leisler was found guilty in April and executed in May, along with Jacob Milburne, his chief aide and son-in-law. New York remained split for years between Leislerians and anti-Leislerians as the oligarchy that had controlled New York before 1689 regained power. Although Newarkers were not directly involved in New York politics, they would have counted themselves among the Leislerians, as shown by their vote in 1694 to admit five Dutch settlers as residents in Newark. At least one, Garret Laydecker (or Lydecker), had a role in Leisler's Rebellion, and likely all were seeking to make a new start among sympathizers.[18]

In 1692, the proprietors of East Jersey reclaimed their former right of government and restored Andrew Hamilton as deputy governor. Landowners who had resisted Leisler gained places on Hamilton's council, but the anti-Leislerian vituperation that characterized New York politics in the 1690s was largely absent in East Jersey, perhaps due to Hamilton's temperament and negotiating skill. William Lawrence of Hackensack, who had been a member of Leisler's Committee of Safety along with John Curtis and Henry Lyon, even served as speaker of the assembly in 1693.[19]

CHAPTER 13

Change and Conflict

Newark reached its first quarter-century as a town just as the East Jersey proprietors reasserted their right of government in 1692, following the Glorious Revolution. Most first-generation leaders had died, and a dreadful wave of deaths in the fall of 1694 claimed nine other men, including Thomas Johnson, who had played such an instrumental role in the 1680s.[1] A new group assumed leadership, including Azariah Crane, only eighteen when he signed the agreements in 1667; John Treat, two years younger than Azariah Crane; and Theophilus Pierson, just eight years old when Abraham Pierson Sr. moved his family to Newark, but like the others, now in his prime.

This new generation of leaders remained dedicated to the founding principles of Newark and no doubt still thought of themselves as New Englanders. They handled a more limited scope of responsibilities, restricted now to carrying out powers delegated by acts of the provincial assembly and traditional tasks such as paying ministers, setting township tax rates, and providing for the poor. After Newarkers compromised with the proprietors over land titles in 1693, the town meeting no longer had responsibility for allocating unappropriated land or admitting new inhabitants. Nonetheless, Newark was still a New England town that regulated when "cattle shall have Liberty to go into the Neck and when they shall be prohibited" and aimed for consensus when working through conflict, including within the Newark church. Having accepted the proprietors' compromise on land titles, Newarkers found that their interests diverged from those of other New Englanders, especially Elizabethtown residents, who continued to assert their rights vigorously under their original Nicolls patent. However, the two towns would still rise "with one voice" in 1699 to protest an extraordinary provincial tax.[2]

Scottish Covenanters

Newark remained largely a closed, agrarian community of New Englanders, leavened by Scots with similar Calvinist religious beliefs. The first Scots to arrive in

Newark were Presbyterian Covenanters, men and women who had been imprisoned following the failure in 1685 of Argyll's Rising to overthrow King James and then banished to "his majesty's plantations abroad" for refusing to swear the oath of allegiance to James or recognize him as head of the Church of Scotland. Peter Russell, a Covenanter who had been tortured with burning matches after attempting to escape prison in Dunnottar Castle, joined Margaret Forest, James Muirhead, and about thirty others in protesting their "unjust sentence of banishment" and calling King James "a man that is a sworn enemy to religion, an avowed papist, whom by our covenants we are bound to withstand" as head of the Scottish church. Russell, Forest, and Muirhead all eventually made their way to Newark.[3]

George Scot of Pitlochie, author of *The Model of the Government of East Jersey in America*, a promotional tract, agreed to transport more than one hundred Covenanter prisoners to East Jersey on the *Henry and Francis*, along with settlers paying their own way and still other passengers willing to work as indentured servants for four years to pay off their voyage and become eligible for twenty-five acres of land at the end of their term. Scot planned to cover his costs by selling the prisoners into indentured servitude. However, the seventeen-week voyage proved disastrous due to fever, fetid meat, and foul weather. Sixty passengers died while crossing the Atlantic, including Scot, members of his family, and twenty-two prisoners. The *Henry and Francis* finally reached Perth Amboy at the start of winter, but as Peter Russell recorded, another prisoner, "Janett Simintowne [Symington,] died after we cam Ashor & we buried hir & severall others ther."[4] According to an early account, the Covenanter prisoners were treated harshly when they came ashore at Perth Amboy, but Newarkers soon came to their aid: "A little way up the country there was a town where there was a minister settled, and the inhabitants there were very kind to them. When they had information of the prisoners' circumstances, they invited all who were able to travel, to come and live with them, and sent horses for such as were not, and entertained them that winter freely, and with much kindness." Nineteenth-century historian William Whitehead "supposed" the town to be Woodbridge, but it was almost certainly Newark since neither Woodbridge nor Elizabethtown had a settled minister in December 1685. Indeed, Peter Russell wrote to his family about "New wark where we live and hath lived since the midle of Januarie." In another letter, he added, "The towne we are now in is called new wark, wher the people hath bein kynd & charatable to us."[5]

By spring many of the Covenanters made their way to New England ("severall of us are gon . . . to New Ingland"), but at least five were still in Newark. Russell informed his family that Margaret Forest and he were staying "in ane house with Mistris Percone [Pierson] the ministers mother" and that "John Smith & Jeames Muirhead & Gawin Muirhead is with us in this towne." All were Covenanters from the central lowlands of Scotland; John Smith and James Muirhead had sailed with Peter Russell on the *Henry and Francis*, while Margaret Forest and Gawin Muirhead arrived on different ships. They had feared being sold into indentures or worse. On a visit to Woodbridge, they rejoiced that James and John Edward "had com from Carolina & that they wer frie & Also thosse that wer sent to Gamyca [Jamaica] before us was frie also." In a brief note, John Smith assured his brother and sister "we are not sold as slaves." However, Richard Hutton, captain of the *Henry and Francis*, sued several prisoners in East Jersey's Court of Common Right for their passage; as John Smith noted, "we are perseued By the Laws of the province for our fraught [freight]." Only Hutton's failure to appear at a court hearing in June kept him from winning his case.[6]

The Covenanters were the first group of "strangers" accepted in Newark since its founding two decades earlier. Deeply grounded in their faith (Russell sent a blessing to his parents, "Now peace mercie & grace be to you from our father the God of all mercie & grace & the Lord jesus christ & his holy spirit to be your comforter leader & teacher") and well educated (Smith ended his note with the Latin phrase *Sic subsenbitur*, "So it will be understood"), they shared with Newarkers a similar Bible-inflected way of expressing their Calvinist beliefs. Their tales about persecution at the hands of the Stuart king likely influenced Newarkers' decision three years later to provide active support for the Glorious Revolution.

They also prepared the way for other Scots to settle in Newark. In the 1690s, Mary Bond, widow of Stephen Bond, sold land to Scots Robert Campbell and James Clisby, while Samuel Plum sold a fifty-three-acre plot to John Meadie. John Cockburn purchased 205 acres "within the bounds of Newark" in 1695, including a twenty-five-acre tract along the Passaic River where his house was located. Patrick Falconer, son of Sir John Falconer, stood out from the rest. He settled first in Woodbridge, but in 1688, at age twenty-nine, he was welcomed to Newark, where he bought a home lot and more than thirty-seven acres of upland and meadow from Henry Lyon. In Newark, he was chosen as collector of funds in January 1691, having already been granted the honorific "Mr" at age thirty-one. He grew particularly close to Abraham Pierson Jr., even leaving him and his daughter Abigail legacies when he died suddenly in 1692.[7]

Conflict in Newark's Church

Abraham Pierson Jr. left Newark in spring 1692, soon after Falconer's death, having served the town as a minister for more than two decades, first as assistant to his father and then alone after his father's death in 1678. There are no records indicating why Pierson returned to Connecticut, but tradition suggests it had to do with his taking accommodative steps toward the Presbyterian church order. Perhaps Pierson and Falconer, a Scots Presbyterian, discussed church governance, comparing Presbyterian with Congregational forms of church organization and building on earlier conversations Pierson no doubt had with the Covenanters. The issue was then in the air: In 1691, Presbyterian and Congregational ministers in London reached an amicable agreement reconciling the differences in church order and even suggesting a new term, United Brethren, "to reduce all distinguishing Names." In a key section, the London ministers agreed that "pastors ought to have frequent meetings together, that by mutual Advice, Support, Encouragement, and Brotherly intercourse, they may strengthen the hearts and hands of each other in the ways of the Lord." Some Newarkers, however, continued to advocate for a strictly independent form of Congregational church government, insisting on lay control over local church decisions without recourse to ministers from other congregations to mediate disputes or ensure adherence to doctrine. This strict view of Congregationalism may have generated sufficient controversy to cause Pierson to leave Newark. As nineteenth-century minister Jonathan Stearns suggested in his history of the Newark church, "The people were liable, from their early history to be too strenuous on points of ecclesiastical government; and the minister may have erred in attempting to introduce in such a community, modifications for which the body of people were not prepared."[8]

Although early Newark church records did not survive, town records provide some insights. The first hint of dissension in the church was the vote at the town meeting on January 2, 1688, "to pay the Minister by Contribution" rather than as part of the town rate, as in prior years. At the town meeting a week later, fifty-one men pledged, "all being called by name," to pay their share of Pierson's eighty-pound salary, including all those elected that year as townsmen, constable, clerk, or treasurer. However, John Treat and Thomas Ludington, both sufficiently senior to be among the twelve men chosen by the town three months later to negotiate with the proprietors for a land settlement, did not sign the pledge. Were they merely absent from the January meeting, or were they among a few raising questions about Pierson? It is impossible to know without the church records. Once Pierson decided to leave, he parted amicably, and the town agreed to make up arrears in his salary.[9]

Newarkers were tribal in many ways, not least in choosing their ministers. They preferred men they knew or who were related to people they knew. Without a settled minister for the first time since the founding of Newark twenty-five years earlier, they turned to John Prudden, the son of the founding minister of Milford and thus personally known since childhood to many of them. Prudden had been Pierson's classmate at Harvard before serving a church in Jamaica, Long Island, for many years. In August 1692, the Newark town meeting, having apparently consulted with the church, unanimously agreed to call Prudden as Newark's minister. Perhaps chastened by Pierson's departure, they pledged to "freely and readily submit themselves to him and to his Dispensations and Administrations . . . as God shall assist and direct him therein by his Word and Spirit." It is noteworthy that Thomas Ludington, who had not joined the pledge to pay his share of Pierson's salary, was a member of the committee that negotiated a compensation package with Prudden.[10]

Prudden remained Newark's minister for the next seven years, but in 1699 he wished to be relieved of some or all his duties. Early in the year, the town voted to "treat and agree with" Jabez Wakeman to help Prudden "carry on the Work of the Ministry" during the coming year. Wakeman, a grandson of one of the founders of New Haven Colony, had visited his Kitchell cousins in Newark after completing three years of study at Harvard. Newarkers perhaps thought they could retain Prudden's services if they provided him with an able assistant; if Wakeman did not accept their invitation, then they were willing to consider "some other." It appears Wakeman did not immediately agree to stay in Newark, and during the next few months Prudden pressed his request to be released from his covenant to serve the Newark church. Newarkers did not accede to his request. By June, the town agreed to send for "the hon'rd and revered Counsel of Elders" to review and mediate "the Issue of late Difficulties." The ministers, unnamed but presumably from Connecticut or Long Island, apparently took Prudden's side. Having been corrected, the town voted "their full Compliance with, and Acquiescence in that Issue" and agreed "to defray the whole Charge of [the ministers'] Journey and Trouble, till they return." The town also voted to pay Prudden's arrears "due to him by our particular Subscriptions" and asked him to continue in his ministry "till God shall favor us with some other Supply." Prudden remained on good terms with Newarkers, farming, teaching school, and filling Newark's pulpit as needed between pastorates, until his death in 1725.[11]

At the same time that the town asked Prudden to remain a little longer, they formed a committee to "join with such as the Church shall appoint" to search for his replacement, "to be on Trial, in order to Settlement in the pastoral Office in this Place." Again, they turned to Jabez Wakeman, but it took some months to achieve unanimity, perhaps reflecting the critical importance Newarkers placed on the minister's role in the life of the town. They wanted to get it right, and for two years it was the primary topic at town meetings. Despite the halting start to his ministry, Wakeman won over the congregation during the next four years. Then, in late 1704, tragedy struck. Wakeman's two-year-old son came down with dysentery and died on October 29, followed by Wakeman himself nine days later, just twenty-six years old. His early death was a blow to the subsequent development of the town, just as Patrick Falconer's had been a dozen years earlier.[12]

Political Ferment

After securing their land titles with the proprietors in 1693 and gaining new grants in 1694, Newarkers focused on local issues in their town meetings, such as "preventing Harm by Swine," allowing a sawmill so long as "any of the Inhabitants have Boards, as cheap as others and before Strangers [nonresidents]," and looking for "a well qualified Man for a School Master." In contrast, Elizabethtown residents remained in ferment over land titles, continuing to claim their Nicolls patent provided both a clear title and freedom from paying quitrents. They brought a case in the Court of Common Pleas in Perth Amboy in May 1695, which delivered a verdict in favor of the proprietors. They then appealed the verdict to London, where it was reversed. Nonetheless, the proprietors persisted in denying the validity of the Nicolls patent. In response, sixty-five Elizabethtown residents, claiming to be "groaning under . . . great Oppressions" of the proprietors, petitioned King William to be brought under New York's government and "to grant to the Court of Justice at New York, a Power to Judge all Causes in . . . East New-Jersey." In sending the petition, Elizabethtown residents seized on the persistent vulnerability of the proprietors regarding their right to govern. Newarkers did not join Elizabethtown in their extraordinary petition to be part of New York, perhaps fearing putting their land titles at new risk, since the petition called Governor Hamilton, with whom Newark had negotiated its settlement, "a pretended Governor."[13]

However, several years later Newark's interests again overlapped with Elizabethtown, in opposition to a finance bill urged by governor Jeremiah Basse. The proprietors had recalled Governor Hamilton in 1697, under the mistaken impression that his having been born in Scotland, not England, made him ineligible to serve. Basse was sent as his replacement, but he was not nearly so skilled a political leader as Hamilton. His effort to establish Perth Amboy as a freeport separate from New York stirred up fierce opposition from Governor Bellomont in New York—just as prior efforts had going back to Philip Carteret's time as governor. In November 1698, as a test case, Basse had the *Hester*, a small ship that he owned with his brother-in-law, loaded with a cargo of barrel staves without paying customs fees. Informed of this affront, Governor Bellomont sent his customs collector and a company of forty men to seize the ship and convey it to New York. Basse declined to pay New York customs and have the ship restored to him, preferring instead to appeal the case to London. To generate public support for his position, Basse convened the assembly, now called the House of Representatives, for the first time since becoming governor. Newarkers were immediately suspicious. The town meeting elected John Treat and Jasper Crane Jr. as their deputies and formed a committee of the most senior leaders of Newark to advise them.[14]

The House of Representatives convened on February 21, 1699, in Perth Amboy. Basse's proposed "Act for Redressing a Force of our Neighbour Province," which, despite its title, was a bill to raise £675, the largest finance bill in New Jersey's history up to that point, stirred great controversy. Its vaguely stated intent was "to remonstrate the injuries already done us [i.e., the seizure of the *Hester*], but also to avoid the like incursions in the future." The house approved the act before adjourning on March 13.[15] Newarkers exploded in protest when they learned the details of the finance act. At a town meeting on April 11, they thanked Treat and Crane "for not consenting to the passing" of the act and complained that the funds were to be raised by bills of exchange "obtained at extraordinary Rates" and then left "to be disposed to such Uses as a few Men . . . shall think fit." "With one Voice," Newarkers resolved not to pay the tax, and "as one Man" to resist any efforts to collect it.[16]

Once again in opposition, Newarkers wrote to other towns asking them to combine "in Hindering the execution of so unreasonable an act and to remonstrate our grievances." Elizabethtown joined Newark in opposing the legislation and endorsing a letter drafted by Lewis Morris, a well-educated and hot-headed young man who had been removed from the provincial council by Governor Basse, that expanded the scope of resistance to include opposition to Basse himself. Scottish settlers also joined the revolt against Basse and the so-called anti-proprietary members of the House of Representatives. Residents of Perth Amboy agreed at their town meeting on April 25 to sign the letter, following an impassioned appeal by Lewis Morris, George Willocks, and Thomas Gordon (the latter two were Scottish members of the Board of Proprietors, upset that for the first time unimproved lands would be taxed). On June 1, Freehold, a small town settled a decade earlier by Scots, became the fourth and last town to endorse the letter, although by that point the controversy had already crested. Newark's opposition to the act was sincere and deeply felt, but Lewis Morris and others seized on their opposition to orchestrate the wider campaign to weaken Basse.[17]

Events in East Jersey soon veered close to anarchy. A few days before the House of Representatives reconvened in May 1699, Basse attempted to get the upper hand by calling Morris and Willocks before a Court of Common Right and ordering them to put up £300 security for good behavior. When they refused, he had them imprisoned for denying the authority of the court. Men from Elizabethtown, including Benjamin Price, a justice of the peace, and Isaac Whitehead, town clerk, then took things into their own hands. They broke into the Woodbridge jail very early in the morning on May 13, armed "with Clubbs Staves & other weapons," and released Morris and Willocks from confinement. Basse's council consulted with a committee from the house about how best to respond, and at first they jointly agreed to prepare a bill to suppress insurrections. After further consideration, however, house members demurred from becoming involved in punishing Morris and Willocks or taking steps to amend the finance act, since they "differed in their Opinions." Newarker John Treat was a member of several house delegations that consulted urgently with the Council during this period, including the meeting when they discussed suppressing insurrections, so he knew well what Basse and the Council wanted. He likely supported the house's recommendation to Basse on May 18 to adjourn the session without taking further action, and he was probably among the members who departed with Speaker Harriman early in the morning of May 19, depriving the house of a quorum and thus making it unable to conduct business. Newarkers achieved their specific objective of stopping the finance act, since it appears that it was never put into effect. In addition, as historian Eugene Sheridan noted, Basse was "thoroughly discredited in East Jersey" and soon returned to England.[18]

In due course, the proprietors sent William Hamilton back to East Jersey to serve a second term as governor, but conditions remained tense and chaotic. Elizabethtown residents remained restless and ready to take extralegal measures to challenge the proprietors and force recognition of their land titles based on the Nicolls patent. The temporary alliance between Morris, Willocks, and the towns of Newark, Elizabethtown, Perth Amboy, and Freehold split apart. Morris and Willocks, joined by the Woodbridge town meeting, defended the new Hamilton government, while Elizabethtown linked with so-called anti-proprietary towns that had supported Basse and opposed the Scottish element among the proprietors. Newarkers adopted a low profile in this ongoing dispute, not wanting to put their land titles at risk, and focused more on securing a minister for their church. Nevertheless, they were caught in the middle of violent standoffs during the final two years before East and West Jersey became a royal colony.[19]

Newark leaders were on the receiving end when Elizabethtown residents disrupted court proceedings early in 1700 in a further challenge to proprietary government. On March 12, the Court of Sessions for Essex County convened for its half-yearly meeting in Elizabethtown, with Newarkers John Curtis, John Treat, and Theophilus Pierson joining William Sandford of New Barbadoes and Elias McKeilson of Acquackanonk on the bench as judges. As the court session was getting underway, Samuel Carter of Elizabethtown railed in "an Insolent and contemptious maner" against the authority and power of the court, even bidding presiding judge William Sandford to "kiss his arse." Minutes of the court session record that Carter also "grossly abused" the prosecuting attorney and foreman of the jury, uttering "words and Actions wholly unfitt to be mentioned." The judges ordered Carter held without bail and agreed, "not one dissenting," to report the "violence and Irruption of the Laws" to the governor and Council for their further action, fearing that if not stopped it might lead to "the Ruine of the Collony." The court then adjourned proceedings to the next morning. If the judges hoped for a calmer session, they were disappointed. A sizable contingent of Elizabethtown residents, led by senior leaders of the town, again threw the session into disarray "with unseemly actions and Insolent gestures, which seemed Rather to Looke like a Rebellion than otherwise." A week later, following Elizabethtown's example, residents of Piscataway nailed the doors to their meetinghouse shut to obstruct the Middlesex County court from holding its proceedings. And a week after that, Richard Saltar of Monmouth, a leader of the anti-proprietary party, similarly denied the authority of the Monmouth court.[20]

In April, Governor Hamilton's council learned that more than 220 inhabitants of East Jersey, led by residents of Elizabethtown, Piscataway, and Monmouth, along with several Dutch signers, had sent a remonstrance and petition "home" to King William III. Samuel Plum, perhaps still smarting from the case the proprietors brought against him fifteen years earlier for payment of quitrent arrears, was apparently the only Newarker to sign the petition. The petitioners claimed they had purchased their lands directly from "native Pagans" and had thus gained clear title. Along with a catalogue of other "grievances and oppressions," the petitioners charged that the proprietors, "under pretence and Colour of having bought the Government with the Soile," had illegally sued and ejected several persons from their lands for failure to pay quitrents. In a point-by-point response sent to the Lords of Trade in London, the proprietors argued that the petitioners were wrong in insisting that if the proprietors gave up their right of government—then under negotiation—"their Interest in the Soyle and Quit-Rents . . . must fall with it." What is noteworthy is that Newarkers stayed out of this fight; with one exception, they did not sign the petition, and there is no record of their discussing the issues at a town meeting.[21]

In the fall, the Essex County Court of Sessions convened in Newark's meetinghouse, with John Curtis and Theophilus Pierson serving as judges alongside Elias McKeilson and William Sandford, who presided. In the chaos that ensued, New Englanders in Newark represented authority—ironically for John Curtis since he had challenged Edmund Andros in 1680—and New Englanders in Elizabethtown represented a challenge to authority, with the difference stemming from the security or lack of security of their land titles. As soon as the court session opened, Samuel Carter arrived with about fifty men from Elizabethtown and again challenged the authority of the court to meet, but the judges proceeded to handle a standard misdemeanor case. When the court instructed the constable to take the defendant into custody, a melee broke out in the courtroom. Samuel Carter and two men set upon the constable, while two other men pulled Sandford off the bench. One took Sandford's sword and broke it in pieces, and another punched him, dislodging his hat and wig (both symbols of his office). The other judges, including Curtis and Pierson, were "grossly abused" and had their clothes torn off their backs.

Early the next morning, the judges met at Theophilus Pierson's house in Newark to record the names of the Elizabethtown men in the "rabble." "A greate company" of Elizabethtown men rode on horseback to Pierson's house. They demanded to see John Curtis and William Sandford, calling them rascals who had usurped authority by jailing one Joseph Parmiter. Pierson offered a compromise: If two men provided a sufficient bond for Parmiter's appearance in court, he might be released. The Elizabethtown men refused, saying they would release him themselves. When Pierson asked by what power they could secure Parmiter's release, one man held up his club, saying "by this power" and prompted the other men, "and soe you say all Gentlemen." With that, the other men held up their clubs, shouting "yes, one & all." They rode off to find the sheriff and, after a scuffle, took his keys and then released the prisoner.

Later the same day, the sheriff summoned twenty-four Newarkers to Pierson's house to serve as a jury of inquest and hear depositions from several Newark witnesses about the morning's events, as well as other evidence presented by Pierson. The jury made a presentment of thirty-six men from Elizabethtown for their involvement in the day's events. However, conditions in Essex County and indeed all East Jersey were so unsettled in this period that findings of the inquest were not presented to a grand jury until two years after the Jerseys had been reunited and become a royal colony.[22]

End of Proprietary Government

The Twenty-Four Proprietors surrendered their right of government early in 1702, after more than two years of administrative review by the Board of Trade in London. With the death of King William in March, the execution of the surrender document was delayed to April 15; two days later Queen Anne accepted it. Lewis Morris and his allies hoped that William Hamilton would be appointed governor of the new royal colony of New Jersey, but the London imperium recommended that someone "wholly unconcern'd in the Factions which have divided the Inhabitants of those Parts" be appointed. In due course, the queen named Lord Cornbury, governor of New York, to the additional office of governor of New Jersey. His detailed instructions for New Jersey, more than a hundred in number, finally reached him in July 1703, and he published them in Perth Amboy the following month. The proprietors had been stripped of their right of government, but they retained their right of soil together with all quitrents. Existing land titles were confirmed unless the land was left unimproved. The newly combined East and West Jersey assembly was reduced to twenty-four members, with two seats reserved for Perth Amboy and ten at-large members for the rest of East Jersey. Only men with at least 1,000 acres of land could serve in the assembly, and only freeholders with one hundred acres of land could vote for a member of the assembly—in stark contrast to Newark's founding principle of widespread suffrage of male church members. With these new requirements, Newark did not again have direct representation in the assembly until 1716.[23]

Cornbury's instructions called for him to protect the liberty of conscience for Protestants but, at the same time, encourage the spread of Anglican churches in the colony, instructions he carried out with zeal. Following Jabez Wakeman's death in 1704, the Newark town meeting took care to petition Cornbury for license "to get and settle a Man in the Work of the Ministry of the Gospel"—a step never deemed necessary during the proprietary period. Cornbury issued licenses to preach but intended them to be "local and limited"—that is, for only the place noted in the license. Non-Anglicans soon complained that "if a People want a Minister, they must have a license to call one, whither from New-England or Europe, [and] a License to admit Ministers to attend any Ordination, and limited for number." Cornbury was especially adamant about restricting preaching by "strowling" ministers who moved from place to place. When Francis Makemie, an Ulster Scots minister considered the founder of Presbyterianism in America, preached without a license in New York, Cornbury brought charges against him. While he was still in prison awaiting trial, Cornbury ordered an investigation of a similar, though private, religious meeting in Newark at Jasper Crane Jr.'s house, attended by Samuel Melyn, Elizabethtown's minister. Justice William Sandford examined Crane, Melyn, and another man, under oath, "to discover what Discourse they had with sundry of their friends." He found nothing to prosecute, but the fact that he took depositions caused outrage: "No men are safe in their most private Conversations, if most intimate Friends can be compelled upon Oath to betray one anothers Secrets."[24]

Under the new government, Newarkers were subject to a royal governor, a council made up of proprietors and large landowners, and an assembly that excluded the voices of common freeholders. Although the proprietors had given up their right to government, they extended their control over civil and military affairs through their participation on the governor's council. In negotiating the transfer of power to the royal governor, the proprietors secured the right for the council to nominate and approve local and county officials, including magistrates, judges, clerks, coroners, sheriffs, and militia officers. For decades, men attending the Newark town meeting on January 1 had elected a wide array of officers, but now their votes were limited to selecting overseers of the poor, fence viewers, "sheep Masters," and assessors for the town rate. After New Jersey became a royal colony, Newarkers still held occasional town meetings, but not as intended when Newark was first settled thirty-five years earlier.[25]

Conclusion

On April 27, 1713, Robert Hunter affixed his seal as governor of New Jersey and New York to a charter formally recognizing the Township of Newark. At a town meeting a year earlier, Newarkers had voted to seek the charter, claiming in their petition that the "want of a Charter or Pattent of Incorporation [placed them] under Sundry Inconveniences and Disorders." The charter, modeled on one granted to the new settlement of Amwell, New Jersey, a few years earlier, provided only modest privileges. "The Limits and Bounds" of the Newark tract, freshly surveyed and including both the lands "purchased from the Indians" in July 1667 and the extension to the ridge of First Mountain acquired eleven years later, were confirmed—but not the "over the mountain" purchase in 1702. Ten named trustees and their successors elected by Newark freeholders were permitted to call annual town meetings to fill several named positions by majority vote: five overseers for managing common lands in the Neck, two constables, one overseer of the poor, and one overseer of highways. The charter's key benefit was clarifying the town's authority to fence and manage common lands in the Neck. In return, the trustees were required to pay an annual rent of five shillings "on the feast day of the Annunciation of the Blessed Virgin Mary"—a high church Anglican reference that must have given pause to Calvinist Newarkers.[1]

This royally approved township charter was not at all the New England township the founders of Newark had intended in 1666. They planned a township that would carry out "civil and town affairs according to God and Godly government," with control over distributing land, admitting new inhabitants, holding town courts, choosing ministers, and electing militia officers. Nor was it what they had wanted twelve years later when they petitioned Governor Carteret and the council for a charter, "with as good Privileges as our Neighbors at Woodbridge have." Newark's 1713 charter was a pale reflection of the charter secured by the founders of Woodbridge in 1669 by submitting to the authority of the proprietors and governor Philip Carteret. Their charter incorporated items from the articles they had negotiated when Woodbridge was first settled: boundaries of their township tract, permission to make successive divisions of land to associates and freeholders, power to admit other inhabitants by majority vote, authority to establish courts for small civil matters and misdemeanors, freedom to choose magistrates to assist judges, the right to nominate candidates for justice of the peace and militia office, and liberty of conscience in choosing their own ministers. In return, Governor Carteret required Woodbridge to set aside 1,000 acres at Amboy Point for the proprietors (some 2,000 acres fewer than the one-seventh share stipulated in the concessions). He also mandated that each Woodbridge inhabitant have his landholdings surveyed by the surveyor general, patent them individually, and pay annual halfpenny per acre rents. Woodbridge residents were also directed to take an oath of allegiance to the king and a second oath of fidelity to the proprietors. In addition, the Woodbridge patent required all freeholders to contribute to the support of the minister chosen "by pluralitie of voices" but allowed freeholders to maintain any other minister at their own charge "without being molested or disturbed for the same."[2]

Newark's founders wanted a stricter version of a New England township than the founders of Woodbridge, and they were reluctant to cede much authority to Governor Carteret. When they secured permission to acquire the Newark tract, they negotiated an exception to the requirement in the concessions to set aside one-seventh of the tract for the proprietors, so they could retain control over who would be admitted as associates to live among them. They were willing to pay quit-rents collectively, but not individually, so the town could control both the initial distribution of land and subsequent sale or lease of landholdings to strangers. For ten years, they strongly resisted taking out individual land patents. Convinced of the "true Religion and worship of God" expressed in the Congregational way, they could not accept the prospect of residents maintaining different churches. Most importantly, they had agreed in their fundamental agreements to restrict civic, judicial, and militia offices to "some or other [members] of the Congregational Churches" and allow only church members the right to vote in elections for these offices. In their view, proprietary government was not godly government.

In the beginning, Newark's founders hoped that New Haven Colony could be largely reconstituted in New Jersey following the disappointment of seeing their colony subsumed within Connecticut after the Restoration of Charles II. They may have been discouraged when the New Haven group decided not to join the Milford group in settling in New Jersey in 1666, but they still had hopes of acquiring more land for establishing other townships on the same basis as Newark. It was only after the collapse of their 10,000-acre New Barbadoes investment in 1674, and their subsequent failure to acquire the Acquackanonk tract, that the town petitioned Governor Carteret and the council for a patent modeled on the one granted to Woodbridge nine years earlier. By that point, however, Carteret had no incentive to grant any favors to Newark, especially since Newarkers had joined in displacing him in the rebellion of 1672.

When Newarkers petitioned again for a charter in 1680, they still aimed to "enlarge and settle our Town bounds," this time with "that Land and Meadow called Poquanuck." However, the governor and council would not consider their request until all Newark landholders took out individual patents and made up their arrears in quitrent payments. Newarkers had lost any leverage they held in the early years when the proprietary government was keen to attract new settlers. After 1681, the Scottish proprietors were more organized and efficient in requiring land patents and collecting quitrents than Carteret's government had been. That put more pressure on Newarkers, who then focused just on securing their land titles, without seeking any privileges. By 1693, they were ready to accept Governor Hamilton's compromise of an additional one hundred acres for each "old settler" in return for all landowners patenting their lands and paying arrears in quitrents. As a result, the town meeting ceded control over admitting new inhabitants and making grants of land within the Newark tract.[3]

Newarkers did not give up their commitment to the New England township model easily. In the first two decades, the town meeting remained committed to the fundamental agreements, going so far as to choose two men in November 1685 "to go from House to House of those as have not subscribed to our fundamental Covenant, and return their answer to the Town." Yet, the scope of their town government gradually diminished. In the early years, the town meeting chose two magistrates with both civil and judicial authority. A new structure was implemented in 1674, with seven townsmen elected annually "to carry all Town Business, according to the best of their Judgments for the Good of the Town," but the town meeting explicitly reserved three types of decisions for themselves: disposing of land, admitting inhabitants, and determining the method of levying the town rate, although in practice selecting a minister was also reserved for the full town meeting. These were the core functions of a New England township that Newarkers were most reluctant to give up. In 1682, the town meeting confirmed the townsmen structure, "provided it infringe not on any of the three things prohibited in the Town Book," and it remained in place through 1694, succeeded briefly by "select men." In 1696, the townsmen were replaced by trustees for common lands and streets of Newark on behalf of "the Old Settlers of the Towne of Newark," named initially by the Board of Proprietors. The creation of the trusteeship marked the final separation between the original land association and the town meeting.[4]

If the general assembly passed laws related to township practice, the Newark town meeting readily implemented them, in contrast to directives and proclamations by the governor and council. Representation mattered, and Newark deputies participated actively when the assembly met. In 1676, when the general assembly passed legislation establishing monthly courts in the towns for "small Matters," the town meeting took care to choose three judges "by Papers" (by comparison, deputies were elected at the same meeting "by Vote with Hands"). The same year, the town also established the offices of Packer of Meat and Sealer of Leather, "according to the order of the General Assembly." Similarly, the town meeting implemented later legislation regarding rates, swine, fence viewing, and schoolmasters.[5]

Challenges to the closed and collective nature of Newark's original township model also developed within the community. Tensions were apparent in 1681, when the town meeting attempted to deal with "inconsiderate receiving and entertaining of Strangers amongst us." With uncharacteristically legalistic language, the town meeting voted that without permission no one could "receive or entertain" anyone "of what Age or Quality soever" who hoped to settle in Newark; nor was any landowner, "by Right of Inheritance or otherwise," permitted to sell or lease any home lot or parcel of land to a stranger; nor was any stranger permitted to "stay or abide above one month" without license, subject to a stiff five-pound penalty plus "all damages that may grow by such Entertainments." It was no doubt a losing battle. Similarly, drawing on New England precedents and perhaps reflecting an increasing aridity in faith, the town meeting aimed to reinforce respect for authority and relative status within the community by developing a seating plan for church services in the meetinghouse that would place persons "according to Office, Age, Estate, Infirmity and Desent or Parentage." Poor attendance at town meetings irritated leaders in 1684, with the town records noting that lack of attendance hindered town business and that those "as do attend are much damnified by loosing their Time." To improve attendance, they instituted a new system for imposing fines "for late Coming, total Absence, or irregular going away before the Meeting be dismissed." When Newark was formed, voting and holding town offices were restricted to church members, but the policy lapsed at some point. Perhaps it was in 1678, when Governor Carteret ordered that only those who had patented their lands be permitted to vote; the change most likely had taken place no later than 1688, when for the first time Abraham Pierson Jr.'s salary was paid "by Contributions," rather than through a town-wide tax.[6]

During the proprietary period, Newarkers learned that establishing and maintaining a New England township, even with careful planning and clear intent, required more than a community of settlers who subscribed to a set of fundamental agreements. It required multiple townships organized in similar ways and supported by a governor and colonial legislature drawn from those townships, as existed in Massachusetts and Connecticut until Edmund Andros imposed the Dominion of New England in 1686. With the proprietary government at odds with the New England ideal, New England–style townships could not flourish. Newarkers were isolated. They failed to acquire additional tracts of land where new towns could have formed with similar aims. While they had allies in Elizabethtown and Piscataway, those towns' reliance on the Nicolls patents for their land titles led to differences in tactics. Woodbridge residents shared a New England background, but their early acceptance of both the headright system and proprietary government took them in another direction. The ethnic fault lines in New Jersey among English, Dutch, and Scottish settlers and the heterogeneous religious views of Anglicans, Quakers, Baptists, and Calvinists posed an insuperable challenge. Newarkers brought their New England values and religious beliefs to a new land, but they failed to sustain the godly government they had tried so hard to establish.

Yet, Newarkers remained New Englanders with communitarian instincts and a collective approach to distributing land and making decisions. Their dedication to mutuality remained strong. They aimed for a wide sharing of responsibility for township tasks and worked methodically to achieve consensus when addressing issues, evident in their frequent formation of ad hoc committees. When they eventually relented to proprietary pressure to patent their landholdings, it was an accommodation on their part; they were not persuaded that their approach had been wrong. They reverted to form when they acquired the Newark Mountain, or "over the mountain," tract in March 1702 from Taphow and other Native leaders. Just as in 1666, Newarkers created a new land association and secured subscriptions from a group of 101 investors (nearly all original settlers or their children, including one woman, Elizabeth Ogden) subscribing for 117 shares. All investors promised to pay for the land "and all Such Charges as shall Necessarily Accrue . . . according to our proportion by our Subscription." In due course, individual plots of land were distributed to the subscribers based on their number of shares. In 1719, the settlers formed the Newark Mountain Society church, which remained an independent Congregational church until 1748, well after other local churches (including Newark) had affiliated with the Philadelphia Synod of the Presbyterian Church to offset the rise of Anglicanism after New Jersey became a royal colony.[7]

In making the Newark Mountain acquisition, Newarkers first sought a grant from the Board of Proprietors, but—similar to 1666—they proceeded to acquire the land directly from Natives Americans when the board was unable or unwilling to make a grant, either because it was in disarray or hesitant to make major land grants at a time when the future of the proprietary structure was under negotiation in London. Native American leaders, in turn, were ready to negotiate directly with groups seeking land. The Newark Mountain tract was just one of several "Indian title" deals that took place at the turn of the eighteenth century. Native leaders criticized the Board of Proprietors for surveying tracts of land without permission and then issuing "patents for it without asking our Consent, much less Compacting with us for it." Taphow, one of the sachems, viewed Newarkers and their allies as "benefactors" who had come to his aid against the proprietors "in times of Greatest Necesity." If Taphow's deed of gift in 1701 to a group of men from Newark and Elizabethtown for a tract of land on the south branch of the Passaic River is to be believed, he admired their "industry and Labour" in "subduing this wilderness."[8] While that phrase was likely inserted by the beneficiaries of the deed of gift, it reflects the divide between New Englanders and the gentry on the Board of Proprietors over the "origins and nature of property." As historian Brendan McConville pointed out in his study of eighteenth-century land disputes in New Jersey, the gentry "conceptualized property as flowing from institutional authority and maintained that the empire's legal system was the ultimate arbiter of property rights. [After 1740, New Englanders and others] came increasingly to assert that property was the product of labor and possession . . . protected by natural law."[9] But it is evident from Taphow's deed that Newarkers were already thinking in those terms at the turn of the eighteenth century.

Newark Mountain and other nearby settlements continued relatively undisturbed for three or four decades until James Alexander, Robert Hunter Morris, and David Ogden, gentry as well connected and powerful as any in New Jersey at the time, and all affiliated with the Board of Proprietors, challenged Indian titles.[10] In 1743, the three men secured grants from the Board of Proprietors for an extensive tract that overlapped the Newark Mountain tract, and then took forceful steps to assert their ownership rights. They offered three options to settlers who lacked proprietary title: take a lease for one year without any rent and then deliver the land; enter a three-year lease with a yearly rent; or purchase the farm for a price per acre set by the new owners. None of these options was acceptable to most farmers, who thought the land was already theirs through Indian title and their work on the land.[11]

Newarkers long responded with spirited resistance when their community was challenged, forming committees, joining in petitions, and sometimes taking more direct action—especially if landholdings were at issue.[12] In 1744, a committee drawn from members of the Newark Mountain Society church, many of them children or grandchildren of original Newark settlers, coordinated the response to the efforts of Alexander, Morris, and Ogden. A year later, in an action reminiscent of the extralegal tactics used by Elizabethtown residents in 1700, a group of farmers forcefully released one of their associates, arrested for cutting timber on land to which he did not have a clear title, from the Newark jail. Another crowd took similarly violent action three months later, using axes to break into the Newark jail and release men who had been arrested following the first action.[13] Over the coming months and years, the land disputes and jail breaks spread to other counties, alarming the gentry-controlled government and Board of Proprietors. To buttress both their plea to strengthen the militia and proposal to have troops sent from England, the board drew parallels to Bacon's rebellion in Virginia in 1676, reporting that the "insurrection" in Essex County was spreading across New Jersey and over the border into New York and Pennsylvania. However, the overwhelming majority of Newarkers, perhaps as many as 80 percent, supported the Newark Mountain settlers in their efforts to retain their landholdings. As late as 1750, over four hundred men from Newark and "parts adjacent" signed a petition to King George II on behalf of the Newark Mountain settlers and against the Board of Proprietors.[14]

The century-long contest over land policy in New Jersey, from the proprietary period to the American Revolution, was a continuous, if evolving, contest between the original two models for development: the community-based township/land association model with small farms versus the authoritarian headright system reframed to favor large estates for gentry and aspiring aristocrats. New Englanders had settled in a new land. They failed to sustain their New England way of godly self-government, but as a community, they remained determined to defend both their land and their rights.

Acknowledgments

Scholarly work on early New Jersey and the settlement of Newark is, for the most part, decades old. When I came across a previously unknown letter by governor Philip Carteret from August 1666 in the collection of the New Jersey Historical Society, I realized that a fresh study was not only needed, but untapped materials might be available. I am grateful to James Amemasor for guiding me through the society's extensive holdings and encouraging me to continue my research. Steven Tettamanti, executive director of the New Jersey Historical Society, kindly gave permission to reproduce items as illustrations in this book.

Newark is well served by the librarians and archivists who staff the Newark Public Library's Charles F. Cummings New Jersey Information Center. Tom Ankner, Vanessa Castaldo, Greg Guderian, and Beth Zak-Cohen answered with dispatch all my questions and requests for materials, while often offering their own insights and encouragement. I am deeply grateful.

By reviewing archival resources, usually page by page, and asking questions from a different perspective, I aimed to place Newark's story within the context of not just proprietary New Jersey, but New England, New York, and the British Atlantic as well. I am grateful to the staff at the New Jersey State Archives, New York State Archives, Connecticut State Archives, and Rutgers University Special Collections for providing access to primary sources in their care. I am also grateful to Artyom Anikin for translating a document in the Colve Papers at the New York State Archives and examining other items for me. Through the timely assistance of Natalie Borisovets and Mark Krasovic, both of Rutgers-Newark, I accessed digitized copies of UK State Papers for America and the West Indies.

The staff of the Massachusetts Historical Society facilitated my research among the extensive Winthrop Family Papers in their care; I found many documents, more even than I had hoped, related to Newarkers. Karen Gallagher and Wiebke McGhee of the North Lanarkshire Archives in Scotland provided scans of two letters by Scottish Covenanters who lived in Newark after their harrowing passage across the Atlantic as prisoners. George Musser helped me understand the location of landholdings described in early land deeds and alerted me to "Indian" deeds held by Princeton University Special Collections. I have learned much about the Dutch in the Middle Colonies from historian Firth Fabend, and I benefited from her reading of an early draft of my chapter about the Dutch reconquest in 1672. David William Voorhees, director of the Jacob Leisler Institute for the Study of Early New York History, answered my questions and pointed me to further resources that document the involvement of Newarkers in Leisler's Rebellion.

Warren Grover, who cofounded the Newark History Society with the late Charles Cummings and me in 2002, took a close interest in my research. I am pleased that my book will join his pathbreaking *Nazis in Newark* in drawing attention to Newark's place in the larger American experience. Gail Malmgreen, the ever-vigilant director of the Newark Archives Project online database, was quick to point out possible new sources. Peter Mickulas of Rutgers University Press provided essential advice and guidance while I prepared my book manuscript. Bob Hartman quickly responded to my call for help and expertly prepared a key image for use in the book.

Finally, I am grateful for the forbearance of my son Eliot and daughter Emma as I disappeared into the seventeenth century for weeks on end, absorbed in trying to make sense of people from a pre-Enlightenment world so different from our own. My wife Gloria's pertinent and probing questions often sparked more careful analysis, and this book is better because of her.

Chronology

1660 May	Restoration of Charles II as King of England.
1664 June	James, Duke of York, grants land soon called New Jersey to Sir George Carteret and Lord Berkeley as proprietors.
1664 August	English capture New Amsterdam from Dutch and name it New York.
1665 February	Proprietors issue their concession and agreement to guide settlement of New Jersey and appoint Philip Carteret as governor; he arrives in late July.
1666 May	Settlers from New Haven Colony negotiate purchase of the Newark tract from the Hackensack, a Munsee Lenape tribe. Land is soon surveyed for six-acre home lots.
1667 June	Sixty-four settlers approve fundamental agreements establishing the township. Terms of the land purchase are confirmed with the Hackensack in July.
1668 February	First division of upland in Newark; first division of meadow follows a year later.
1668 May	First meeting of New Jersey's general assembly.
1672 May	Rebellion displaces governor Philip Carteret; assembly names James Carteret as "president."
1673 August	Dutch recapture New York and New Jersey during Third Anglo-Dutch Trade War.
1673 November	Dutch confiscate Nathaniel Kingsland's New Barbadoes estate and sell it to a Newark-led group.
1674 March	Lord Berkeley sells his half-share of New Jersey, leading to separate West Jersey propriety; Sir George Carteret retains his half-share and is confirmed as proprietor of East Jersey in July.
1674 October	Treaty of Westminster ending the Third Anglo-Dutch Trade War takes effect in the colonies, returning New York and New

	Jersey to the English; Philip Carteret returns as governor and imposes strict controls on townships, starting with Newark; New Barbadoes acquisition is soon reversed.
1675–1676	King Philip's War in New England; deadliest war in colonial America raises alarm in Newark.
1676 August	First group of Newarkers agree to individual land patents.
1680 March	New York governor Edmund Andros assumes nominal control of East Jersey; Philip Carteret regains authority a year later.
1681 October	Assembly claims rights under Magna Carta in the "Revolution of 1681."
1682 February	Sir George Carteret's executors sell East Jersey to twelve investors led by William Penn. After each of the new proprietors sells a half-share, the group is known as the Twenty-Four Proprietors.
1685 February	Following the death of Charles II, the Duke of York succeeds his brother to the English throne as James II.
1688 August	Dominion of New England proclaimed in East New Jersey; proprietary government is suspended.
1689 June	During the Glorious Revolution, William and Mary are proclaimed in New York by Jacob Leisler and other militia leaders; Committee of Safety is formed, including a representative from Newark.
1692	Proprietary government is reestablished in East Jersey.
1693 February	Newarkers reach a compromise with the Board of Proprietors over land titles; "old settlers" receive new one-hundred-acre grants, but the town meeting gives up power to admit inhabitants and allocate land.
1702 April	Queen Anne accepts the proprietors' surrender of their right of government; East Jersey and West Jersey are unified as the royal colony of New Jersey.
1713 April	Newark is granted a royal charter.

Notes

INTRODUCTION

1. King Charles II to John Berry, December 9, 1672, *The Grants, Concessions, and Original Constitutions of the Province of New Jersey* (LS), ed. A. Leaming and J. Spicer (Somerville, NJ, 1881), 38–39; Alexander Bryan to John Winthrop Jr., May 1, 1673, Winthrop Family Papers (WP), Massachusetts Historical Society, Ms. N-262. Bryan reported that a vessel from Milford met the ship carrying Bollen off Southampton, Long Island, and helped to guide it toward New York City: "They cam out of England in December and came by Fyall and tooke in some wine there"; LS, 40–41, the petition is not extant.

2. Jasper Crane and Abraham Pierson to John Winthrop Jr., May 14, 1673, WP.

3. Crane and Pierson to Winthrop, June 14, 1672, WP; John Winthrop Jr. and Samuel Wyllys to Sir George Carteret, July 2, 1673, WP; *Massachusetts Historical Society Collections*, 3rd series, vol. 10 (1849), 84–85.

4. William Whitehead, *East Jersey Under the Proprietary Governments* (Newark, 1875), 64–67.

5. John E. Pomfret, *The Province of East Jersey, 1609–1702* (Princeton, NJ: Princeton University Press, 1962), 73.

6. John Allen Latschar, "East New Jersey, 1665–1682: Perils of a Proprietary Government" (PhD diss., Rutgers University, 1978), 267.

7. Richard P. McCormick, *New Jersey from Colony to State, 1609–1789* (Newark: New Jersey Historical Society, 1981), 27.

8. William Jones (1624–1706), former deputy-governor of New Haven Colony, informed New Haven's General Court on December 4, 1665, about "the busines of Delaware, & the articles were read to the towne & the towne told th[a]t there was a Committee for the ordering of th[a]t affayre." These articles are not extant, but Governor Carteret's response to them, February 27, 1666, is printed in *Archives of the State of New Jersey* (NJA), 1st Series, 1–42 (Trenton, NJ, 1880–1949), 1:51–54; Philip Carteret and James Bollen to Sir George Carteret and Lord Berkeley, August 3, 1666, Stevens Family Papers, MG409, Box 1, Folder 1, New Jersey Historical Society (NJHS); Timothy J. Crist, "Turbulent Tymes in a New Colony: Philip Carteret's Letter to the Proprietors, August 3, 1666," *New Jersey Studies* (2021): 99–102, https://doi.org/10.14713/njs.v7i2.251, accessed January 13, 2025; Newark Town Records (NTR), published as *Records of the Town of Newark, New Jersey* (Newark: NJHS, 1864, reissued 1966), 29 (February 3, 1669/70).

9. Articles Agreed and Concluded Upon Between [Philip Carteret and John Pike, Daniel Pierce, and Abraham Tappan], May 21, 1666, Ferdinand John Paris Papers, MG244, Box 5, folder 3, NJHS; Joseph Dally, *Woodbridge and Vicinity* (New Brunswick, NJ, 1873), 9.

10. Alan Taylor, *American Colonies* (New York: Viking, 2001), 170–171; William Haller Jr., *The Puritan Frontier: Town-Planting in New England Colonial Development, 1630–1660* (New York: AMS Press, 1968), 18, 35; NTR, 3 (undated); Claire Priest, *Credit Nation: Property Laws and Institutions in Early America* (Princeton, NJ: Princeton University Press, 2021), 51; NTR, 13 (January 1668/69).

11. John Frederick Martin, *Profits in the Wilderness: Entrepreneurship and the Founding of New England Towns in the Seventeenth Century* (Chapel Hill: University of North Carolina Press, 1991), 248–249.

12. Richard Nicolls, *The Conditions for New-Planters in the Territories of His Royal Highness the Duke of York* (Cambridge, MA, 1665), https://quod.lib.umich.edu/e/evans/N00058.0001.001/1:1?rgn=div1;view=fulltext, accessed January 13, 2025; Nicolls allowed for quitrents but did not impose them: "The Purchasers are free from all manner of Assessments or Rates for five years after their Town-plot is set out, and when the five years are expired, they shall only be liable to the publick Rates, and Payments according to the Custome of other Inhabitants both *English* and *Dutch*"; Richard Nicolls to Edward Hyde, Earl of Clarendon, July 30, 1665, and April 7, 1666, *The Clarendon Papers* (New York, 1870), 75, 119.

13. The Concession and Agreement of the Lords Proprietors of the Province of New Caesarea, or New Jersey, to and with All and Every the Adventurers and All Such as Shall Settle or Plant There, LS, 12–26; Settlers who accompanied Philip Carteret on his voyage to New Jersey received larger allotments of 150 acres for themselves, family members, and able servants; indentured servants who sailed with them would receive 75 acres for their own account at the end of their period of service; Priest, *Credit Nation*, 23.

14. King Charles II granted territory between the west side of the Connecticut River and the east side of Delaware Bay to his brother James, Duke of York, in March 1664. The Duke of York, in turn, granted the land between the Hudson and Delaware Rivers to Carteret and Berkeley on June 23 and 24, 1664, through a lease-and-release transaction. The English captured New Netherland, including what became New Jersey, from the Dutch in September 1664, although the English fleet had sailed in May. Carteret, Berkeley, and William Coventry, members of a special Privy Council committee, provided advice on seizing the Dutch territory. "The New Jersey Venture," *Societe Jersiaise Annual Bulletin*, 18 (1964): 429–436, https://societe-jersiaise.org/digital-publications/bulletin?file=../bulletin-pdfs/ABSJ1964-web.pdf, accessed December 14, 2020; McCormick, *New Jersey from Colony to State*, 16, 18; Pomfret, *East Jersey*, 27–33; Maxine Lurie, "New Jersey: The Unique Proprietary," *Pennsylvania Magazine of History and Biography*, 111, no. 1 (1987): 78–79. The concessions and Philip Carteret's commission and instructions from the proprietors are printed in NJA, 1:20–25, 28–43; David Ogg, *England in the Reign of Charles II* (Oxford: Oxford University Press, 1967), 250.

15. G. R. Balleine, "Sir George Carteret," *Societe Jersiaise Annual Bulletin*, 17 (1957): 55, https://societe-jersiaise.org/digital-publications/bulletin?file=../bulletin-pdfs/ABSJ1957-web.pdf, accessed December 14, 2020; G. R. Balleine, *All for the King: The Life Story of Sir George Carteret* (St. Helier, Jersey: Société Jersiaise, 1976), 39–57.

16. Cecil T. Carr, ed., *Select Charters of Trading Companies, AD 1530–1707*, Selden Society, vol. 28 (London, 1913): 172–192; Berkeley also invested in the African and Fishing companies. Barry M. Gough, "The 'Adventurers of England Trading Into Hudson's Bay': A

Study of the Founding Members of the Hudson's Bay Company, 1665–1670." *Albion* 2, no. 1 (1970): 35–47; Balleine, *All for the King*, 148–159.

17. Frederick W. Ricord and William Nelson, eds., *Journal of the Governor and Council, Vol. I 1682–1714* (Trenton, NJ, 1890), 144.

18. In addition to "New Jersey: The Unique Proprietary," Maxine N. Lurie's contributions include "New Jersey: The Long Lived Proprietary," in *Constructing Early Modern Empires* (Leiden, Netherlands: Brill, 2007), 327–356, and "The Reality of Empire: New Englanders on the Ground in Seventeenth Century East Jersey," *New Jersey Studies* 3, no. 2 (2017): 1–26; Brendan McConville, *These Daring Disturbers of the Public Peace: The Struggle for Property and Power in Early New Jersey* (Ithaca, NY: Cornell University Press, 1999).

19. Edward Paul Rindler, "The Migration from New Haven Colony to Newark, East Jersey: A Study of Puritan Values and Behavior, 1630–1720" (PhD diss., University of Pennsylvania, 1977); Kenneth A. Lockridge, *A New England Town: The First Hundred Years, Dedham, Massachusetts, 1636–1736* (New York: Norton, 1970); Philip J. Greven Jr., *Four Generations: Population, Land and Family in Colonial Andover, Massachusetts* (Ithaca, NY: Cornell University Press, 1970); Sumner Chilton Powell, *Puritan Village: The Formation of a New England Town* (Hanover, NH: Wesleyan University Press, 1970).

20. Latschar, "East New Jersey."

21. Mary Beth Norton, *Founding Mothers & Fathers: Gendered Power and the Forming of American Society* (New York: Vintage, 2011), 12, 298.

CHAPTER 1 — BEFORE NEWARK

1. Newark Town Records (NTR), published as *Records of the Town of Newark, New Jersey.* (Newark: New Jersey Historical Society [NJHS], 1864; reissued 1966), 1–8 (undated). Robert Treat, Micah Tompkins, Edward Riggs, and Stephen Freeman were from Milford. Tompkins and Treat had moved with their families from Wethersfield to Milford; Tompkins was an original settler of Milford in 1639, and Treat became town clerk in 1640 and later served as an assistant in the General Court of New Haven Colony. Samuel Swaine, who with Richard Harrison and Thomas Blatchly represented settlers from Branford, had also lived in Wethersfield; Harrison and Blatchly had lived in New Haven before helping to settle Branford. Samuel Kitchell represented the interests of potential settlers from Guilford. Thomas Morris of New Haven, who signed the covenant forming New Haven township in 1639, was joined by Richard Beckly and Thomas Johnson. Marshall Harris, *Origin of the Land Tenure System in the United States* (Ames: Iowa State College Press, 1953; reprinted 1970), 278.

2. Mathew Gilbert to Peter Stuyvesant, Milford, November 8, 1661. Gilbert was a deputy governor of New Haven Colony. In *Documents Relating to the History and Settlement of the Towns Along the Hudson and Mohawk Rivers*, ed. Berthold Fernow (Albany, 1881), 208.

3. Isabel Macbeath Calder, *The New Haven Colony* (1934, reprinted by Archon Books, 1970), 216–217, 222–223.

4. "Propositions . . . to be Presented to the Much Honored Gouvernor of the New Netherlands," November 8, 1661; "Answer of the Director-General and Council to the Foregoing Propositions," November 28, 1661; "Further Answer to the Proposals of Robert Treat, Philipp Graves and John Gregory of New-Haven Concerning the Settlement of Achter Cull," May 30, 1662; "Concession to be Granted to the Englishmen, Who Desire to Settle on the Kil van Kol," July 20, 1663, all in Fernow, *Documents*, 209–211, 221–222, 281–282.

5. Directors in Holland to Stuyvesant, March 26, 1663, Fernow, *Documents*, 239–240.

6. Robert Treat to Stuyvesant, Milford, June 29, 1663; Stuyvesant to Robert Treat, July 20, 1663; Council minutes of meeting with Oratam, July 20, 1663, all in Fernow, *Documents*, 266–267, 280–282; Robert C. Black III, *The Younger John Winthrop* (New York: Columbia University Press, 1966), 246–251; Calder, New Haven Colony, 231–240.

7. William Jones to Richard Nicolls, December 20, 1664, in *Documents Relative to the Colonial History of the State of New-York* (DCHNY), ed. J. R. Brodhead, B. Fernow, and E. B. O'Callaghan, 1–15 (Albany, 1853–1887), 1:82; Calder, New Haven Colony, 253; Jasper Crane led an unsuccessful effort by New Haven Colony in 1651 to expand to the Delaware River. Stuyvesant detained Crane and another leader in New Amsterdam until they promised to abandon the undertaking. Crane petitioned the commissioners of the United Colonies for relief from detention. David Pulsifer, ed., *Records of the Colony of New Plymouth, in New England* (Boston, 1859), 9:210–212 (mis-transcribed as "Jasper Graine"); Calder, New Haven Colony, 191–195; C. A. Weslager, *The English on the Delaware: 1610–1682* (New Brunswick, NJ: Rutgers University Press, 1967); Stuyvesant to the governor of Massachusetts, justifying his actions, April 1651, DCHNY, 12:69–70.

8. Jones informed New Haven's General Court on December 4, 1665, about "the busines of Delaware, & the Articles were read to the towne & the towne told that there was a Committee for the ordering of that affayre." Franklin Bowditch Dexter, "New Haven Town Records, 1662–1684," *Ancient Town Records* (New Haven, CT: New Haven Colony Historical Society, 1919), 2:155.

9. Philip Carteret, February 27, 1665/66, *Archives of the State of New Jersey* (NJA), 1st Series, 1–42 (Trenton, NJ, 1880–1949), 1:51–54; Robert Treat and John Gregory had been dispatched by New Haven Colony on February 10, 1666, to gain changes to the agreement. Calder, New Haven Colony, 254; Carteret refers to the "county" where the people from New Haven would settle, suggesting that he used the Virginia and Maryland headright system or the English county model as his frame of reference. In contrast, Governor Nicolls of New York apparently used townships as his frame of reference. Richard Nicolls to the Duke of York, ca. 1665, DCHNY, 3:105.

10. Dexter, "New Haven Town Records," 155, 176; Philip Carteret to the Proprietors, August 3, 1666, Timothy J. Crist, "Turbulent Tymes in a New Colony: Philip Carteret's Letter to the Proprietors, August 3, 1666," *New Jersey Studies*, vol. 7, no. 2 (2021): 100, https://doi.org/10.14713/njs.v7i2.251, accessed January 13, 2025.

11. Alan Taylor, *American Colonies* (New York: Viking, 2001), 170; Leonard W. Larabee, "Milford, Connecticut: The Early Development of a Town as Shown in Its Land Records" [New Haven]: Tercentenary Commission of the State of Connecticut, by Yale University Press, 1933), 9; Samuel Maverick, "A Briefe Description of New England;" *Proceedings of the Massachusetts Historical Society*, 2nd series (1884–1885), 1:245.

12. Calder, New Haven Colony, 251–252; Town of Milford to John Winthrop Jr., March 11, 1667, Winthrop Family Papers (WP), Massachusetts Historical Society, Ms. N-262; Jasper Crane to John Winthrop Jr., March 19, 1667, WP.

13. Abraham Pierson to John Winthrop Jr., June 14, 1666, WP.

14. John Davenport to John Winthrop Jr., June 14, 1666, WP.

15. John Davenport (1597–1670), ill and almost seventy in the fall of 1665, likely felt unable to withstand the rigors of a new settlement. He moved instead to Boston, where he died on March 15, 1670.

16. While Carteret and the proprietors later "insisted that settlers . . . clear Indian titles by paying out of their own pocket" (Maxine N. Lurie, "The Reality of Empire: New Englanders on the Ground in Seventeenth Century New Jersey," *New Jersey Studies: An*

Interdisciplinary Journal, vol. 3, no. 2 [2017]: 12), it is evident from Carteret's letter that in 1666 he contemplated clearing Indigenous titles to land himself.

17. While most settlers of Elizabethtown were from Long Island, nine men among the sixty-five residents who took an oath of allegiance in February 1666 were from New Haven, and one was from Stamford. Edwin Hatfield, *History of Elizabeth, New Jersey; Including the Early History of Union County* (New York, 1868), 56–57.

18. New Haven Colony commissioned Robert Treat and John Gregory in February 1666 to handle a second round of negotiations with Carteret about settling on the Delaware. Calder, New Haven Colony, 254.

19. Newark Town Records have several references to "Articles": NTR, 14 (January 1668/69, "Two Courts in our Town Yearly . . . according to Our Articles"), 26–27 (January 26, 1669/70, common lands and highways, "so far as Our Articles will allow," and "the Articles should be copied out, at a Town Charge"), and 29 (February 3, 1669/70, "as by their Legall purchase and Articles doth and May Shew").

20. Carteret to the Proprietors, August 3, 1666, Crist, "Turbulent Tymes," 100–101. In negotiations over the possible Delaware River settlement, Carteret insisted that "the 500 Acres Allotted to the Lords cannot be altred, it being a great deal less than they Intended by their Concessions," NJA, 1:52.

CHAPTER 2 — TRUE OWNERS OF THE LAND

1. Deposition of Robert Treat, March 13, 1687/8, Elizabethtown Bill in Chancery (EBC), published as *A Bill in the Chancery of New-Jersey, at the Suit of John Earl of Stair, and Others, Proprietors of the Eastern-Division of New-Jersey; Against Benjamin Bond, and Some Other Persons of Elizabethtown* (New York, 1747), 118; *The Minutes of the Board of Proprietors of the Eastern Division of New Jersey* (MBPEDNJ), ed. George J. Miller, Maxine N. Lurie, and Joanne R. Walroth, 1–4 (Perth Amboy and Newark, 1949–1985), 2:274–275. The settlers of Newark agreed to "make one township . . . according to God and a Godly Government" on May 21, 1666. They likely took this necessary first step before unloading their goods on the bank of the Passaic. Five days later, Carteret provided Treat with an introduction to Oratam, the Hackensack sachem, so it is likely the confrontation took place between those dates. Newark Town Records (NTR), published as *Records of the Town of Newark, New Jersey* (Newark: New Jersey Historical Society [NJHS], 1864, reissued 1966), 1 (undated). The Hackensack likely challenged the settlers with a show of weapons, but they may also have communicated with some shared language. The Hackensack had experience trading with the Dutch in New Amsterdam, and the settlers had learned some of the Quiripi language during their two decades of interactions with the Quinnipiac in New Haven Colony. Quiripi and Munsee are both Eastern Algonquian dialects. Paul Otto, *The Dutch-Munsee Encounter in America: The Struggle for Sovereignty in the Hudson Valley* (New York: Berghahn Books, 2006), 138; Robert S. Grumet, *The Munsee Indians: A History* (Norman: University of Oklahoma Press, 2009), 40.

2. Grumet, *Munsee Indians*, 4, 17, 19, 38; Otto, *Dutch-Munsee Encounter*, 2, 16. On the use of the term "Munsee," see 20–22n7.

3. Otto, *Dutch-Munsee Encounter*, 143–148. For an impressionistic account of the Peach War, see Donna Merwick, *The Shame and the Sorrow: Dutch-Amerindian Encounters in New Netherland* (Philadelphia: University of Pennsylvania Press, 2006), 220–227.

4. Otto, *Dutch-Munsee Encounter*, 163.

5. Grumet, *Munsee Indians*, 70–72 and passim; George H. Budke, *Indian Deeds: 1630 to 1748* (typescript, Library Association of Rockland County, 1975), 7. A similar crossover

point in West Jersey between the Indigenous and European populations was not reached until perhaps forty or fifty years later. Jean R. Soderlund, *Separate Paths: Lenapes and Colonists in West New Jersey* (New Brunswick, NJ: Rutgers University Press, 2022), 65.

6. Grumet, *Munsee Indians*, 84.

7. Sachems sold Staten Island a second time in 1657 and a third time in 1670.

8. Paul Otto, "Review of *The Munsee Indians: A History by Robert S. Grumet and Daniel K. Richter*," *American Historical Review* 115, no. 4 (2010): 1141; Berthold Fernow, ed., *Documents Relating to the History and Settlement of the Towns Along the Hudson and Mohawk Rivers* (Albany, 1881), 280; W. H. Shaw, *History of Essex and Hudson Counties, New Jersey*, vol. 1 (Philadelphia, 1884), 358.

9. Deposition of Robert Treat, March 13, 1688, EBC, 118; Robert J. Miller, "The Doctrine of Discovery in American Indian Law," *Idaho Law Review* 42, no. 1 (2005): 15–33; Wendy Warren, *New England Bound: Slavery and Colonization in Early America* (New York: Liveright Publishing, 2016), 89–90.

10. *Archives of the State of New Jersey* (NJA), 1st Series, 1–42 (Trenton, NJ, 1880–1949), 1:55–56.

11. Timothy J. Crist, "Turbulent Tymes in a New Colony: Philip Carteret's Letter to the Proprietors, August 3, 1666," *New Jersey Studies*, vol. 7, no. 2 (2021): 94–95; EBC, 118; NJA, 1:55–56; John Menta, *The Quinnipiac: Cultural Conflict in Southern New England*, Yale University Publications in Anthropology, vol. 86 (New Haven: Peabody Museum of Natural History, 2003), 135.

12. Samuel Edsall recalled in 1688 that "by order of Governour Phillip Carteret and upon request of the inhabitants of Newark, I did for them purchase of the Hackingsack Indians a parcel of land," MBPEDNJ, 2:275–276; EBC, 117, 118; "Governor Phillip Carterets Disbursements to the Indians for the Purchase of a Tract of Land up the Raritan River," including "One Anker of Rum [i.e., 10 gallons] Expended at 4 Severall meetings of the Christians and Indians . . . £3:—:—.", October 20, 1677, Minutes of the Governor and Council of New Jersey (MGC), NJSA, SEA00001, 28–29; Carteret also spent five pounds on "provisions" at the meetings. Deposition of Joseph Harrison, October 1, 1742, EBC, 116.

13. Grumet, *Munsee Indians*, 122–125. As Ives Goddard pointed out in his review of Grumet's *First Manhattans*, Grumet rarely provided evidence for equating the same person with different names; Goddard questioned Grumet's conclusions: "These equations are informed by no linguistic knowledge or philological method and are simply presented as if they were obvious on inspection." *New York History* 92, no. 4 (2011): 296.

14. NTR, 278–280. The purchase price was included in the "Town Rate" allocated to settlers of Newark by the town treasurer, NTR, 12 (September 10, 1668).

15. EBC, 188; Budke, *Indian Deeds*, 34A–34D; NTR, 278–280; East Jersey Deeds (EJD), NJSA, SSTSE023, 1 (Part B): 269–270 (69–70 on verso). Newark settlers noted that when they asked Carteret to reimburse them for the purchase of the land, he refused.

16. The boundaries are outlined in the deed of sale. Samuel Edsall also described them in a deposition taken on March 5, 1688, MBPEDNJ, 2:275–276. A fathom is a standard length of wampum about six feet in length containing approximately 360 beads. In correspondence with Henry Oldenberg in 1669, John Winthrop Jr. noted that "the white [wampum] is by the Indians account at six a penny; of the black they account a penny, and was so far for many yeares among the English as current at that rate . . . but now it passeth at the rate as they can agree in trading it." John Winthrop Jr. to Henry Oldenberg, October 4, 1669, Winthrop Family Papers (WP), Massachusetts Historical Society, Ms. N-262. The Elizabethtown associates paid 400 fathoms of white wampum, 200 fathoms of black

wampum, twenty fathoms of trade cloth, two made coats, two guns, two kettles, ten bars of lead, and twenty hands of gunpowder; Samuel Edsall and James Bollen witnessed the final payment for the Elizabethtown tract on October 28, 1666. In the mid-eighteenth century, an individual associated with the proprietors estimated the value at £60.15s. Elizabethtown purchase, Ferdinand John Paris Papers, MG244, Box 5, Folder 3, New Jersey Historical Society (NJHS).

17. Recent observers have asserted without evidence that the Hackensack were "attacked" by the settlers and not compensated for the land, in what they argue is the first instance of racial injustice in Newark's history. See Kevin Mumford, *Newark: A History of Race, Rights, and Riots in America* (New York: New York University Press, 2007), 13–14.

18. Paul Otto noted that "the importance of maintaining good relations with others pervaded their [i.e., Munsee] society," *Dutch-Munsee Encounter*, 15. See also Jason R. Sellers, "History, Memory, and the Indian Struggle for Autonomy in the Seventeenth-Century Hudson Valley," *Early American Studies* (2015): 714–742.

19. Philip Carteret to the Proprietors, August 3, 1666, in Crist, "Turbulent Tymes," 94, 100. Using the values Carteret assigned to different goods in determining his £42.6s.6d payment for the Raritan River tract purchase in August 1677, Newarkers paid roughly £140 for the Newark tract, not including the value of twenty pistols, ten swords, fifty knives, twenty hoes, and three troopers coats for which Carteret's account does not provide a value—almost two-and-a-half times the amount paid for the much larger Elizabethtown tract. "Disbursements to the Indians," MGC, 29.

20. Although "upper commons" was not regularly applied to Harriet Tubman Square until the late eighteenth century, it is the only one of the seven areas noted in the town records in February 1670 as "Town Commons" that is in the upper (or north) end of the town. NTR, 26 (January 25 and 26, 1669/70).

21. Budke, *Indian Deeds*, 47E; NTR, 55 (August 10, 1674), 61 (November 22, 1675), 78 (May 3, 1680); MGC, 17 (April 5, 1676); "That Wereas the Governor and Councell have this 3 Yeares kept a tract of Land Called Haquiquenanck Intending It for the Newark men and Seeing the Indians will not sell it Unto them," MGC, 31 (May 2, 1678).

22. NTR, 71 (March 1, 1677/78 and March 30, 1678) and 280–281 (land deed); Budke, *Indian Deeds*, 34E. James Bollen, Hendrick Drogestradt, and Samuel Harrison served as witnesses.

23. Newarkers fit the definition of settler colonists: "Settler colonialism is different from other forms of colonialism in that settlers come with the intention of making a new home on the land, a homemaking that insists on settler sovereignty over all things in their new domain." Eve Tuck and K. Wayne Yang, "Decolonization Is Not a Metaphor," *Decolonization: Indigeneity, Education & Society* 1, no. 1 (2012): 5.

24. Originally transcribed as "Watseson," NTR, 73 (February 13, 1678/79), allocating the land to Samuel Dod.

25. Perro is recalled today in the name of nearby Parrow Street.

26. Deposition of Jonathan Tichenor, March 22, 1741/42, EBC, 113; deposition of Ebenezer Lindsley, March 22, 1741/42, EBC, 112. In 1679–1680, Charles Wolley listed 150 fighting men among the Tappans and twice that among the Minisinks, "two days journey" to the west, but only "very few" among the Navesink; he did not mention the Hackensack or the Raritan. Charles Wolley, *A Two Years' Journal in New York and Part of Its Territories in America* (n.p.: Applewood, 2010, reprint of 1902 edition), 65; Otto, *Dutch-Munsee Encounter*, 167.

27. A. Leaming and J. Spicer, eds., *The Grants, Concessions, and Original Constitutions of the Province of New Jersey* (LS) (Somerville, NJ, 1881), 88.

28. Order of Governor Philip Carteret, October 5, 1675, MGC, 9. Earlier that year, Carteret had restricted the sale of strong liquors to Indians by one John Gray, "living remote from any towne or Neighbourhood, by which meanes the[y] Commit many outrages," April 2, 1675, MGC, 2.

29. S. W. Adams and H. Reed Stiles, *The History of Ancient Wethersfield* (New York: Grafton Press, 1904), 65–67.

30. Alexander Bryan Sr. to John Winthrop Jr., September 27, 1668, WP. The general assembly appointed two men to meet with "the Sachem of the Indians that killed the Indian boy at Elizabeth Town," LS, 88.

31. NTR, 51 (September 24, 1673). Hackensack sachem and chiefs met with Colve on September 13; Mohawks also sent a delegation. J. R. Brodhead, B. Fernow, and E. B. O'Callaghan, eds., *Documents Relative to the Colonial History of the State of New-York* (DCHNY), vols. 1–15 (Albany, 1853–1887), 2:606–607, 633.

32. Joseph A. Conforti, *Saints and Strangers: New England in British North America* (Baltimore: The Johns Hopkins University Press, 2006), 111; Philip Carteret, "Instructions for the Military Officers," July 15, 1675, EJD, 3:117; Order of Governor Philip Carteret, October 22, 1675, MGC, 10; William Sandford was commissioned as captain of Newark's militia, aided by John Ward as lieutenant and Joseph Johnson as ensign. LS, 103, 125; NTR, 61 (January 10, 1675/76).

33. Gawen Lawrie to the Scottish Proprietors, March 26, 1684, in William Whitehead, *East Jersey Under the Proprietary Governments* (Newark, 1875), 427.

34. Franklin Bowditch Dexter, ed., *New Haven Town Records, 1649–1662* (New Haven: New Haven Colony Historical Society, 1917), 188–189; Leonard Bacon, *Thirteen Historical Discourses* (New Haven, 1839), 347.

35. Abraham Pierson to Commissioners of the United Colonies of New England, August 24, 1664, digitized by Yale Indian Papers Project, https://findit.library.yale.edu/yipp/catalog/digcoll:3998, accessed October 24, 2021. Pierson's annual payment from commissioners of the United Colonies reached thirty pounds per year; it was abated to fifteen pounds in 1667 when he moved to Newark, then discontinued. "Acts of the Commissioners of the United Colonies of New England," in *Records of the Colony of New Plymouth,* ed. David Pulsifer and Nathaniel B. Shurtleff, vols. 1–12 (Boston: 1855–1861), 227, 277, 296, 318, 331; Charles Hervey Townshend, "The Quinnipiack Indians and Their Reservation," *Papers of the New Haven Colony Historical Society* (New Haven: New Haven Historical Society, 1900), 6:179–182. John Menta, *Quinnipiac*, 37–39.

36. Ebenezer Hazard, *Historical Collections; Consisting of State Papers* (Reprinted, Freeport, NY: Books for Libraries Press, 1969), 2:397–398; Pulsifer and Shurtleff, *Records of . . . New Plymouth*, 10:288.

37. The catechism, underwritten by the Society for the Propagation of the Gospel in New England, was printed by Samuel Green in Cambridge. J. Hammond Trumbull asserted that Pierson knew little of the "inflectional and conjugational forms" of Quiripi: "Some Helps for the Indians: A Catechism by the Rev. Abraham Pierson," *Collections of the Connecticut Historical Society* (Hartford: Connecticut Historical Society, 1895), 3:10.

38. Trumbull, "Some Helps for the Indians," 24–25; 38–39; 51–52.

39. *Centinal of Freedom* [Newark], November 9, 1796.

40. For Lenape stories about "the coming of the whites," see Camilla Townsend and Nicky Kay Michael, *On the Turtle's Back: Stories the Lenape Told Their Grandchildren* (New Brunswick, NJ: Rutgers University Press, 2023), chapter 6.

41. Crist, "Turbulent Tymes," 95, 100–101.

42. "He pretty well understood the Indian Language," deposition of Ebenezer Lindsley, March 1, 1741/42, EBC, 112; "Being capable in his younger years to understand and talk the Indian Language," deposition of Jonathan Tichenor, March 22, 1741/42, EBC, 113.

43. Deposition of Joseph Harrison, October 1, 1742, EBC, 116. For a map of "Indian Period Tribes, Trails Villages," see John P. Snyder, *The Story of New Jersey's Boundaries,1606–1968* (Trenton: New Jersey Geological Survey, reprinted 2004), 2.

44. Whippany deed to Daniel Dod and Samuel Harrison, April 1, 1694, West Jersey Deeds B, part 2: 651, NJSA; "Deed from Nantzeckim, Awoonemo, and Charahkoon to Theophilus Pierson for Land in Essex County, New Jersey, Along the Passaic River," August 8 and 15, 1700, James Alexander Papers, Box 6, folder 55, Princeton University Library; West Jersey Deeds, O:151, NJSA; "Deed from Tapehow, Rarawakon, Waweyask, Pequacheek, Powas, Nonzacum, Owanamus, and Orewandeca to Edward Earle, Jr. for Land in Morris and Somerset County, New Jersey, Along the Passaick River," December 31, 1701 and November 29, 1709, James Alexander Papers, Box 6, folder 56, Princeton University Library; West Jersey Deeds, O:145, NJSA; Earle was granted one-sixth ownership of the tract, while ten other men had a one-twelfth share, including Newarkers Theophilus Pierson, Jasper Crane, George Harrison, John Morris, Eliphalet Johnson, John Cooper, Robert Young, Daniel Dod, and William Brant. In 1701, Newarkers negotiated with Taphow, Loantiquo, and Manshum for the large "over the mountain" tract directly to the west of the original Newark tract, between the top of First Mountain and the south branch of the Passaic River, this time paying about £130. "Over the Mountain" tract, March 1701/2, deed lost in a fire at Jonathan Pierson's house on March 7, 1744/45, reconstructed March 14, 1744/45, and confirmed by King Quichtoo, King Tishowasqamin, Saphoo, and Yaupis, James Alexander Papers, Box 6, folder 59, EJD, E-3:105–107. George Musser plotted these tracts, "Partition of Lenapehoking: Indian Deeds for Essex County," https://www.eastjerseyhistory.org/statichtml/Indian%20deeds.jpg, accessed January 13, 2025.

45. Shaw, *History of Essex and Hudson Counties*, 2:855; Anita Bakshi, ed., *Our Land, Our Stories: Excavating Subterranean Histories of Ringwood Mines and the Ramapough Lunaape Nation* (n.p.: Design for Public History, 2022); "State of the Facts Concerning the late Riots at Newark," Ferdinand John Paris Papers, MG 244, Box 4, Folder 7, NJHS.

CHAPTER 3 — GODLY GOVERNMENT

1. "Capt. Bulling was att our towne goeing to the new plantation," Alexander Bryan to John Winthrop Jr., Milford, June 8, 1666, Winthrop Family Papers (WP), Massachusetts Historical Society, Ms. N-262.

2. Newark Town Records (NTR), published as *Records of the Town of Newark, New Jersey* (Newark: New Jersey Historical Society [NJHS], 1864, reissued 1966), 1–2 (undated). It was expected that at least five committee members "might remain or be in the place" during the early months.

3. Some men came from other towns for the meeting, including John Harrison and John Johnson from New Haven, Ebenezer Camfield from Norwalk, and Thomas Lyon from Fairfield.

4. All signed except Thomas Lyon, who signed with his mark, an "L."

5. The other verses were Exodus 18:21, Deuteronomy 17:15, and Jeremiah 36:21.

6. NTR, 2–3 (undated). Of the eleven committee men in May 1666, only Richard Beckly withdrew and did not subscribe to the fundamental agreements.

7. William M. Lamont, *Godly Rule: Politics and Religion, 1603–1660* (London: Macmillan and Co., 1969).

8. Mathew Gilbert to Peter Stuyvesant, Milford, November 8, 1661, in *Documents Relating to the History and Settlement of the Towns Along the Hudson and Mohawk Rivers*, ed. Berthold Fernow (Albany, 1881), 208.

9. John Davenport, excerpt from his "MS. Life of Mr. Cotton," in Thomas Hutchinson, *A Collection of Original Papers Relative to the History of the Colony of Massachusets-Bay* (Boston, 1769), 161. Cotton's compilation was printed in 1641 in London as *An Abstract of the Laws of New England*, https://www.mass.gov/doc/an-abstract-of-the-laws-of-new-england/download, accessed January 13, 2025; Michael P. Winship, "Godly Republicanism and the Origins of the Massachusetts Polity," *William and Mary Quarterly* 63, no. 3 (2006): 427–462; Avihu Zakai, "Theocracy in New England: The Nature and Meaning of the Holy Experiment in the Wilderness," *Journal of Religious History* 14, no. 2 (1986): 133–151; Shira Wolosky, "Biblical Republicanism: John Cotton's 'Moses His Judicials' and American Hebraism," *Hebraic Political Studies* 4, no. 2 (2009): 104–127; Richard J. Ross, "Puritan Godly Discipline in Comparative Perspective: Legal Pluralism and the Sources of 'Intensity,'" *American Historical Review* 113, no. 4 (2008): 975–1002.

10. William Smith Pelletreau, comp., *The First Book of Records of the Town of Southampton* (Sag-Harbor, NY, 1874), 18–22.

11. Hutchinson, *Collection of Original Papers*, 161.

12. The pamphlet also informed debates in Massachusetts about how to respond to the king's demands for major ecclesiastical and civil changes in the colony. Adrian Chastain Weimer, *A Constitutional Culture: New England and the Struggle Against Arbitrary Rule in the Restoration Empire* (Philadelphia: University of Pennsylvania Press, 2023), 81, 83.

13. [John Davenport], *A Discourse About Civil Government in a New Plantation Whose Design Is Religion* (Cambridge, MA, 1663), Wing D358. While the title page credits John Cotton, it has been attributed to John Davenport by various authorities, from Cotton Mather to Leonard Bacon and Bruce Steiner. Leonard Bacon, *Thirteen Historical Discourses . . . First Church in New Haven* (New Haven, CT, 1839), 289–292; Bruce E. Steiner, "Dissension at Quinnipiac: The Authorship and Setting of a Discourse About Civil Government in a New Plantation Whose Design Is Religion," *New England Quarterly* 54, no. 1 (1981): 14–32; Isabel Calder argued for John Cotton as the author. Isabel M. Calder, "John Cotton and the New Haven Colony," *New England Quarterly* 3, no. 1 (1930): 82–94.

14. Davenport, *Discourse About Civil Government*, 7, 8; Zakai, "Theocracy in New England," 137.

15. Davenport distinguished "between a Common-wealth already settled, and a Common-wealth yet to be settled . . . wherein men are free to chuse what Form they shall judge best." In that second category of "yet to be settled," he distinguished, on the one hand, "between Places, where all, or the most considerable part of first and free Planters, profess their desire and purpose of entering into Church-fellowship according to Christ, and of enjoying in that State all the ordinances in purity and peace" and, on the other hand, "those Places where all or the most considerable part of the first and free Planters are otherwise minded, and profess the contrary." *Discourse About Civil Government*, 9, 12.

16. "Civil Power is primarily conversant" with "the things of this life, [such] as Goods, lands, Honour, [and] the liberties and Peace of the outward man." In contrast, "church Power" is focused on "the things of God, [such] as the Souls and Consciences of men, the doctrine and Worship of God, [and] the Communion of the Saints." Therefore, Davenport argued that power over spiritual matters should not be put into the hands of civil magistrates, and that church officers should not be "distracted" from their responsibilities "by Secular intanglements." He made a further distinction between church officers and church members, concluding that "magistrates [should] be chosen out of free burgesses,

and by them, and that those free burgesses [should] be chosen out of such as are members of these Churches," because they "are fitter to judge and determine according to God, then other men." In addressing the roles of women and servants, he noted, "The Church so considered is a Spiritual Political Body, consisting of divers Members Male and Female, Bond and Free; sundry of which are not capable of Magistracy, nor of Voting in the choice of Magistrates, inasmuch as none have that Right and Power but free Burgesses, among whom Women and Servants are not reckoned, though they may be, and are Church-members." *Discourse About Civil Government*, 3, 5, 7, 11.

17. Davenport argued that if non–church members were denied their rights, "this were indeed to have the Common-wealth swallowed up of the Church." *Discourse About Civil Government*, 11–12.

18. NTR, 2 (undated). This fundamental agreement mirrors one adopted in New Haven on June 4, 1639, although it goes further by extending to "any Chief Military Trust or Office." Charles J. Hoadly, ed., *Records of the Colony and Plantation of New-Haven, from 1638 to 1649* (Hartford, CT, 1857), 17.

19. John Davenport, *The Power of Congregational Churches Asserted and Vindicated* (London: 1672), 10.

20. Davenport, *Discourse About Civil Government*, 7; NTR, 2.

21. Alexander MacWhorter, *A Century Sermon, Preached in Newark, New-Jersey, January 1, 1801; Containing a Brief History of the Presbyterial Church in That Town* (Newark, 1807), 6.

22. Jonathan F. Stearns, *First Church in Newark. Historical Discourses, Relating to the First Presbyterian Church in Newark* (Newark, 1853), 24.

23. Abraham Pierson arranged for John Bowers to "serve out his yeare" preaching in Branford. Bowers's son Nathaniel was called as Newark's fifth minister in 1705. The Branford town meeting assessed "those that are Removed out of the Towne" [i.e., moved to Newark] for their share of the twelve pounds due Mr. Bowers "for preaching from the tim that Mr Person wente away from Brainford." Remaining Branford residents, including five who signed Newark's fundamental agreements, felt it necessary in January 1668 to reaffirm their commitment to "Congregationall principles as to Church order" and to reconstitute their church. The five were Jasper Crane, John Ward, Samuel Plum, Edward Ball, and Thomas Blatchly. Blatchly, a merchant, was admitted to Guilford in 1668 and did not move to Newark; his son Aaron moved to Newark and received a home lot and divisions of land before returning to Guilford in 1683. "Town of Branford, Conn. Deeds," vol. 1, 1645–1679), 1:317, microfilm image 166; 1:319, microfilm image 167 (January 20, 1667[8]); and 1:335, microfilm image 175, https://www.familysearch.org/search/catalog/157834?availability=Family%20History%20Library, accessed January 13, 2025.

24. Kenneth A. Lockridge, *A New England Town: The First Hundred Years, Dedham, Massachusetts, 1636–1736* (New York: Norton, 1970), 24; David A. Weir, *Early New England: A Covenanted Society* (Grand Rapids, MI: William B. Eerdmans, 2005), 9–10, 99; Edmund S. Morgan, *Visible Saints: The History of a Puritan Idea* (Ithaca, NY: Cornell University Press, 1965), 64; Isabel Macbeath Calder, *The New Haven Colony* (1934, reprinted by Archon Books, 1970), 32–34.

25. In both New Haven and Milford, civil covenants were made on June 4, 1639, while the churches were formed ten weeks later. Calder, New Haven Colony, 83–86. For the text of the Milford covenant, see Federal Writers Project, *History of Milford, Connecticut, 1639–1939* (Bridgeport, CT: Milford Tercentenary Committee, 1939), 6n.

26. Abraham Pierson to John Winthrop Jr., September 27, 1667, "I am upon my remove (if God grant health and life)," *Collections of the Massachusetts Historical Society*, third

series, vol. 10 (1849), 69; John Davenport Jr. to John Winthrop Jr. He had received two letters from "my Father[-in-law] Pierson" and learned "of theire health, after sicknes, and especially one of my wives sisters, 15 yrs. Old, who was neare unto death, but God was merciful to her and them in recovering her againe." October 28, 1667, WP.

27. NTR, 7 (undated), 22 (December 3, 1669), 33 (December 29, 1670), 55 (October 31, 1674).

28. NTR, 21 (June 23, 1669), 24 (January 1, 1669/70). In 1676, the town gave Edward Ball "liberty to take the Elder's Lott." NTR, 65 (November 21, 1676).

29. Gerald F. Moran, "Religious Renewal, Puritan Tribalism, and the Family in Seventeenth-Century Milford, Connecticut," *William and Mary Quarterly* 36, no. 2 (1979): 240.

30. Edward Paul Rindler, "The Migration from New Haven Colony to Newark, East Jersey: A Study of Puritan Values and Behavior, 1630–1720" (PhD diss., University of Pennsylvania, 1977), 381. He added that half of those who did not serve were among the youngest male settlers. No Newark settlers were noted as "dismissed" from the church in Milford to the church in Newark, suggesting there was no church in Newark to dismiss them to at the time they moved. Years later, however, the Milford church recorded that "Major Robert Treat was dismissed from the Church of Christ at Neworke to this Church," July 5, 1674[?]. First Church of Christ (First Congregational) Milford Records, Connecticut State Archives, microfilm reel #615.

31. NTR, 4 (undated), 10–11 (September 10, 1668). Pierson had been paid every half year in a similar in-kind manner in Branford: "For every milch Cow hee shall have 2 pound of butter in part of pay once every yeare and the Rest of his pay to make up the full sume of 30lbs for his first holfe yeare to be paide in beefe or porke or Indian Corne or wampum: for the second holfe yeare hee shall have his pay in wheate and pease good and movable according to the generall Currant price that it then goes at when it is due." "Town of Branford, Conn. Deeds," 1:31; microfilm image 22 (September 22, 1650).

32. NTR, 11–12 (September 10, 1668).

33. NTR, 18 (April 17, 1669) and 34 (January 2, 1670/71). In 1714, the floor planks were recycled for "making a floor in the Schoolhouse in the Midle of the Town," NTR, 124 (September 28, 1714).

34. NTR, 11 (September 10, 1668). New Haven's church was 50 feet square, and Milford's church was 40 feet square. Calder, New Haven Colony, 90; Newark's meetinghouse was not lath-and-plastered until 1675, NTR, 60 (August 28, 1675).

35. NTR, 22 (July 28, 1669) and 43 (March 4, 1671/72). Pierson suffered from kidney stones and other urinary ailments starting in 1668, and he sought medical advice from John Winthrop Jr. and various doctors in New York. He described his symptoms in several letters to Winthrop: September 30, 1668; February 2, 1668/69; June 3, 1669; September 22, 1670; and May 4, 1671, John Davenport Jr. wrote to Winthrop in March 1669, "We are much troubled, hearing that my Father Pierson, is so afflicted with the stone," undated [after March 24, 1669], WP.

36. "We have none that hath a settled Preacher that follows no other Imployment, save one Town Newwark." Gawen Lawrie to the Scots proprietors, March 26, 1684, William Whitehead, *East Jersey Under the Proprietary Governments* (Newark, 1875), 426. Abraham Pierson Jr. remained in Newark until 1692.

37. NTR, 3–4 (undated). Items recorded in the town records were not dated during the period when the town was led by a committee rather than an elected town government.

38. NTR, 3–4 (undated). The town records do not record any instance of this fundamental agreement needing to be enforced.

39. Anne Yale Eaton, wife of governor Theophilus Eaton, challenged theological and social norms and was finally expelled from the New Haven church in 1645. Lilian Handlin, "Dissent in a Small Community," *New England Quarterly* 58, no. 2 (1985): 193–220.

40. The tradition about "Milford" was reinforced by a reference in George Scot, *The Model of the Government of East New-Jersey* (1685), reprinted in Whitehead, *East Jersey*, 405.

41. Jonathan Stearns advocated for "New Work," since the town motto of Newark-on-Trent, where Abraham Pierson is reputed to have lived after university, is "Novum Opus." Stearns, *First Church in Newark*, 21. On the meanings of "new" for New England, see John McWilliams, *New England's Crises and Cultural Memory: Literature, Politics, History, Religion, 1620–1860* (Cambridge: Cambridge University Press, 2004), 10. See also Isaiah 43:19.

42. Lockridge, *New England Town*, 16–17; John Frederick Martin, *Profits in the Wilderness: Entrepreneurship and the Founding of New England Towns in the Seventeenth Century* (Chapel Hill: University of North Carolina Press, 1991), 295–303.

43. Calder, New Haven Colony, 74; Rindler, "Migration," chapter 1; Richard E. Pierson and Jennifer Pierson, *Pierson Millennium* (Westminster, MD: Heritage Books, 2004), 51–52. Hans Albers was the only Dutch or German original settler of Newark.

44. On the course of study at Cambridge University, see Samuel Eliot Morison, *The Founding of Harvard College* (Cambridge: Harvard University Press, 1935), chapter 3.

45. Edwin Hatfield, *History of Elizabeth, New Jersey; Including the Early History of Union County* (New York, 1868), 56–57.

46. NTR, 9 (February 6, 1667/68). A quarter of New Haven settlers in 1639 were addressed as "Mr," but only Rev. Peter Prudden was accorded that status among Milford settlers. Rindler, "Migration," 8–9, 22.

47. Rindler, "Migration," 39, 333–335.

48. Mary Beth Norton, *Founding Mothers & Fathers: Gendered Power and the Forming of American Society* (New York: Vintage, 2011), 38, 41.

49. In Whitehead, *East Jersey*, 437.

CHAPTER 4 — FOR THE GOOD OF THE TOWN

1. *Correspondence of Hartlib, Haak, Oldenburg & Others of the Founders of The Royal Society with Gov. Winthrop of Connecticut 1661–1672* (Boston, 1878), 34–35.

2. "Newark Town Book 1691," MG267, file 3, f. 1, New Jersey Historical Society (NJHS); Timothy J. Crist, "Turbulent Tymes in a New Colony: Philip Carteret's Letter to the Proprietors, August 3, 1666," *New Jersey Studies* (2021): 91. Treat's reference to "Neworke" suggests he recorded the entry in late 1667, after the town had agreed on the name "Newark."

3. Claire Priest, *Credit Nation: Property Laws and Institutions in Early America* (Princeton, NJ: Princeton University Press, 2021), 4; Joseph A. Conforti, *Saints and Strangers: New England in British North America* (Baltimore: The Johns Hopkins University Press, 2006), 49.

4. Newark Town Records (NTR), published as *Records of the Town of Newark, New Jersey* (Newark: NJHS, 1864, reissued 1966), 9 (February 6, 1667/68), 24 (January 1, 1669/70), 49 (May 26, 1673). John was born about 1635, Deliverance in 1642, Azariah in 1649, and Jasper Jr. in 1651. Jasper Crane was still in Branford in January 1668; he did not sell his lands there until March 1668. "Town of Branford, Conn. Deeds," vol. 1, 1645–1679), 1:232, microfilm image 124, https://www.familysearch.org/en/search/film/008140452?cat=157834, accessed January 13, 2025.. Transfer of title to Azariah and Jasper Jr. of 154 acres in thirteen parcels; after this transfer, Jasper Sr. and his wife Alice retained ownership of only their fourteen-acre house lot in Newark, August 16, 1675, East Jersey Deeds (EJD), NJSA,

SSTSE023, 1:143; Crane willed his house lot to his daughter Hannah, who was married to Thomas Huntington; EJD, 3:173; NTR, 8; "Newark Town Book 1691," 11. When Delivered Crane died without issue, his landholdings were split among his brother John, his brother-in-law Thomas Huntington, and Azariah and Jasper Crane jointly. "Newark Town Book 1691," 63. On December 7, 1697, Azariah and Jasper "cast lots for the land given to us by our father" to divide their ownership interests; the parcels to which each one gained full title are listed in the "Newark Town Book 1691," 216; Ellery Bicknell Crane, *Genealogy of the Crane Family: Descendants of Benjamin Crane, or Wethersfield, Conn., and John Crane, of Coventry, Conn.; Also of Jasper Crane, of New Haven, Conn. and Newark, N.J., and Stephen Crane, of Elizabethtown, N.J., with Families of the Name in New Hampshire, Maryland and Virginia* (Worcester, MA: Press of Charles Hamilton, 1900), 301; Greven provides an example from Andover, Massachusetts, of a younger son staying with his father's household until receiving his inheritance at his father's death. Philip J. Greven Jr., *Four Generations: Population, Land and Family in Colonial Andover, Massachusetts* (Ithaca, NY: Cornell University Press, 1970), 81n11; Conforti, *Saints and Strangers*, 49.

5. NTR, 4–5 (undated). The two "middle Highways," today's Broad and Market Streets, were each "eight Rods wide" (about 136 feet), and other roads four rods (about 68 feet) wide.

6. Leonard W. Larabee, *Milford, Connecticut: The Early Development of a Town as Shown in Its Land Records* (New Haven: Tercentenary Commission of the State of Connecticut, by Yale University Press, 1933), 4; Edward Paul Rindler, "The Migration from New Haven Colony to Newark, East Jersey: A Study of Puritan Values and Behavior, 1630–1720" (PhD diss., University of Pennsylvania, 1977), 120.

7. John Cotton, *An Abstract of the Laws of New England* (London, 1641), 6.

8. NTR, 5, 6 (undated), 22 (December 3, 1669); "Newark Town Book 1691," 4 (Baldwin), 11 (Crane). Jasper Crane was later granted two additional acres taken from the lot that had been set aside for William Leete, plus a half-acre in the front, "in all ten acres and a half." On the New England practice of drawing lots, see Sumner Chilton Powell, *Puritan Village: The Formation of a New England Town* (Hanover, NH: Wesleyan University Press, 1963), 84–85.

9. "Their Streets are laid out too large, and the Sheep in the Towns are mostly maintained in them; They are so large that they need not trouble to pave them." Gawen Lawrie to the Scots proprietors, March 26, 1684, William Whitehead, *East Jersey Under the Proprietary Governments* (Newark, 1875), 426.

10. NTR, 6–7 (undated). In time, there were seven gates in a larger common fence. NTR, 84 (October 19, 1681).

11. "Newark Town Book 1691," 3. The chair is now in the collection of the Yale University Art Gallery.

12. I have used the term "associates," rather than "proprietors" as employed elsewhere in New England, to refer to original investors in the Newark land purchase to avoid confusion with the New Jersey and East Jersey proprietors. Newarkers used "associates" in their first covenant in May 1666, in the deed of sale for the Newark tract, and again in the 1670s when a group of investors from Newark formed to purchase the Barbadoes Neck tract.

13. Roy Hidemichi Akagi emphasizes the communal nature of these land companies in *The Town Proprietors of the New England Colonies: A Study of Their Development, Organization, Activities and Controversies, 1620–1770* (Gloucester, MA: Peter Smith, 1963, reprint of 1924 ed.), while John Frederick Martin stresses the entrepreneurial aspects in *Profits in the Wilderness: Entrepreneurship and the Founding of New England Towns in the Seventeenth Century* (Chapel Hill: University of North Carolina Press, 1991).

14. Martin discusses the meaning of "inhabitant" in New England towns, *Profits in the Wilderness*, 218–228.

15. NTR, 7 (undated). Hadley, Massachusetts, formed in this period and similar to Newark in its origins, required a three-year residency before land could be sold. Akagi, *Town Proprietors*, 36.

16. NTR, 6 (undated). Since William Leete, former governor of New Haven Colony and future governor of Connecticut, and John Gregory provided capital for the purchase of the Newark tract, they were both included in the first division of uplands and meadows in 1668. In December 1669, the town permitted Jasper Crane and his son Delivered Crane to take up land "formerly laid out for John Gregory, if he had come to our Town." NTR, 22 (December 3, 1669).

17. John Winthrop Jr. to Richard Nicolls, April 3, 1667, Winthrop Family Papers (WP), Massachusetts Historical Society, Ms. N-262. Governor Carteret complained to the proprietors in August 1666 about efforts by New York to impose a 10 percent customs duty, even on families bound from New England for New Jersey with provisions and household goods; this was "a great discouragement" to the settling of the province. Crist, "Turbulent Tymes," 93, 99.

18. Davis's estate was assessed at £289, at the top of the middle third of assessments. NTR, 8 (undated), 9 (February 5, 1667/68), 14 (March 5, 1668/69), 29 (February 3, 1669/70).

19. NTR, 83 (January 21, 1680/81), 90 (January 1, 1682/83), 91 (May 11, 1683), 97 (March 9, 1684/85), 107 (January 1, 1693/94).

20. NTR, 14 (March 5, 1668/69). He was "accommodated, after the Proportion of an Hundred Fifty Pound Estate," NTR, 21 (June 23, 1669). Martin notes a similar use of "estate given in" in New Haven and Norwalk records, *Profits in the Wilderness*, 154–155.

21. NTR, 14 (March 5, 1668/69), 26 (January 26, 1669/70), 30 (February 3, 1669/70), 48 (May 26, 1673). Two acres of Leete's home lot had already been allocated to Jasper Crane, on top of his eight-acre home lot. In 1671, the town meeting allowed William Leete three pounds "towards his Disbursements on his place . . . besides what his fence shall Be Apprised At." NTR, 22 (December 3, 1669). Pierson's admission as "a planter in the Town," with the right to take part in land divisions with an estate of £250, was delayed until the next month. NTR, 34 (January 2, 1670/71).

22. NTR, 91 (May 11, 1683).

23. NTR, 83 (January 21, 1680/81). The importance of land records, both for confirming title and noting boundaries, was underscored in late 1670 when the town asked Robert Treat to "enter Both the First and Second of Land, into the Book of records." NTR, 32 (December 12, 1670).

24. John Davenport Jr. to John Winthrop Jr., February 12, 1667/68, WP; NTR, 8 (undated), 9 (February 6, 1667/68); John Davenport Jr. to John Winthrop Jr., January 22, 1667/68, WP.

25. Martin, *Profits in the Wilderness*, 156–161; Larabee, *Milford*, 4.

26. NTR, 7–8 (undated); inventory of the estate of Lawrence Ward, April 18, 1670, EJD, 3:47–48; will of Hugh Roberts, 26 February 1670/71, EJD, 3:49.

27. The four men who deserted their lots were Thomas Harrison, Mr. Webster, Goodman Cole, and Joseph Horton. The six men admitted as late as November 1972 were Alexander Munrow, John Browne Jr., Abraham Pierson Jr., Daniel Dod, Jonathan Sargant, and Samuel Lyon. NTR, 8 (undated), 9 (February 6, 1667/68). Jonathan Sargant was admitted as a planter in January 1670, "if he will Abide in the Town and follow his Trade; Provided he pay his Shear to the purchase for what he hath, as others Have Done." NTR, 29 (January 25 and 26, 1669/70); Samuel Lyon was admitted as a planter and granted the tai-

lor's lot in November 1672. NTR, 45 (November 14, 1672); Martin, *Profits in the Wilderness*, 156–158; Akagi, *Town Proprietors*, 108; Rindler, "Migration," 122–125.

28. NTR, 8–9 (undated). Treat "motion'd To the Town that he might have all that Lay on this Side of the Creek, Against his Land near Home, which was Granted fully unto Him."

29. "Note Here—that Micah Tompkins, Jonathan Tompkins, Ephram Pennington, Zachariah Burwell, Ephraim Burwell, John Brooks and George Day desired and had Liberty to Take up their first Division of upland, if it be there to be had, in the Little Neck by Goodman Tompkins; and Hugh Roberts his division at the rear of his Home Lot; and Mr. Person and Mr. Camfield a part of their Divisions in the Neck on this side Goodman Roberts; Viz, Mr. Person for One Hundred, and Mr. Camfield for Two Hundred pound." NTR, 9 (February 6, 1667/68).

30. The "place agreed upon by the said Agents of the Towns for to Begin the Dividing bounds, is from the Top of a Little round hill, named divident hill; and from Thence to run upon a North West Line, Into the Country." NTR, 10 (May 20, 1668).

31. The list of men who drew lots and the numbers they drew was later inserted in the town records. NTR, 24 (January 1, 1669/70); Salt hay could feed cattle for local consumption and for trade. *Conforti*, Saints and Strangers, 85.

32. NTR, 15 (March 9, 1668/69).

33. NTR, 21 (June 10 and 23, 1669). The town confirmed the committee's decisions on July 28, 1669.

34. NTR, 27 (January 25 and 26, 1669/70).

35. NTR, 36–38 (February 21, 1670/71). A separate allocation of less valuable bogs took place in 1671 among those who wanted it.

36. NTR, 59 (May 18, 1675) and 86 (December 12, 1681); Larabee, *Milford*, 9. Charles T. McGrath mapped many of the parcels allocated in this division in "Newark Mountain: Third Division of Land, ca., 1696" (Rockaway, NJ: 2005). Newark land records show that some men received more than forty acres (e.g., Samuel Kitchell [sixty-nine acres] and Edward Ball [fifty acres]), but that may have been due to sizing. A fourth division was discussed at a town meeting in February 1687 but was not carried out; there is no record of it in the town records or land records. NTR, 101 (February 7, 1686/87).

37. Larabee, *Milford*, 5; Rindler, "Migration," 144–151; Andover, Massachusetts, started shifting away from the open-field system in the 1650s. Greven, *Four Generations*, 42, 52–53.

38. Powell, *Puritan Village*, 85, 91.

39. NTR, 16 (March 9, 1668/69). The town also set the day "when to Burn About the Fences," NTR, 35 (February 20, 1670/71). The following year, three men were deputized "to Burn the Woods this present year," NTR, 43 (March 4, 1671/72). In 1673, men were warned that they would be fined if they set fire to the meadow before March 10, "by Gunning or any other ways," NTR, 48 (February 28, 1672/73).

40. NTR, 18 (April 17, 1669). NTR, 42 (January 1, 1671/72).

41. NTR, 73 (February 12, 1678/79). Rindler, "Migration," 371–379. For land divisions and open-field farming in Piscataway and Woodbridge, both settled at the same time as Newark; see Michael J. Gall, "Once Upon a Time in a Nucleated Village: English Land Use and Town Planning in Seventeenth-Century East Jersey," *Bulletin of the Archaeological Society of New Jersey* 66 (2011): 33–46; Michael J. Gall, "'An Earthly Tabernacle': English Land Use and Town Planning in Seventeenth-Century Woodbridge, New Jersey," *Northeast Historical Archaeology* 43, no. 1 (2014): 3.

42. NTR, 15–16 (March 9, 1668/69).

43. NTR, 17 (March 30, 1669).

44. NTR, 29 (February 3, 1669/70). Neither Bollen's nor Carteret's letter is extant.

45. NTR, 30 (March 24, 1669/70). The proprietors' concessions required in specie quit-rents payments, but Carteret accepted in-kind payment from the residents of Woodbridge; see John Allen Latschar, "East New Jersey, 1665–1682: Perils of a Proprietary Government" (PhD diss., Rutgers University, 1978), 236n22.

46. NTR, 30 (March 20, 1670/71). The "rate for the half penny an acre" noted in the town records in January 1673 refers to a town rate ordered the prior November. NTR, 45 (November 14, 1672) and 47 (January 31, 1672/73).

47. "Newark Town Book 1691." The Newark town records indicate that the wife of Robert Denison picked second, but the town book lists the home lot under her husband. In contrast, the town records report that the sixth lot went to Edward Riggs, but the town book notes the lot going to Elizabeth Riggs.

48. William Blackstone, cited by Marylynn Salmon, *Women and the Law of Property in Early America* (Chapel Hill: University of North Carolina Press, 2016), 200. Female indentured servants and enslaved persons were even more limited in their personhood.

49. Sale of a parcel of land, "with the consent of Mary Rose the wife of said Samuel Rose witness my hand, Mary Rose [her mark]," to John Crane. "Newark Town Book 1691," May 4, 1692; Salmon, *Women and the Law of Property*, xv, 15; Mary Beth Norton, *Founding Mothers & Fathers: Gendered Power and the Forming of American Society* (New York: Vintage, 2011), 84.

50. Cornelia Hughes Dayton, *Women Before the Bar: Gender, Law, and Society in Connecticut, 1639–1789* (Chapel Hill: University of North Carolina Press, 1995), 40–41. Norton, *Founding Mothers*, 156–157.

51. Norton, *Founding Mothers*, 139–140.

52. Will of Stephen Freeman dated June 14, 1675, and proved October 22, 1675, EJD, 3:119.

53. Will of Hugh Roberts dated February 26, 1670[1], and proved November 22,1671, EJD, 3:49.

54. Will of Samuel Swaine, March 17, 1681/82, "Newark Town Book 1691," 37.

55. Elizabeth Ward "passed over" seven acres of upland and nine acres of meadow "with her full consent" to "John Ward, a dish turner," as well as most of her home lot and four acres of meadow to John Catlin, "agreed and consented unto by his Aunt Elizabeth Ward—widow—to be accorded unto him for his own, he making good the condition with her that is expressed in the letter of administration for his part thereof, which is to provide for the one half of his said Aunts comfortable maintenance during the term of her life as his cousin John Ward dishturner is to do for the other half according to agreement within themselves & to their said Aunt." *Newark Town Book*, 22.

56. Will of Joseph Browne, December 17, 1689, "Newark Town Book 1691," 20.

57. Agreement between Elizabeth Lyon and her son Thomas Lyon, August 10, 1704, "Newark Town Book 1691," 280, in Daniel Clark's transcription.

58. Salmon, *Women and the Law of Property*, 6.

59. Will of Sarah Davis, March 27, 1691, "Newark Town Book 1691," 33; Norton, *Founding Mothers*, 155.

60. Conforti, *Saints and Strangers*, 53.

CHAPTER 5 — FIRST SETTLERS AND SLAVERY

1. F. W. Ricord and W. Nelson, eds., *Journal of the Governor and Council, Volume I: 1682–1714* (JGC), vol. 13 in *Archives of the State of New Jersey* (NJA) (Trenton, NJ, 1890), 189–203; Graham Russell Gao Hodges, *Black New Jersey: 1664 to the Present Day* (New Brunswick, NJ: Rutgers University Press, 2019), 12–13; East Jersey Deeds (EJD), New Jersey State Archives (NJSA), SSTSE023, 3:33–34 (March 15, 1669/70). Nicolaes Varlet was a

member of Carteret's Council. On the Varlet family's involvement with enslavement, see Nicole Saffold Maskiell, *Bound by Bondage: Slavery and the Creation of a Northern Gentry* (Ithaca, NY: Cornell University Press, 2022), 40–44. On fire as a form of protest by enslaved persons, see Wendy Warren, *New England Bound: Slavery and Colonization in Early America* (New York: Liveright Publishing, 2016), 196–201.

2. On at least two occasions, Carteret's indentured servants ran away. "Governor Captt. Carteret hath several of his servants that are Runn away from him, and they Coming into this Collony [Connecticut], the people here abouts are so farr from Examaning and Stopping of them, that they doe not only Relieve them butt help to Convay them away." James Bollen to John Winthrop Jr., June 6, 1666, Winthrop Family Papers (WP), Massachusetts Historical Society, Ms. N-262; "A Hue and Crye After 4 Servants Belonging to Governor Cartwright," in *Books of General Entries of the Colony of New York, 1664–1673*, vol. 1, ed. Peter R. Christoph and Florence A. Christoph (Baltimore: Genealogical Publishing Company, 1982),191; *Archives of the State of New Jersey* (NJA), 1st Series, 1–42, Trenton, NJ, 1880–1949, 21:252.

3. EJD, 3:1–3 (reverse).

4. EJD, 3:1 (reverse); EJD, 1 (Part B) 86; EJD, A:41, D:5–9, 2:1; New Jersey State Archives (NJSA), "Early Land Records, 1650–1900s," https://wwwnet-dos.state.nj.us/DOS_ArchivesDBPortal/EarlyLandRecords.aspx, accessed March 9, 2024. At his death in 1691, Sandford owned eleven slaves ("boy Jak," his wife, and their two children, valued at seventy pounds; Peter, Tony, and Thomas, together valued at ninety pounds; Jack Lily and his wife, forty-five pounds; a woman named Jude, twenty-five pounds; and Sampson, twenty-five pounds). Chris Schopfer and Sharon Olson, "The Will and Inventory of William Sandford," *Genealogical Magazine of New Jersey*, 22, no. 1 (2017): 46–49.

5. William Whitehead, *East Jersey Under the Proprietary Governments* (Newark, 1875), 271, 275.

6. A. Leaming and J. Spicer, eds., *The Grants, Concessions, and Original Constitutions of the Province of New Jersey* (LS) (Somerville, NJ, 1881), 237, 254–255; Maskiell, *Bound by Bondage*, 68–69; Paul Axel-Lute, "The Law of Slavery in New Jersey: An Annotated Bibliography," A6, New Jersey Digital Legal Library, https://archive.ph/h6Ta8, accessed March 25, 2024.

7. LS, 376–381 ("An Act for the Redressing a Force of Our Neighbour Province").

8. On Monmouth County, see Graham Russell Hodges, *Slavery and Freedom in the Rural North: African Americans in Monmouth County, New Jersey, 1665–1865* (Madison, WI: Madison House, 1997).

9. Trevor Burnard, Introduction, in *Planters, Merchants, and Slaves: Plantation Societies in British America, 1650–1820* (Chicago: University of Chicago Press, 2015); Newark Town Records (NTR), published as *Records of the Town of Newark, New Jersey* (Newark: New Jersey Historical Society [NJHS], 1864, reissued 1966), 7 (undated but 1667).

10. David W. Blight, *Yale and Slavery: A History* (New Haven, CT: Yale University Press, 2024), 37; Leonard Bacon, *Thirteen Historical Discourses* (New Haven, CT, 1839), 388. For mention of Davenport's servants, see Francis J. Bremer, *Building a New Jerusalem: John Davenport, a Puritan in Three Worlds* (New Haven, CT: Yale University Press, 2012), 236; Simeon E. Baldwin, "Theophilus Eaton: First Governor of the Colony of New Haven," *Papers of the New Haven Colony Historical Society* (1908), 7:31.

11. Richard E. Pierson and Jennifer Pierson, *Pierson Millennium* (Westminster, MD: Heritage Books, 2004), 90. Abraham Pierson's estate inventory, EJD, 3:153–155. He bequeathed his "great bible and what other English book she pleaseth to Choose" to his

wife Abigail, "doctor Halls his paraphrase Upon the bible" to his son Thomas, and "a new English bible and a good English book out of Librarie" to all his children still living at home. His son Abraham received the rest of his books "together with the frame belonging to the books," with the stipulation that he pay eight pounds to his sister Mary when she married, as part of her portion from the estate. In 1701, Abraham Pierson Jr. presented several books from his father's collection to help found the Collegiate School in Connecticut, later renamed Yale. "Halls his paraphrase" is likely Joseph Hall, *A Plaine and Familiar Explication (By Way of Paraphrase) of All the Hard Texts of the Whole Divine Scripture of the Old and New Testament* (London, 1633); George William Pierson, *The Founding of Yale: The Legend of the Forty Folios* (New Haven, CT: Yale University Press, 1988), 174, 181–185, 196–197, 203–213; "Town of Branford, Conn. Deeds," vol. 1, 1645–1679), 1:313, microfilm image 165, https://www.familysearch.org/en/search/film/008140452?cat=157834, accessed March 12, 2026.

12. I am grateful to James Amemasor of the New Jersey Historical Society for drawing my attention to the reference to Pierson's servant. Samuel Conger, writing as "Mount Pleasant," transcribed Pierson's will and estate inventory in correspondence in the *Newark Daily Advertiser*, June 10, 1851, 2. He asserted that had Pierson's servant been enslaved, he would have been listed as a "negro man," in the manner enslaved persons were listed at the time in wills and other documents of New Barbadoes planters; it seems more likely that Newarkers in early years would follow New Haven practice (cf. Davenport's "servant") than Barbados practice; Warren, *New England Bound*, 2, 25; The town valued cattle from fifteen shillings to two pounds per head, and horses from fifteen shillings to £2.10s per head, both depending on age, when setting the town rate in 1695. NTR, 108 (January 17, 1694/95); Following King Philip's War, Robert Treat owned Indian captives in Connecticut. Margaret Ellen Newall, *Brethren by Nature: New England Indians, Colonists, and the Origins of American Slavery* (Ithaca, NY: Cornell University Press, 2015), 198.

13. Fletcher's enslaved boy was valued at twenty pounds, Essex Wills, Unrecorded Vol. 6, 51–52, NJSA; Harriman paid forty-eight pounds for Toney and £19.10s for Hagar. Edwin Hatfield, *History of Elizabeth, New Jersey; Including the Early History of Union County* (New York, 1868), 287–288; Samuel Melyn's estate inventory assigned a value of thirty pounds to his enslaved woman, July 19, 1711, Essex Wills, Unrecorded Vol. 5, 253, NJSA; Theophilus Pierson's will, March 10, 1713, Essex Wills, Recorded Vol. 1, 405 and Unrecorded Vol. 5, 65, NJSA. When he prepared his will, he was designated a "gentleman" as a sign of his wealth and status, likely the only early Newarker who earned that recognition; David Pierson's will, A. Van Doren Honeyman, *Calendar of New Jersey Wills, Vol. II., 1730–1750* (Somerville, NJ: Unionist-Gazette Association, 1918), 374.

14. Governor William Burnet to the Lords of Trade, May 9, 1727, enclosing "an account of the Inhabitants of the Province of New Jersey . . . taken in the Year 1726," in *Documents Relative to the Colonial History of the State of New-York* (DCHNY), ed. J. R. Brodhead, B. Fernow, and E. B. O'Callaghan, vols. 1–15 (Albany, 1853–1887), 5:818–819. By comparison, a New York census conducted three years earlier had found that Blacks were 15 percent of the population of 40,584. Peter O. Wacker, *Land & People: A Cultural Geography of Preindustrial New Jersey: Origins and Settlement Patterns* (New Brunswick, NJ: Rutgers University Press, 1975), 190; Graham Russell Hodges, *Root & Branch: African Americans in New York & East Jersey, 1613–1863* (Chapel Hill: University of North Carolina Press, 1999), Table 1; John P. Snyder, "The Story of New Jersey's Civil Boundaries, 1606–1968" (Trenton, NJ: Bureau of Geology and Topography, 1969), 125, https://www.nj.gov/dep/njgs/enviroed/oldpubs/bulletin67.pdf, accessed March 25, 2024.

15. Axel-Lute, "Law of Slavery in New Jersey," A8; enslaved people were not permitted to stay in other houses over two hours without their owner's consent, and if found over five miles from their owner's residence they were to be apprehended as runaways. They were also not permitted to carry guns or take dogs into the woods for hunting. NTR, 123 (May 25, 1713).

16. Clarke's estate inventory, Essex County Wills (1697–1727), reel 367:55, NJSA; Allen (367:85), Hatfield (367:137), Halsted (367:209), Levy (367:498), Scot (367:287), Plassy (367:319); Wills for Tuttle, Richard Clarke, Robertson, Bryant, and Rousby are listed in *Calendar of New Jersey Wills, Vol I. 1670–1730*, ed. William Nelson (Paterson, NJ: Press Printing and Publishing, 1901).

17. John Curtis's will, September 11, 1704, and inventory, October 1, 1705, Essex Wills, Unrecorded Vols., 4:267–268, 5:189, NJSA. Azariah's Crane's will, February 10, 1721/22, proved January 12, 1730/31, EJD, B:35; Essex Wills, B:183, NJSA; Joanna Crane's estate inventory, 1720/21, Essex County Wills (1697–1727), reel 367:162, NJSA; Joanna Crane's son Joseph (1676–1726) owned "one Neagro Girll" appraised at forty-five pounds (including her bedding), reel 367:341. There is no mention of enslaved people in the wills of Newark leaders and significant property owners John Ward Sr., Samuel Plum, Thomas Richards, John Treat, and John Gardner; inventories of their estates have not survived.

18. Warren, *New England Bound*, 118, 155–158; Stephen Wickes, *History of the Oranges in Essex County, N.J., From 1606 to 1806* (Newark, 1892), 140–143.

19. Peter Russell to Robert Russell, March 18, 1686, North Lanarkshire Archives, U21/433/172. For examples of "hue and cry" issued by Edward Ball as Newark town attorney on behalf of Elizabethtown owners of indentured servants, see *The Andros Papers: 1679–1680*, ed. Peter R. Christoph and Florence A. Christoph (Syracuse, NY: Syracuse University Press, 1991), 393 and 408.

CHAPTER 6 — SEEDS OF CONFLICT

1. John Allen Latschar, "East New Jersey, 1665–1682: Perils of a Proprietary Government" (PhD diss., Rutgers University, 1978), 101–103; J. R. Brodhead, B. Fernow, and E. B. O'Callaghan, eds., *Documents Relative to the Colonial History of the State of New-York* (DCHNY), vols. 1–15 (Albany, 1853–1887), 3:105–106; Robert C. Ritchie, *The Duke's Province: A Study of New York Politics and Society, 1664–1691* (Chapel Hill: University of North Carolina Press, 1977), 49–50; Philip Carteret to the Proprietors, August 3, 1666, Timothy J. Crist, "Turbulent Tymes in a New Colony: Philip Carteret's Letter to the Proprietors, August 3, 1666," *New Jersey Studies*, vol. 7, no. 2 (2021): 99, 101–102.

2. Vauquellin returned between December 1667 and May 1668. Latschar, "East New Jersey," 174n45; John Davenport Jr. to John Winthrop Jr., January 22, 1667/68 ["22.11. (67.)"], Winthrop Family Papers (WP), Massachusetts Historical Society, Ms. N-262. Lovelace reached New York in late winter/early spring of 1668; Nicolls sailed to London in early August, four years to the day after his arrival to take New York from the Dutch. John Davenport Jr. to John Winthrop Jr., February 12, 1667/68, and Alexander Bryan Sr. to John Winthrop Jr., August 27, 1668, WP.

3. East Jersey Deeds (EJD), New Jersey State Archives (NJSA), SSTSE023, 3:13 (January 2, 1667/68); Latschar, "East New Jersey," 150–154; Edwin Hatfield, *History of Elizabeth, New Jersey; Including the Early History of Union County* (New York, 1868), 69–70.

4. EJD, 3:12 (October 8, 1667; marginal notation, "This Commission whas delivered Back Where fore void") and 3:15 (May 16, 1668). Crane's appointment confirms he had completed his move to Newark, having sold eleven parcels of land along with his house,

barn, and stables in Branford to Thomas Harrison in March. "Town of Branford, Conn. Deeds," vol. 1, 1645–1679), 1:233, microfilm image 124, https://www.familysearch.org/en/search/film/008140452?cat=157834, accessed March 12, 2026.

5. EJD, 3:31 (December 16, 1669); A. Leaming and J. Spicer, eds., *The Grants, Concessions, and Original Constitutions of the Province of New Jersey* (LS) (Somerville, NJ, 1881), 16, 18; Newark Town Records (NTR), published as *Records of the Town of Newark, New Jersey* (Newark: New Jersey Historical Society [NJHS], 1864, reissued 1966), 13–14 (January 1668/69) and 23 (January 1, 1669/70).

6. EJD, 3:13–14 (April 7, 1668); list of the burgesses for each town, including "Capt. Robert Treat and Mr. Samuel Swarne for Newark, upon Pishawack river," LS, 77; NTR (May 20, 1668), 10.

7. LS, 15–18.

8. John Brackett, representative for Elizabethtown, was from New Haven, while John Ogden, also from Elizabethtown, was familiar with Connecticut's laws; John Bishop and Robert Dennis of Woodbridge had come from Massachusetts. Jacob Melyn, designated by the assembly as treasurer for the tax receipts, had also moved from New Haven. LS, 77; Latschar, "East New Jersey," 179–180; Edgar J. McManus, *Law and Liberty in Early New England: Criminal Justice and Due Process, 1620–1692* (Amherst: University of Massachusetts Press, 1993), 13, 30, 36–38; Ritchie, *Duke's Province*, 34; George L. Haskins, "Influences of New England Law on the Middle Colonies," *Law and History Review* 1, no. 2 (1983): 238–250.

9. LS, 78–80, 84; McManus, *Law and Liberty*, 23, 173–174, Appendix A; "The Duke of York's Laws, 1665–1675," NYCourts.gov, https://www.nycourts.gov/history/legal-history-new-york/documents/charters-duke-transcript.pdf, accessed August 5, 2022. In New England, judges and juries often did not enforce the death penalty for capital offenses—presumably the case in early New Jersey as well; Preston W. Edsall, *Journal of the Courts of Common Right and Chancery of Easy Jersey, 1683–1702* (Philadelphia: American Legal History Society, 1937), 113–120.

10. LS, 81, 84. The general assembly set their next meeting for the first Tuesday of November and then yearly on the same date, with deputies from each town to be chosen annually on January 1—actions taken "according to the Concessions." They also allowed for the governor and council to call a session on "extraordinary occasions . . . as the necessity and weighty Affairs of the Province shall require." Because several members wished to depart at the end of week, the assembly informed the governor that draft laws regarding breach of oaths, false witness, and "prohibiting of all sales of Strong Drink and liquors to the Indians" would be taken up at the next session. EJD, 3:2 (October 16, 1665).

11. Abraham Pierson to John Winthrop Jr., September 30, 1668, WP. Pierson also noted that Lovelace "at the beginning gave order that there should be every fortnight a day of humiliation through all the colony till it please God to abate the sicknes." For Lovelace's order, see Victor Hugo Paltsits, ed., *Minutes of the Executive Council of the Province of New York: Administration of Francis Lovelace, 1668–1673* (MEC), 2 vols. (Albany: State of New York, 1910), 1:20–21.

12. LS, 85–91; the assembly also imposed a new forty-shilling tax on each town and took steps to get Middletown and Shrewsbury to submit to provincial laws. Daniel J. Weeks, *Not for Filthy Lucre's Sake: Richard Saltar and the Antiproprietary Movement in East Jersey, 1665–1707* (Bethlehem, PA: Lehigh University Press, 2001), 50–53.

13. EJD, 1:33–34 (July 4, 1668); New Jersey early land records, https://www.state.nj.us/state/darm/EarlyLandRecordsPDF/SSTSE023_EJ_Liber_1_Part_A_p_0033-0034.pdf, accessed January 13, 2025.

14. Petition of Nathaniel Kingsland, on behalf of himself and William Sandford, to the king and Privy Council, April 6, 1669 [No. 44]; Answer of William, Lord Willoughby to petition of Nathaniel Kingsland, April 23, 1669 [No. 53]; Reply of Nathaniel Kingsland to Lord Willoughby, May 7, 1669 [No. 62], all in *Calendar of State Papers Colonial, America and West Indies: Volume 7, 1669–1674*, ed. W. Noel Sainsbury (London, 1889), 13–26, British History Online, http://www.british-history.ac.uk/cal-state-papers/colonial/america-west-indies/vol7/pp21-26, accessed August 29, 2022.

15. EJD, 1 (Part A): 42–43 (July 20, 1668); EJD, 1 (Part B):69/269–70/270 (July 11, 1667). Sandford's payment (with Newark's payment for its tract, for comparison, in parentheses) was 170 fathoms black wampum, 200 fathoms white wampum (850 fathoms total), seventeen match coats (twenty), sixteen guns (ten), sixty double hands of powder (fifty), ten pair of breeches (ten), sixty knives (fifty), sixty-seven bars of lead (one hundred), one anchor of brandy (two), three half "fats" of beer (four barrels), eleven blankets (four), thirty axes (twenty), twenty hoes (twenty), and two coats of "dorens" (three trooper coats) to Hackensack sachems Anoren, Gosgue, Hanyaham, Kenarenawack, Tamark, and Tantagua, on behalf of themselves "and all others young and olde herein Concerned."

16. EJD, 1 (Part A):130–132 (March 26, 1671), 132–133 (June 1, 1671), 133–134 (May 21, 1673); Kingsland later left one-third of his New Barbadoes holdings to his nephew Isaac Kingsland and the remaining two-thirds to his children. Charles H. Winfield, *History of the Land Titles in Hudson County, N.J., 1609–1871* (New York, 1872), 327.

17. EJD, 3:46–47, 47–48 (June 10, 1669); Alan Taylor, *American Colonies* (New York: Viking, 2001), 215; Richard S. Dunn, "The Barbados Census of 1680: Profile of the Richest Colony in English America," *William and Mary Quarterly* (1969): 11–12; EJD, 3:3 (reverse), for number of Berry's slaves.

18. EJD, 3:28 (August 30, 1669); "His [i.e., Governor Carteret's] ship is now come in from Barbadoes," Abraham Pierson to John Winthrop Jr., September 30, 1668, WP; Nicholas Blake to Joseph Williamson, November 12, 1669, "America and West Indies: November 1669," in *Calendar of State Papers Colonial, America and West Indies: Volume 7, 1669–1674*, 44–46. British History Online, http://www.british-history.ac.uk/cal-state-papers/colonial/america-west-indies/vol7/pp44-46, accessed August 29, 2022.

19. Samuel Maverick to John Winthrop Jr., February 24, 1668/69, and June 29, 1669, *Collections of the Massachusetts Historical Society*, series 4, 7 (1865), 315, 319; Latschar, "East New Jersey," 168; "Conditions Agreed Between His R. H. and B & C," EJD, 3:7 (reverse); Philip Carteret to Rachel Carteret (in French), May 17, 1672, Philip Carteret Collection, C0901, Box 1, folder 2, Princeton University Library.

20. Bollen's grant of 2,000 acres between the Hackensack River and Overpeck Creek, July 30, 1669, EJD, 1 (Part A):61; Vauquellin's 2,000-acre tract, July 30, 1669, EJD, 1 (Part A):60; William Pardon's land grant, July 30, 1669, EJD, 1 (Part A):63; Philip Carteret's grant, June 20, 1669, EJD, 1 (Part A):57.

21. A few years earlier, Newbury residents advocated a more moderate course than other Massachusetts towns by seeking a compromise in response to demands of the restored king. Adrian Chastain Weimer, *A Constitutional Culture: New England and the Struggle Against Arbitrary Rule in the Restoration Empire* (Philadelphia: University of Pennsylvania Press, 2023), 142, 243.

22. Text of Woodbridge charter, Joseph W. Dally, *Woodbridge and Vicinity* (New Brunswick, NJ, 1873), 298–302. The Woodbridge charter was dated June 1 and accepted by the town on August 16, 1669; Latschar, "East New Jersey," 128–129; EJD, 1 (Part A):51–56; Woodbridge Town Records, Liber A, 162 (August 16, 1669), Rutgers University Special Collections (32907021.1). At the Woodbridge town meeting on July 6, John Pike and Sam-

uel Moore were directed to meet with Carteret "to make their objections against the [charter] and get those things Eased," Woodbridge Town Records, 162.

23. Woodbridge Town Records, 162 (July 8, 1669, "Land Due to them by Consessions"), 164 (August 20, 1669, looking out for suitable parcels of land), 165 (August 27, 1669, vote to distribute land according to the more traditional New England method "by their Estates Ratable," but "none Shall have Less than the Concessions"), and 166 (September 10, 1669, vote to revoke decision to distribute land by ratable estate). By 1679, sixty Woodbridge residents had received patents for holdings of 162 acres on average, compared to an average of 103 acres for fifty-six Newark patentees. Latschar, "East New Jersey," 459 (chart 3); Woodbridge also allocated 250 acres to Carteret. Woodbridge Town Records, 174 (March 1, 1669/70).

24. Philip Carteret to Robert Vauquellin, April 4, 1670, and June 13, 1670, recorded in Woodbridge Town Records, 180–181 (November 1, 1670); order of Philip Carteret to John Pike, October 25, 1670, Woodbridge Town Records, 179–180 (November 1, 1670). For Woodbridge's articles, 1666, see Dally, *Woodbridge*, 9–10.

25. Latschar, "East New Jersey," 459. Woodbridge tried first to hire Abraham Pierson Jr. as its minister in June 1669, but Newark thwarted that by hiring him as an assistant to his father. The Woodbridge town meeting then voted in July 1670 to approach Jeremiah Peck, with their fallback "to procure Mr. Samuel Treat to preach with us Six or Twelve Months as our Minister." In November 1670, the town agreed to pay Samuel Treat twenty-one pounds "to Be with us as our Minister, and to preach unto us for the Next Six Months Ensuing." The town voted unanimously in January 1672 to call Treat in a "settled Ministry," but he declined the call. Woodbridge Town Records, 161 (June 8, 1669), 178 (July 5, 1670), 181 (November 16, 1670), 185 (December 5, 1671), 186 (January 2, 1671/72).

26. Abraham Pierson to John Winthrop Jr., February 2, 1668/69, WP; NTR, 21 (July 28, 1669) and 22 (December 3, 1669); EJD, 3:31 (recall of commissions, December 16, 1669; order to Thomas Johnson, December 17, 1669).

27. NTR, 23 (January 1, 1669/70) and 26–27 (January 26, 1669/70).

28. EJD, 3:36 (October 20, 1670, courts in Bergen and Woodbridge); NTR, 4 (undated), 33 (January 2, 1670/71) and 35 (February 20, 1670/71); EJD, 3:40 (February 24, 1670/71).

29. Abraham Pierson to John Winthrop Jr., May 4, 1671 [March 1672?], WP. John Davenport Jr. to John Winthrop Jr., "I received a letter lately from my Father [-in-law] Pierson who writes that at N.Y. . . . he had a returne of his distemper which detained him there 3. Weekes in which time he had experience of the exceeding, abundant love and kindnes of an Alderman there." February 23, 1671/72 ["Boston 23.12.71"], WP.

CHAPTER 7 — REBELLION

1. Newark Town Records (NTR), published as *Records of the Town of Newark, New Jersey* (Newark: New Jersey Historical Society [NJHS], 1864, reissued 1966), 43 (January 22, 1671/2).

2. "Proceeding at a Special Court held at Elizabethtown," *Archives of the State of New Jersey* (NJA), 1st Series, 1–42 (Trenton, NJ, 1880–1949), 1:80–87; East Jersey Deeds (EJD), New Jersey State Archives (NJSA), SSTSE023, 3:78–80; Valot's citizenship and Elizabethtown house lot, EJD, 1 (Part B):14/325–15/324 (February 22, 1669/70).

3. Edwin Hatfield, *History of Elizabeth, New Jersey; Including the Early History of Union County* (New York, 1868), 82.

4. Newarkers selected Jasper Crane and Robert Treat as deputies to the general assembly on September 29, 1671. It was expected that the assembly would convene on October 3, "according to the Governors Warrant," but the session that approved the new legal

framework took place on December 14. NTR, 40 (September 29, 1671); appointment of provost marshal, December 23, 1671, EJD, 3:51, 78–80.

5. "Proceeding at a Special Court," NJA, 1:80–87; EJD, 3:78–80.

6. Samuel Moore was instructed to "distrain . . . the [defendants'] goods and chattels . . . and the same bring to sale [to cover the fines], and return the overplus to the owners." He did not collect the fines before the rebellion of 1672. Council's new order to collect the fines, EJD, 3:105 (December 11, 1674).

7. EJD, 3:64 (December 6, 1672), 3:82 (May 21, 1673), 3:105 (December 11, 1674); Minutes of the Governor and Council of New Jersey (MGC), NJSA, SEA00001, 3 (April 21, 1676); NTR, 65 (November 21, 1676); EJD, 2 (Part A):1 (May 1, 1678); Peter R. Christoph and Florence A. Christoph, eds., *The Andros Papers: 1679–1680* (Syracuse, NY: Syracuse University Press, 1991), 385–386 (September 9, 1680) and 392–395 (September 14 and 23, 1680); "Famous Old Meeker House May Soon Be Destroyed," *Newark Sunday Call*, July 18, 1909.

8. NTR, 43 (March 22, 1672) and 46 (December 9, 1672).

9. John Ogden's order "in his Majesties Name" to arrest William Pardon, EJD, 3:65 (June 25, 1672); Samuel Swaine was "third Man" if Crane or Treat could not serve as deputy. NTR, 42 (January 1, 1671/72).

10. A. Leaming and J. Spicer, eds., *The Grants, Concessions, and Original Constitutions of the Province of New Jersey* (LS) (Somerville, NJ, 1881), 15. On May 13, Newarkers chose Jasper Crane and Samuel Swaine "to Consult with the rest of the representatives of the Country." The council later claimed that some of the deputies avoided taking the oath of assemblymen. EJD, 3:55; NJA, 1:94–97 (July 1, 1672). The assembly proclamation is not extant but is referenced in "A Declaration & Protestation of . . . Philip Carteret . . . & his Councill," May 28, 1672, EJD, 3:53; NJA, 1:89–91.

11. Address of the council to the proprietors, July 1, 1672, EJD, 3:55; meeting of the Executive Council of New York, June 10, 1672, in *Minutes of the Executive Council of the Province of New York: Administration of Francis Lovelace, 1668–1673* (MEC), ed. Victor Hugo Paltsits, 2 vols. (Albany: State of New York, 1910), 1:129–130.

12. *Jersey and the Slave Trade*, a report lodged with the Isle of Jersey assembly in 2020, accepts an analysis by local historian Doug Ford that James Carteret commanded the *Speedwell* in 1663–1664 on an early slaving voyage for the Royal African Company. The crew collected 302 slaves in Benin and transported them to Barbados and St. Kitts for sale. https://statesassembly.gov.je/assemblypropositions/2020/p.78-2020.pdf, accessed August 4, 2023. However, the "Slaves Voyages" database identifies the captain of the *Speedwell* only as "Carteret." It is perhaps more likely that James Carteret, who was then just twenty or twenty-one years old, accompanied the crew on its 392-day voyage, and the captain was another member of the extended Carteret family. Voyage ID 9564, Slave Voyages, https://www.slavevoyages.org/voyage/database, accessed August 4, 2023. He entered the Royal Navy in 1665, serving as a first lieutenant of the *Royal Prince*. Likely through his father's influence, he served as vice admiral of the British Fleet operating against the French in the West Indies in 1667. He commanded the *Foresight* and the *Jersey* before leaving the Navy in 1670. In 1671, he was appointed a landgrave of Carolina with 12,000 acres near the head of the Cooper River. His father later came close to disowning him, leaving him only one hundred pounds a year in his will. "James Carteret: The Black Sheep," *Tony's Musings* blogpost, June 26, 2020, http://tonymusings.blogspot.com/2020/06/james-carteret-black-sheep.html, accessed August 4, 2023; J. Franklin Jameson, Bartlett Burleigh James, and Peter Sluyter, eds. *Journal of Jasper Danckaerts, 1679–1680* (New York: Charles Scribner's Sons, 1913), 66.

13. Philip Carteret to Peter Carteret, May 8, 1672, Philip Carteret Collection, C0901, Princeton University Library. Printed (with modern spelling) in *New Jersey: Autograph Letters from Philip Carteret, First Governor of New Jersey, 1672–1682* (London: Maggs Bros., 1934).

14. "A Declaration & Protestation of . . . Philip Carteret . . . & his Council," May 28, 1672, EJD, 3:53; NJA, 1:89–91; MEC, 1:129–130 (June 10, 1672) and 2:715–717 (June 11, 1672); John Allen Latschar, "East New Jersey, 1665–1682: Perils of a Proprietary Government" (PhD diss., Rutgers University, 1978), 252–254.

15. James Carteret, June 14, 1672, MEC, 2:717–720; declaration by Philip Carteret, July 1, 1672, EJD, 3:55; MEC, 1:138–139 (July 6, 1672); Executive Council to Philip Carteret, June 15, 1672, EJD, 3:57; commission of Samuel Moore, July 1, 1672, NJA, 1:93–94; Latschar, "East New Jersey," 255–263.

16. The petition is not extant, but the proprietors' response, dated December 11, 1672, is printed in LS, 40–41; NTR, 44–45 (June 17, 1672), 45 (August 10, 1672), 62 (February 25, 1675/76).

17. Francis Lovelace to James Carteret, October 13 and 22, 1672, MEC, 2:721–724.

18. Marriage license for James Carteret and Frances Delavall, April 15, 1673, in *Books of General Entries of the Colony of New York, 1674–1688*, ed. Peter R. Christoph and Florence A. Christoph, (Baltimore: Genealogical Publishing Company, 1982), 532; Israel Chauncy to John Winthrop Jr., April 15, 1673, and Alexander Bryan to John Winthrop Jr., April 15, 1673, Winthrop Family Papers (WP), Massachusetts Historical Society, Ms. N-262. Nathaniel Brewster, minister at Brookhaven, Long Island, officiated at the wedding. The war between the English and Dutch was responsible for delays in ships reaching New York. In the period when no ships arrived in New York, seven or eight had reached Boston, and fifty to sixty had arrived in Virginia in convoys. Donald G. Shomette and Robert D. Haslach, *Raid on America: The Dutch Naval Campaign of 1672–1674* (Columbia: University of South Carolina Press, 1988), 164.

19. Alexander Bryan to John Winthrop Jr., May 1, 1673, WP.

20. EJD, 3:64; LS, 39–40.

21. The proprietors also secured a letter from James, Duke of York, to Governor Lovelace in New York, November 25, 1672, confirming that the Nicolls land grants to the founders of Elizabethtown and the Navesink settlements were invalid. LS, 31–32.

22. LS, 32–34.

23. LS, 35–37. In separate "directions for the Governor and Council of New Jersey," December 7, 1672, the proprietors allowed a three-year period for landholders in "Elizabethtown, Newark, Piscataquay, and the two towns of Navesink (i.e., Middletown and Shrewsbury)" to clear their arrears in quitrents due since 1670, besides keeping up with "their growing rent" in current years. LS, 37–38.

24. King Charles II, December 9, 1672, LS, 38–39.

25. Proprietors' letter, December 11, 1672, LS, 40–41.

26. Alexander Bryan to John Winthrop Jr., May 3, 1672, WP.

27. EJD, 3:64. Berry's plan was that once the surveyor general completed his work in Newark, he would turn to Piscataway, Navesink, Elizabethtown, Woodbridge, and finally settlements along the Delaware River before the end of July. This timetable proved much too ambitious.

28. Only two representatives from Bergen and two from Woodbridge attended the assembly in Bergen on June 10 and took oaths of loyalty and fidelity. The assembly adjourned four days later. EJD, 3:83, 84, 86.

29. Jasper Crane and Abraham Pierson to John Winthrop Jr., May 14, 1673, WP.

30. Jasper Crane and Abraham Pierson to John Winthrop Jr., June 16, 1673, WP; NTR, 50 (July 1 and 5, 1673).

31. John Winthrop Jr. and Samuel Wyllys to Sir George Carteret, July 2, 1673, WP, printed in Massachusetts Historical Society *Collections*, 3rd Series, 10:84–85.

32. John Berry to John Winthrop Jr. before July 24, 1673, WP, Massachusetts Historical Society *Collections*, 3rd Series, 10:85. Winthrop noted that he received Berry's letter on July 24.

CHAPTER 8 — REPRIEVE

1. The town meeting also formed a five-member committee "to consider with the messengers from other Towns, about sending a Petition to England." Newark Town Records (NTR), published as *Records of the Town of Newark, New Jersey* (Newark: New Jersey Historical Society [NJHS], 1864, reissued 1966), 50 (July 1 and 5, 1673); "They are at that place [Newark] under many thoughts what the issue of that government will be." Israel Chauncy to John Winthrop Jr., July 2, 1673, Winthrop Family Papers (WP), Massachusetts Historical Society, Ms. N-262.

2. Edwin Hatfield, *History of Elizabeth, New Jersey; Including the Early History of Union County* (New York, 1868), 161–162; James Carteret to Francis Lovelace, June 14, 1672, and Francis Lovelace to James Carteret, September 18, 1672, in *Minutes of the Executive Council of the Province of New York: Administration of Francis Lovelace, 1668–1673* (MEC), ed. Victor Hugo Paltsits, 2 vols. (Albany: State of New York, 1910), 2:717–721.

3. Donald G. Shomette and Robert D. Haslach, *Raid on America: The Dutch Naval Campaign of 1672–1674* (Columbia: University of South Carolina Press, 1988), 140–151. They called it the Battle of Lynnhaven.

4. Shomette and Haslach, *Raid on America*, 155.

5. John Davenport Jr. to John Winthrop Jr., July 29, 1673, WP.

6. Nathan Gold to John Winthrop Jr., August 8, 1673, WP; William Hayes's affidavit, December 2, 1673, in *Documents Relative to the Colonial History of the State of New-York* (DCHNY), ed. J. R. Brodhead, B. Fernow, and E. B. O'Callaghan, vols. 1–15 (Albany, 1853–1887), 3:200–201, 213–214.

7. Shomette and Haslach, *Raid on America*, 158 ("traitor's detailed revelations"), 147 (deserters), 149 (pilots). Lisa Jardine, *Going Dutch: How England Plundered Holland's Glory* (New York: HarperCollins, 2008), 11, 14; Gold to Winthrop Jr. ("then they enquired of one Mr Hopkins"), WP; Hayes's affidavit ("did voluntarily declare"), DCHNY, 213–214.

8. Israel Chauncy to John Winthrop Jr., August 5, 1673, WP; John Sharpe, "An exact account of all proceedings concerning the taking of New Yorke from the English, July the 30th 1673," Massachusetts Historical Society *Collections*, 6th series (1889), 3:437; Shomette and Haslach, *Raid on America*, 165–174.

9. There was a 10-day difference between the "old style" Julian calendar used by the English and the "new style" Gregorian calendar used by the Dutch.

10. Order allowing Elizabethtown, Newark, Woodbridge, and Piscataway to send delegates to surrender to the Dutch, August 12, 1673, New York State Archives (NYSA), NYSA_A1881-78_V23_0001, http://digitalcollections.archives.nysed.gov/index.php/Detail/objects/51715, accessed August 14, 2023. Orders to Bergen and to Middletown and Shrewsbury are items 2 and 3 in the same series.

11. NTR, 50 (August 4, 1673); "After Coll . . . hath already Complyed and the other party is sommoned to appeare next Tuesday." Nathan Gold to John Winthrop Jr., August 8, 1673, WP.

12. "Privileges Granted to the Several Towns in New Jersey," August 18, 1673, NYSA, NYSA_A1881-78_V23_0012, https://digitalcollections.archives.nysed.gov/index.php/Detail/objects/51727, accessed August 14, 2023.

13. Order to inhabitants to nominate magistrates, August 19, 1673. NYSA, NYSA_A1881-78_V23_0019, https://digitalcollections.archives.nysed.gov/index.php/Detail/objects/51727, accessed August 14, 2023; NTR, 50 (August 12, 1673).

14. Appointment of magistrates, August 24, 1673, NYSA, NYSA_A1881-78_V23_0025; commission of schout and secretary of Achter Col, August 23/September 1, NYSA, NYSA_A1881-78_V23_0050, https://digitalcollections.archives.nysed.gov/index.php/Detail/objects/51727, accessed August 15, 2023.

15. Census of the several towns at Achter Col, September 14, 1673. The other counts were Woodbridge (fifty-four), Piscataway (forty-three), Middletown (sixty), and Shrewsbury (sixty-eight). NYSA, NYSA_A1881-78_V23_0069b, https://digitalcollections.archives.nysed.gov/index.php/Detail/objects/51727, accessed August 15, 2023; NTR, 50 (August 30, 1673). While administering oaths of allegiance, the Dutch captains also swore in militia officers for each town. The Newark town meeting had double nominated Samuel Swaine and Thomas Johnson for captain, John Ward and Josiah Ward for lieutenant, and Richard Harrison and Samuel Harrison for ensign at a meeting on August 30; the Dutch swore in Samuel Swaine (captain), John Ward (lieutenant), and Samuel Kitchell (ensign, even though he had not been nominated initially); names of the militia officers, September 14, 1673. NYSA, NYSA_A1881-78_V23_0070, https://digitalcollections.archives.nysed.gov/index.php/Detail/objects/51727, accessed August 15, 2023.

16. NTR, 51 (September 24, 1673). Anthony Colve sent orders to John Ogden by way of Newark, requiring that "the Indian Sachem" for the place where the robbery had taken place be summoned to appear before Colve and give satisfaction. Colve added "that all the Cheife Sachems hereabouts as also those of the Mohacks have bene here to present themselves unto me and that he only Remains Defective." The Hackensack had met with the Dutch leaders three weeks earlier; renewal of peace with the Hackensack Indians, September 3/13, 1673, NYSA, NYSA_A1881-78_V23_0068a; Colve's instructions to Ogden, September 19/29, 1673, NYSA_A1881-78_V23_0118a, 0118b (instructions to Ogden continue on 0119), https://digitalcollections.archives.nysed.gov/index.php/Detail/objects/51727, accessed August 16, 2023.

17. NYSA, NYSA_A1881-78_V23_0058 (September 7, 1673), 0062 (September 9, 1673), 0068b (September 13, 1673), 0069a (September 13, 1673), 0118a, 0118b (October 14, 1673), https://digitalcollections.archives.nysed.gov/index.php/Detail/objects/51727, accessed August 17, 2023. Vauquellin was identified as Robert Lapriere, another name by which he was known. Colve directed Ogden in October to deliver arms and goods inventoried as having belonged to Carteret and instructed Hopkins to examine "uppon what Conditions the Tennants are Seated uppon the plantations of Captain [Philip] Carterett."

18. East Jersey Deeds (EJD), New Jersey State Archives (NJSA), SSTSE023, 1 (Part A):130–132 (grant to Kingsland), 132–133 (sale to Sandford); NTR, 40–41 (September 29, 1671). Putting his finances in order for this investment, Pierson sold his remaining property in Branford, including a house, home lot, orchard, horse pasture, and seven other lots and fields to Edward Barker for £120, with instructions to pay several of Pierson's debts in New Haven and New York, and to apply the balance to his account in "Yorke." "Town of Branford, Conn. Deeds," vol. 1, 1645–1679), 1:413, microfilm image 215, (November 13, 1671). https://www.familysearch.org/en/search/film/008140452?cat=157834, accessed January 13, 2025.

19. Shomette and Haslach, *Raid on America*, 183–186; Winthrop received a copy of the confiscation decree in mid-September, WP; NTR, 50 (September 6, 1673), 51 (September 16,

1673); John Allen Latschar, "East New Jersey, 1665–1682: Perils of a Proprietary Government" (PhD diss., Rutgers University, 1978), 295; NYSA, NYSA_A1881-78_V23_0096a (instructions, October 1, 1673), 0096b (order to sell Major Kingsland's plantation and stock at Achter Col, October 1, 1673), https://digitalcollections.archives.nysed.gov/index.php/Detail/objects/51727, accessed August 19, 2023; William Sandford was confirmed as owner of his land, since he was "an actual inhabitant;" i.e., not an absentee owner. Edward S. Rankin, "The Newark–Elizabethtown–Barbadoes Neck Controversy," *Proceedings of the New Jersey Historical Society* n.s. 11 (1926): 353–364.

20. NTR, 51–51 (October 13 and 25, 1673, and November 17, 1673). The sale price is not recorded.

21. NYSA, NYSA_A1881-78_V23_0433 ("Granted and Conveyed to John Ogden and Other Trustees for Township of Newark the Land Confiscated from Nath Kingsland"), 0433_01 (deed of sale, in Dutch, November 29, 1673), https://digitalcollections.archives.nysed.gov/index.php/Detail/objects/51727, accessed August 19, 2023; English translation of the deed of sale, Charles H. Winfield, *History of the Land Titles in Hudson County, N.J., 1609–1871* (New York, 1872), 325–326.

22. NTR, 54 (January 31, 1673/74), 57–58 ("Conditions and Agreement Between the Town of Newark, and John Catlin and Edward Ball," February 24, 1673/74), 54 (March 19, 1673/74). Ball soon moved to the Neck, and the town gave Ebenezer Dod permission to buy Ball's property in Newark, "provided he subscribe to the fundamental agreements as other Inhabitants have done."

23. Mortgage with Pieter Jacobse Marius, March 23, 1674, NYSA, NYSA_A1881-78_V23_0326 (English translation in Winfield, *Land Titles of Hudson County*, 326–327), 0327 (mortgage with Gabriel Minvielle, March 23, 1674), https://digitalcollections.archives.nysed.gov/index.php/Detail/objects/51727, accessed August 19, 2023.

24. John Davenport Jr. to John Winthrop Jr., April 16, 1674, WP; Shomette and Haslach, *Raid on America*, 292–295, 309–310; "Memorials of what strength will be necessary for the retaking of New York," Philip Carteret, November 3, 1673 (item 1160), and "Opinion and humble advice of the Council for Trade and Plantations to the King, about the retaking of New York," November 15, 1673 (item 1165), "America and West Indies: November 1673," in *Calendar of State Papers Colonial, America and West Indies: Volume 7, 1669–1674*, 530–535, British History Online, http://www.british-history.ac.uk/cal-state-papers/colonial/america-west-indies/vol7/pp530-535, accessed August 19, 2023.

25. Petition of Newark, Elizabethtown, and Piscataway for a confirmation of their rights and possessions, June 29, 1674, NYSA, NYSA_A1881-78_V23_0326, https://digitalcollections.archives.nysed.gov/index.php/Detail/objects/51727, accessed August 19, 2023; NTR, 55 (June 29, July 3, and August 10, 1674); Alexander Bryan to John Winthrop Jr., July 30, 1674, WP.

26. Israel Chauncy to John Winthrop Jr., October 19, 1674, and Alexander Bryan to John Winthrop Jr., October 31, 1674, WP; Shomette and Haslach, *Raid on America*, 312; Edmund Andros, proclamation that all transactions remain valid, November 24, 1674, in *The Andros Papers: 1674–1676*, ed. Peter R. Christoph and Florence A. Christoph (Syracuse, NY: Syracuse University Press, 1989), 34–35.

27. Proclamation by Philip Carteret reversing unauthorized land acquisitions, EJD, 3:104 (December 11, 1674).

28. Alexander Bryan to John Winthrop Jr., October 27, 1674 ("James Cartwright with his wife aboard the other Frigatt[;] delavall hath given him all his intrest at Harlum and is to live their"), WP; Philip Carteret to Peter Carteret (in French), June 25, 1675 ("He runs

about among the farmers, and stays where he can most find drink, and sleeps in barns on the straw"), Philip Carteret Collection, C0901, Princeton University Library; Bartlett Burleigh James and J. Franklin Jameson, eds. *Journal of Jasper Danckaerts, 1679–1680* (New York: Charles Scribner's Sons, 1913), 66.

CHAPTER 9 — HARD TIMES

1. Order by Philip Carteret for a General Court, East Jersey Deeds (EJD), New Jersey State Archives (NJSA), SSTSE023, 3:106–107 (December 11, 1674); Israel Chauncy to John Winthrop Jr., February 15, 1674/75, Winthrop Family Papers (WP), Massachusetts Historical Society, Ms. N-262.

2. EJD, 3:99, notation at the end of Sir George Carteret's "Directions, Instructions and Orders"; Charles II to Sir George Carteret, EJD, 3:98 (June 13, 1674); Elizabethtown Bill in Chancery (EBC), published as *A Bill in the Chancery of New-Jersey, at the Suit of John Earl of Stair, and Others, Proprietors of the Eastern-Division of New-Jersey; Against Benjamin Bond, and Some Other Persons of Elizabethtown* (New York, 1747), 38; John Allen Latschar, "East New Jersey, 1665–1682: Perils of a Proprietary Government" (PhD diss., Rutgers University, 1978), 313–317.

3. Newark Town Records (NTR), published as *Records of the Town of Newark, New Jersey* (Newark: New Jersey Historical Society [NJHS], 1864, reissued 1966), 55 (October 31, 1674).

4. Sir George Carteret, "Directions, Instructions and Orders," July 31, 1674, in *The Grants, Concessions, and Original Constitutions of the Province of New Jersey* (LS), ed. A. Leaming and J. Spicer (Somerville, NJ, 1881), 50–56; EJD, 3:94–98. The same day, Sir George Carteret commissioned Philip Carteret once again as governor, LS, 58–60.

5. Peter R. Christoph and Florence A. Christoph, *The Andros Papers, 1674–1676* (Syracuse, NY: Syracuse University Press, 1989), 16. Sir George Carteret to the Council, August 18, 1674, and the Council to Sir George Carteret, November 7, 1674, EJD, 3:99; EBC, 41.

6. EJD, 3:104–107; William Jones to John Winthrop Jr., February 6, 1674/75, WP; NTR, 61 (January 1, 1675/76, election of members of the town's monthly court for "small matters").

7. NTR, 56 (December 11, 1674); William Jones to John Winthrop Jr., February 6, 1674/75, WP; Seth Tompkins to John Winthrop Jr., March 29, 1675 ("Leaving the reporte of our afflicted state & Condition to the information of our Honoured friend Mr Willys"), WP.

8. NTR, 56 (February 20, 1674/75) and 59 (March 8, 1674/75).

9. EJD, 1:135ff. Latschar, "East New Jersey," Chart 3, "East New Jersey Land Patents: 1665–1682;" NTR, 67 (February 7, 1676/77); EJD, 1, part B, 270 (March 2, 1676/77); "The Surveyor Generall hath not finished the Surveys of the several townes," Minutes of the Governor and Council of New Jersey (MGC), NJSA, SEA00001, 5–6 (August 25, 1675). There are numerous Newark surveys in EJD, 2, Part B, dated August 19, the day before Jasper Crane took out the first patent.

10. EJD, 3:102 (oath of a constable) and 105 (Johnson sworn in by James Bollen).

11. EJD, 3:104.

12. NTR, 56–57 (February 28, 1674/75), 59 (March 19, 1674/75), 62 (February 7, 1675/76), and 71 (May 1, 1678, "after lecture"); Kenneth Scott, ed., *Minutes of the Mayors Court of New York, 1674–1675* (Baltimore, Genealogical Publishing Co., Inc., 1983), 39; Colve delegated his power of attorney to Bayard before departing. Christoph and Christoph, *Andros Papers, 1674–1676*, 31–32.

13. NTR, 56 (February 20, 1674/75) and 58 (March 8, 1674/75); MGC, 5 (June 15, 1675), 7 (August 25, 1675), 9 (October 7, 1675). The town cooperated with the efforts of Catlin and Ball by securing the bill of sale for Kingsland's estate from Jacob Melyn and providing a copy of the contract for transfer of part ownership to them.

14. NTR, 62 (January 21, 1675/76), 66–67 (January 1, 1676/77). The town was responsible for the £103.6s.8d that Catlin and the others had borrowed at 10 percent interest to make their first-year payment. For the next five years, there are frequent references in the town records to efforts to settle the purchase debt. NTR, 68 (October 5, 1677), 69 (February 6, 1677/78), 70 (October 22, 1677), and 78 (May 3, 1680). The effort to make John Catlin and his associates whole created similar challenges. NTR, 63 (April 17, 1676); MGC, 19 (petition of Catlin and the others; order to Sandford and Pardon, May 10, 1676), 17 (town meeting order, April 5, 1676), 22 (Sandford's report to the council, June 15, 1676). As one of the patentees who put up capital in 1673, Stephen Freeman personally borrowed forty pounds from Pieter Jacobse Marius, the same Dutch merchant who later loaned over forty-three pounds to Catlin and his associates. That debt became a burden for his widow Hannah after his death in June 1675. Sensitive to her situation, the town meeting specifically excluded "the Widow Freeman" from the levy imposed in April 1676 to reimburse John Catlin and his associates. A final settlement of all remaining issues was not reached until early 1682. EJD, 3:119–120 (inventory and administration for Freeman's estate, noting £15.12s.9d "debts due from the estate"); NTR, 63 (April 17, 1676), 79 (September 3, 1680), 80 (September 27, 1680), 81 (January 4, 1680/81), and 87 (December 19, 1681, and January 1 or 2, 1681/82); Peter R. Christoph and Florence A. Christoph, eds., *The Andros Papers: 1679–1680* (Syracuse, NY: Syracuse University Press, 1991), 382, 385.

15. Order by the governor and council, October 24, 1678, MGC, 40.

16. MGC, 17 (April 5, 1676), 29 (April 4, 1678); NTR, 61 (January 1, 1675/76), 71 (March 30, 1678; Abraham Pierson helped draw up the petition that was delivered to the governor on April 2, 1678).

17. EJD, 3:117 (July 15, 1675).

18. MGC, 14–15 (December 13, 1675); the lists of names are not extant.

19. MGC, 5–7 (August 25, 1675); NTR, 60 (September 10, 1675).

20. LS, 98–111.

21. MGC, 14 (October 22, 1675); in summoning the assembly, Carteret noted "inhabitants In Generall" had shown their willingness to patent their lands, "the Compleating there of being hindred only by the Impossibility of the surveyor perfecting the surveyes for the present." NTR, 60–61 (October 26, 1675), 61 (January 1, 1675/76); LS, 93–111.

22. NTR, 63–64 (June 5, 1676); LS, 112–118.

23. LS, 119–137. Assembly sessions took place in October 1676 (including declaring a day of Thanksgiving for being spared King Philip's War); October 1677 (including repeal of the prohibition on selling arms to Indians, a measure opposed by both of Newark's deputies); October 1678 (including a provision that no man in the province shall be "deprived of the benefit of common law, and a free process therein, as of right belongs to every free English subject"); April 1679; May 1679 (in Middletown and Piscataway on different days); and November 1679 (including declaring a day of Thanksgiving for the deliverance of England "from that horrid plot of the Papists," escape from "that infectious disease of the small pox," and safety "from the trouble of the Indians"). Thomas Johnson served as a deputy to each assembly. He was joined by John Ward (1675 and 1676), Thomas Richards (1677), Samuel Swaine (1678), and John Curtis (1679). NTR, 60–61 (October 26, 1675), 61 (January 1, 1675/76), 65 (January 1, 1676/77), 68 (January 1, 1677/78), and 72 (January 1, 1678/79).

CHAPTER 10 — TRANSITIONS

1. Dumas Malone, ed., *Dictionary of American Biography*, vol. 14 (1962), 587–588; Richard E. Pierson and Jennifer Pierson, *Pierson Millennium* (Westminster, MD: Heritage Books, 2004), 89–90; Cotton Mather, *Magnalia Christi Americana* (Hartford, CT, 1855), 1:398; Mary Grey Lundie Duncan, *Memoirs of . . . Matthias Bruen* (New York, 1831), 12–14.

2. Newark Town Records (NTR), published as *Records of the Town of Newark, New Jersey* (Newark: New Jersey Historical Society [NJHS], 1864, reissued 1966), 72–75 (September 30, 1678, February 12, 1678/79, February 13, 1678/79, and February 19, 1678–79); East Jersey Deeds (EJD), New Jersey State Archives (NJSA), SSTSE023, 2:28, 108.

3. Philip Carteret and Council to Sir George Carteret, April 5, 1676, Minutes of the Governor and Council of New Jersey (MGC), NJSA, SEA00001, 18; Robert C. Ritchie, *The Duke's Province: A Study of New York Politics and Society, 1664–1691* (Chapel Hill: University of North Carolina Press, 1977), 112.

4. Mary Lou Lustig, *The Imperial Executive in America: Sir Edmund Andros, 1637–1714* (Madison, NJ: Fairleigh Dickinson University Press, 2002), 61, 109; G. R. Balleine, *All for the King: The Life Story of Sir George Carteret* (St. Helier, Jersey: Société Jersiaise, 1976), 165.

5. Edmund Andros to Philip Carteret, March 8, 1679/80, in *The Grants, Concessions, and Original Constitutions of the Province of New Jersey* (LS), ed. A. Leaming and J. Spicer (Somerville, NJ, 1881), 673; proclamation of Sir Edmund Andros against Philip Carteret, March 13, 1679/80, in *The Andros Papers: 1679–1680*, ed. Peter R. Christoph and Florence A. Christoph (Syracuse, NY: Syracuse University Press, 1991), 243–244; Philip Carteret to Edmund Andros, March 20, 1679/80, LS, 674–675; *Archives of the State of New Jersey* (NJA), 1st Series, 1–42 (Trenton, NJ, 1880–1949), 1:296–297; John Allen Latschar, "East New Jersey, 1665–1682: Perils of a Proprietary Government" (PhD diss., Rutgers University, 1978), 395–397.

6. NTR, 79 (March 29, 1680); Philip Carteret to Edmund Andros, March 29, 1680, LS, 676–677.

7. NJA, 1:299–302; Philip Carteret's arrest warrant, May 1, 1680, in *Books of General Entries of the Colony of New York, 1674–1688*, ed. Peter R. Christoph and Florence A. Christoph (Baltimore: Genealogical Publishing Co., Inc., 1982), 209; Philip Carteret to Mr. Coustier, July 9, 1680, LS, 678; Philip Carteret to James Bollen, July 9, 1680, LS, 683–685; Bartlett Burleigh James and J. Franklin Jameson, eds., *Journal of Jasper Danckaerts, 1679–1680* (New York: Charles Scribner's Sons, 1913), 241; Latschar, "East New Jersey," 399–400; NTR, 78 (May 3, 1680); NJA, 21:44.

8. Official record of the trial by Matthias Nicolls, May 27 and 28, 1680, LS, 678–679; Danckaerts, *Journal*, 239, 240–244.

9. Return of deputies for Newark, May 24, 1680, *Andros Papers, 1679–1680*, 283–284, 286. Andros's charge to the assembly, June 2, 1680, LS, 680–681; answer of the assembly to Andros, June 2, 1680, and resolution of the assembly confirming privileges, June 2, 1680, *Andros Papers, 1679–1680*, 287–288; council minutes relating to the assembly, June 2–12, 1680, *Andros Papers, 1679–1680*, 296–299.

10. Curtis was identified in a draft warrant as "late of Hempstead on Long Island labourer," but the fact that he was arrested and examined in Newark suggests that he was the Newark leader. For warrants and depositions, *Andros Papers, 1679–1680*, 290–292, 294, 301, 357–358. Taylor was arrested in New York, but the charges were dismissed after he gave security. Proceedings of the New York Council, August 13, 1680, NJA, 1:322. Andros was quick to use arrests to suppress dissent; when Samuel Moore and Samuel Dennis of Woodbridge resisted Andros's orders related to establishing courts, they were arrested in early

August, held in prison for two weeks, and then released once they capitulated. *Andros Papers, 1679–1680*, 331, 358, 363–364, 371.

11. Latschar, "East New Jersey," 420–421; NJA, 1:337–345 (indenture dated September 10, 1680, but apparently signed on October 16, 1680); Sir John Werden to Sir Edmund Andros, November 6, 1680, NJA, 1:345; proclamation by Philip Carteret, March 2, 1680/81, LS, 685–686; Anthony Brockholls to Philip Carteret, April 14, 1681, April 18, 1681, and May 14, 1681, *Books of General Entries*, 216–218.

12. NTR, 83 (July 18, 1681); "Acts of the General Assembly, at Elizabeth Town," July 23, 1681, LS, 137–138; Philip Carteret to Lady Elizabeth Carteret, July 30, 1681, LS, 687; NJA, 1:353; Richard P. McCormick, "The Revolution of 1681 in East Jersey: A Document," *Proceedings of the New Jersey Historical Society*, 71, no. 2 (1953): 112, 123; MGC, 49.

13. McCormick, "Revolution of 1681," 111–113; "Proceedings of the Governor and Council, and the Assembly of New Jersey," NJA, 1:354–355; J. R. Brodhead, B. Fernow, and E. B. O'Callaghan, eds., *Documents Relative to the Colonial History of the State of New-York* (DCHNY), vols. 1–15 (Albany, 1853–1887), 3:293–295.

14. "Proceedings," NJA, 1:354–365; DCHNY, 3:293–300; Latschar, "East New Jersey," 440–447; William Whitehead, *East Jersey Under the Proprietary Governments* (Newark, 1875), 98–99; John E. Pomfret, *The Province of East Jersey, 1609–1702* (Princeton, NJ: Princeton University Press, 1962), 124–128; Claribel F. Young, "Imperial, Proprietary and Freeholder Objectives in the English Settlement of New Jersey, 1664–1682: A Study in Cross Purposes and the Resulting Development of Pluralist Government" (PhD diss., Rutger University, 1989), 232–256.

15. McCormick, "Revolution of 1681," 111–113; MGC, 44, 49; NTR, 87 (January 1 or 2, 1681/82); Young, "Imperial," 256–259.

16. Pomfret, *East Jersey*, 129–132; Elizabeth Carteret to Rachel Carteret, December 14, 1682, Philip Carteret Collection, C0901, Princeton University Library.

CHAPTER 11 — COMPROMISE

1. "The Scots have taken a right course, They have sent over many servants, and are likewayes sending more; They have likewayes sent over many poor Families. . . . this will raise the price of the Land here, and is the reason that several from New York bounds come to me, to take up Land." Gawen Lawrie to a friend, March 26, 1684, William Whitehead, *East Jersey Under the Proprietary Governments* (Newark, 1875), 288.

2. John E. Pomfret, *The Province of East Jersey, 1609–1702* (Princeton, NJ: Princeton University Press, 1962), 130–136; Ned C. Landsman, *Scotland and Its First American Colony, 1683–1765* (Princeton, NJ: Princeton University Press, 1985), 103–109, 122; Barclay's copy of Matthias Nicolls's account, acquired at auction by the State of New Jersey in 2005, was transcribed by Joseph R. Klett in "Account of East Jersey's Seven Settled Towns, Circa 1684," *Genealogical Magazine of New Jersey* 80 (2005): 106–114, without attribution to Matthias Nicolls or reference to the similar version in Scot's *Model*, in Whitehead, *East Jersey*, 271–277. Scot notes, "This was the Condition of the Province Anno, 1680, Given under the hand of Captain Nicholls, Secretary of the Duke in New York."

3. Gawen Lawrie to the Scots Proprietors, March 26, 1684, Whitehead, *East Jersey*, 291; Peter Watson to John Watson, August 20, 1684, Whitehead, *East Jersey*, 303.

4. Thomas Rudyard to B. G., May 30, 1683, Whitehead, *East Jersey*, 281; Gawen Lawrie to the East Jersey Proprietors, March 2, 1684, Whitehead, *East Jersey*, 285; Gawen Lawrie to the Scots Proprietors, March 26, 1684, Whitehead, *East Jersey*, 290; John Reid to a friend in Edinburgh, September 1, 1684, Whitehead, *East Jersey*, 295; John Condit to Thomas Jef-

ferson, December 30, 1802, Founders Online, http://founders.archives.gov/documents /Jefferson/01-39-02-0209, accessed November 13, 2023.

5. Newark Town Records (NTR), published as *Records of the Town of Newark, New Jersey* (Newark: New Jersey Historical Society [NJHS], 1864, reissued 1966), 90 (March 22, 1682/83); F. W. Ricord and W. Nelson, eds., *Journal of the Governor and Council, Volume I: 1682–1714* (JGC), vol. 13 in *Archives of the State of New Jersey* (NJA) (Trenton, NJ, 1890), 35. Residents of Piscataway took similar action, Piscataway Town Records, 3 (October 26, 1683), Rutgers University Special Collections, MC 1359 (typescript, accn. 2099).

6. George J. Miller, Maxine N. Lurie, and Joanne R. Walroth, eds., *The Minutes of the Board of Proprietors of the Eastern Division of New Jersey* (MBPEDNJ), 4 vols. (Perth Amboy and Newark, NJ, 1949–1985), 1:21. Groome calculated Newark's annual quitrent as £11.3s.9½d, with total arrears in 1683 of £139.19s.10½d. Arrears were £1,153.7s.7d for out plantations, £339.0s.6¾d for Shrewsbury, £116.0s.4d for Woodbridge, and £78.10s.7d for Piscataway. The figures for Elizabethtown and Middletown are not extant.

7. Samuel Groome to the East Jersey Proprietors, August 11, 1683, Whitehead, *East Jersey*, 283; NTR, 95 (May 30, 1684, and December 22, 1684); John E. Pomfret, "Governor Gawen Lawrie's 'Brief Account,' 1686," New Jersey Historical Society *Proceedings*, new series, vol. 75 (April 1957): 98–111. For Berry's resistance to paying quitrents, see John E. Pomfret, "The Apologia of Governor Lawrie of East New Jersey, 1686," *William and Mary Quarterly* 14, no. 3 (July 1957): 344–357. The original concessions called for one-seventh of all land grants to be set aside for the proprietors, but governor Philip Carteret had waived that requirement when he approved the Newark tract in 1666; see chapter 1.

8. Newark's arrears were £178.15s.6½d, with only £19.15s.9½d having been paid; the amounts for other towns were Shrewsbury (£441.18s.2½d), Elizabethtown (£284.2s.¼d), Middletown (£247.7s.5½d), and Piscataway (£109.8s.2d), MBPEDNJ, 1:21; David S. Lovejoy, *The Glorious Revolution in America* (New York: Harper & Row, 1972), 212–213.

9. MBPEDNJ, 1:21; NTR, 54 (March 19, 1673/74), 87 (January 6, 1681/82), 90 (February 5, 1682/83).

10. MBPEDNJ, 1:56–57 (April 10, 1685). Newarkers were unfortunate in presenting their petition immediately after inhabitants of Elizabethtown presented a similar petition offering only a twenty-pound annual quitrent payment for a much larger area, putting the board on guard. The board considered Elizabethtown's proposal "ridiculous."

11. NTR, 97 (June 3, 1685, and August 13, 1685); MBPEDNJ, 1:93 (October 15, 1685). Suits were brought against Samuel Plum, Samuel Kitchell, and William Camp in August 1685 and against Abraham Pierson Jr. in February 1686. *Journal of the Courts of Common Right and Chancery of East Jersey*, ed. Preston W. Edsall (Philadelphia: The American Legal History Society, 1937), 204, 207, 217 (August 1685, February and March 1686). Pierson's answer to the bill of inquiry was deemed "insufficient" by the court, and he was given one month to "to putt in a more sufficient Answer." At its March session, the court found against Pierson and charged him court costs. The disposition of the cases against Plum, Kitchell, and Camp is not recorded.

12. NTR, 97 (November 7, 1685), 99 (April 18, 1686), 100–101 (January 24, 1686/87), 101 (February 7, 1686/87, fourth division of land), 102 (April 30, 1688); depositions of Robert Treat, March 13, 1687/8, and Samuel Edsall, March 5, 1687/88, MBPEDNJ, 2:274–276. The board ordered distraints on the property of all East Jersey residents in arrears for their quitrents, MBPEDNJ, 1:154 (March 10, 1686/86, distraint order), 170–171 (April 12, 1688).

13. NTR, 106 (date not recorded); MBPEDNJ, 1:200–201 (February 28, 1692/93).

14. MBPEDNJ, 1:204 (August 9, 1693), 207 (December 8, 1693); East Jersey Deeds (EJD), New Jersey State Archives (NJSA), SSTSE023, O:104, 110–113 (grant to John Curtis), O:103–104

(grant to John Gardner), O:106 (grant to Azariah and Jasper Crane), O:144, 158 (grant to John Treat), https://wwwnet-dos.state.nj.us/DOS_ArchivesDBPortal/EarlyLandRecords.aspx, accessed November 18, 2023.

15. MBPEDNJ, 1:209 (April 20, 1694).

16. MBPEDNJ, 1:209–210 (April 20, 1694), 215 (May 18, 1695), 223 (April 10, 1696); EJD, O:105–106, 153.

17. "Account of the Quitt Rents of the Province of East Jersey, 1696," NJHS, MG 217.

18. NTR, 106 (undated, but early 1693), 107 (January 1, 1693/94, and March 5, 1693/94). MBPEDNJ, 1:112–113 (February 11, 1685/86, similar offer to the residents of Piscataway), 200 (February 28, 1692/93), 204 (August 3, 1693), 223 (February 20, 1695/96, Zophar Beach's patent).

19. MBPEDNJ, 1:222 (April 10, 1696); EJD, F:166–168 (December 10, 1696); NJHS, MG 217.

CHAPTER 12 — TURBULENT TIMES

1. Newark Town Records (NTR), published as *Records of the Town of Newark, New Jersey* (Newark: New Jersey Historical Society [NJHS], 1864, reissued 1966), 90 (February 5, 1682/83). F. W. Ricord and W. Nelson, eds., *Journal of the Governor and Council, Volume I: 1682–1714* (JGC), vol. 13 in *Archives of the State of New Jersey* (NJA) (Trenton, NJ, 1890), 22, 29–30, 34, 40–41, 53, 58, 65, 82, 94; John Ward of Newark was also made a justice of the peace. A. Leaming and J. Spicer, eds., *The Grants, Concessions, and Original Constitutions of the Province of New Jersey* (LS) (Somerville, NJ, 1881), 254–255 (An Act Against Trading with Negro Slaves), 273–274 (An Act to Regulate Treaties with the Indians).

2. LS, 262–265 (A Bill to Regulate Abuses in Taking up Horses); John E. Pomfret, *The Province of East Jersey, 1609–1702* (Princeton, NJ: Princeton University Press, 1962), 177; NTR, 94 (February 25, 1683/84).

3. NTR, 92–93 (January 1, 1683/84; Thomas Johnson and John Curtis chosen as deputies), 95–96 (January 1, 1684/85; Thomas Huntington and John Curtis chosen as deputies), 97 (January 1, 1685/86), 100 (January 1, 1686/87; only John Curtis selected as deputy), 101 (January 2, 1687/88; only John Curtis selected as deputy); LS, 288–289 (An Act Concerning Swine), 293 (An Act for the Court of Common Right to be held at Perth Amboy), 294 (An Act for Rates for Highways); JGC, 143 (April 6, 1686), 187 (June 19, 1688, and September 28, 1692).

4. J. R. Brodhead, B. Fernow, and E. B. O'Callaghan, eds., *Documents Relative to the Colonial History of the State of New-York* (DCHNY), vols. 1–15 (Albany, 1853–1887), 3:361–361 (July 15, 1685), 428 (order of the Lord of Trade about port of entry, August 14, 1687); LS, 306–309 (An Act for a Tax to Withstand Invasion).

5. Formed in 1686, the Dominion of New England originally encompassed Massachusetts, Connecticut, Rhode Island, New Plymouth, Maine, and New Hampshire. DCHNY, 3:536–542, 550–554, 567; JGC, 187 (June 19, 1688, and September 28, 1692); Mary Lou Lustig, *The Imperial Executive in America: Sir Edmund Andros, 1637–1714* (Madison, NJ: Fairleigh Dickinson University Press, 2002), 138–140, 161, 166; Alfred S. T. Goodrick, intro., *Edward Randolph: Including His Letters and Official Papers from the New England, Middle, and Southern Colonies in America, with Other Documents Relating Chiefly to the Vacating of the Royal Charter of the Colony of Massachusetts Bay, 1676–1703* (Boston: Printed for The Prince Society by John Wilson & Son, 1898–1909), 6:263–265 (Edward Randolph to William Blathwayt, October 2, 1688).

6. Steve Pincus, *1688: The First Modern Revolution* (New Haven, CT: Yale University Press, 2009), 6, 122, 154; David S. Lovejoy, *The Glorious Revolution in America* (New York: Harper & Row, 1972), 254.

7. Lovejoy, *Glorious Revolution*, 239–245, 251–252; Pincus, *1688*, 224–225; David William Voorhees, "'In Behalf of the True Protestants Religion': The Glorious Revolution in New York" (PhD diss., New York University, 1988), 118–122. Both Monmouth and Argyle were executed, and Argyle's brother, Lord Neil Campbell, was exiled to East Jersey, where he served briefly as deputy governor in 1686.

8. For Leisler's correspondence with Melyn, see Peter R. Christoph, ed., *The Leisler Papers, 1689–1691* (Syracuse, NY: Syracuse University Press, 2002), 243, 249; see also "Jacob Melyen, Letterbook, 1691–1696," American Antiquarian Society; Evan Haefeli, "Dutch New York and the Salem Witch Trials: Some New Evidence," *Proceedings of the American Antiquarian Society* 110, no. 2 (2000): 277–308; for Leisler's correspondence with William Jones, see DCHNY, 2:7–9; Voorhees, "'In Behalf of the True Protestants Religion,'" 171; "Address of the Militia of New-York to William and Mary," June 1689, DCHNY, 3:583–584; on Leisler, see David William Voorhees, "'To Assert Our Right Before It Quite Be Lost:' The Leisler Rebellion in the Delaware River Valley," *Pennsylvania History: A Journal of Mid-Atlantic Studies* 64, no. 1 (1997): 5–27, and "The 'Fervent Zeale' of Jacob Leisler," *William and Mary Quarterly* 51, no. 3 (1994): 447–472, https://doi.org/10.2307/2947438, accessed January 13, 2025.

9. Lovejoy, *Glorious Revolution*, 255–257; "Abstract of What Is Acted by the Committe of Safety in New Yorke" (minutes; submission, The National Archives, Kew, CO 5/1081 1689/06/27-1689/08/17), http://www.colonialamerica.amdigital.co.uk.proxy.libraries.rutgers.edu/Documents/Details/CO_5_1081_020, accessed November 27, 2023; Randall Baker, *A Perfect Babel of Confusion: Dutch Religion and English Culture in the Middle Colonies* (New York: Oxford University Press, 1989), 30–32; Firth Haring Fabend, "The Pro-Leislerian Farmers in Early New York: A 'Mad Rabble' or 'Gentlemen Standing Up for Their Rights?'" *Hudson River Valley Review* 20 (2006): 79–90.

10. "Abstract" (June 27, 1689), 106–107.

11. "Abstract" (June 27, 1689), 109–111; Stephen Van Cortland to Francis Nicholson, August 5, 1689, DCHNY, 3:609.

12. "Abstract" (June 28, 1689), 116.

13. "Abstract" (June 28, 1689), 115.

14. "Abstract" (July 24, 1689), 126; Nicholas Bayard, one of Leisler's fiercest opponents, noted "Great endevours have also been made . . . to overthrow All civil Government . . . as in the late province of New Jersie . . . by sending of messengers and letters to some of the military Officers and factious men, inticing them to follow their steps; but all . . . are agreed to remain steady." Nicholas Bayard to Francis Nicholson, July 23, 1689, DCHNY, 3:598. On Johnstone, see Ned C. Landsman, *Scotland and Its First American Colony, 1683–1765* (Princeton, NJ: Princeton University Press, 1985), 122.

15. "Abstract" (July 24, 1689), 126; Jacob Leisler to Gilbert Burnet, January 7, 1689/90, and March 31, 1690, DCHNY, 3:656, 701; *Leisler Papers*, 406–407; Stephen Van Cortland, one of the New York aldermen displaced by Leisler, informed Edmund Andros that former governor Andrew Hamilton, Richard Townley, Andrew Bowne, William Pinhorne, and other "new Jarsay Gentlemen" did not dare to visit New York while Leisler retained control. Stephen Van Cortland to Edmund Andros, May 19, 1690, DCHNY, 3:716.

16. Lovejoy, *Glorious Revolution*, 315–316, 319; *Leisler Papers*, xx-xxi, 133 ("Peskatoway men"), 500 (payment of £5.5.0 to Henry Lyon), 501 (payment to Newark soldiers Philip Morris, Samuel Potter, and Benjamin Harrison); NTR, 104 (January 5, 1690/91); Patrick Falconer was chosen by the town meeting "to receive and make payment of this Money of the Soldiers." Piscataway and Woodbridge town records do not mention events related to the Glorious Revolution.

17. NTR, 104 (March 25, 1689/90); Woodbridge Town Records, Liber A, 229 (April 5, 1690), Rutgers University Special Collections (32907021.1). In November 1691, Henry Lyon sought reimbursement from Woodbridge for "his Charge with the Indians." The Woodbridge town meeting approved a payment to Lyon of £1.5s, Woodbridge Town Records, 232 (November 25, 1691); Woodbridge still owed the money more than a year later, Woodbridge Town Records, 233 (December 10, 1692); "Remonstrance of the Inhabitants of East Jersey to the King, Against the Acts of the Proprietors," 1700, NJA, 2:323.

18. Lovejoy, *Glorious Revolution*, 338–339, 354–357, 362–363; Lydecker, a former resident of New York, appeared in Leisler's accounts, *Leisler Papers*, 167, 169, 171, 481; NTR, 107 (March 5, 1693/94); eleven men were admitted as planters at that meeting. In 1696, the proprietors' quit rent account for Newark noted "Hendrick Hendricks van rand" (owning 44 acres), "Tunis Jansen" (120 acres), "Hance Hendrickson alias Speare" (105 acres), "Bastian Van Giesen" (136 acres), and "Jasper Nishipat and Gerrit LDycken" (20 acres). Other Dutch landowners were Johannes Van Gieson (68 acres), Widow Rulifson (60 acres), Isaac Van Gieson (68 acres), and Cornelius and Johannes Tunisons (60 acres). Isaac Van Gieson subsequently sold his land to Jacob Joralemon, NJHS, MG 217. For the location of these tracts, see "Essex Map, ca 1700," www.eastjerseyhistory.org, accessed February 25, 2024.

19. Pomfret, *East Jersey*, 276–307.

CHAPTER 13 — CHANGE AND CONFLICT

1. Joseph Brown made his will on October 20, 1694, John Ward Sr. on October 31, Thomas Johnson on November 2, John Denison on November 3, John Crane Sr. on November 4, Stephen Bond on November 6, and Ebenezer Canfield on November 11; all these wills were proved on November 20 or 21, 1694. Two other men, Ephraim Pennington and Thomas Lyon, died intestate in this period. East Jersey Deeds (EJD), New Jersey State Archives (NJSA), SSTSE023, D:144–153; *Archives of the State of New Jersey* (NJA), 1st Series, 1–42 (Trenton, NJ, 1880–1949), 21:215–217, 221.

2. Jonathan F. Stearns, *First Church in Newark. Historical Discourses, Relating to the First Presbyterian Church in Newark* (Newark, 1853), 96–97; Samuel H. Congar, "Genealogical Notices of the First Settlers of Newark," in *Proceedings Commemorative of the Settlement of Newark, New Jersey, on Its Two Hundredth Anniversary, May 17th, 1866* (Newark, NJ, 1866), 106–153; Newark Town Records (NTR), published as *Records of the Town of Newark, New Jersey* (Newark: New Jersey Historical Society [NJHS], 1864, reissued 1966), 108–109 (January 1, 1695/96), 109–110 (August 10, 1696), and 114 (April 11, 1699).

3. Robert Wodrow, *The History of the Sufferings of the Church of Scotland* (Glasgow, 1836), 4 vols., 4:221–222, 331–333. Deeply devout, Russell considered "the safftie off my hand in denottar [Dunnottar] from the fyr for it is now all well" among the "wonderous markes of the Lord." Peter Russell to Robert Russell, March 18, 1686, Orbiston Letters, North Lanarkshire Archives, U21/433/172; the letter is catalogued as 1688, but internal evidence suggests that it was written in 1686.

4. William A. Whitehead, *Contributions to the Early History of Perth Amboy* (New York, 1856), 23–32; Wodrow, *Sufferings*, 4:221–222, 331–333; Peter Russell to Robert Russell, March 18, 1686, Orbiston Letters, U21/433/172, "Thomas russall died by the way." On Thomas Russell and Janet Symington as Covenanters, see Wodrow, *Sufferings*, 4:332.

5. Wodrow, *Sufferings*, 4:333; Whitehead, *Perth Amboy*, 32; Ned C. Landsman, *Scotland and Its First American Colony, 1683–1765* (Princeton, NJ: Princeton University Press, 1985), 139, 309n16; Peter Russell to Robert Russell, March 18 and May 1686, Orbiston Letters, U21/433/164, 172. The town of Woodbridge soon called Rev. Archibald Riddell, who had

sailed on the *Henry and Francis*, as their minister, and he "showed much kyndness" to many of the Scots who had sailed with him, including Peter Russell when he visited Woodbridge to dispatch his letters.

6. Peter Russell, March 18 and May 1686, and John Smith to his brother and sister, appended to Peter Russell's letter, May 1686, Orbiston Letters, U21/433/164; Wodrow, *Sufferings*, 4:151, 331–332; Whitehead, *Perth Amboy*, 32–34.

7. Letters of Peter Russell, March 18 and May 1686, Orbiston Letters, U21/433/164, 172; Quitrent records, NJHS, MG 217; Patrick Falconer's will, February 27, 1691/92, Unrecorded Wills, Vol. 4, 279, and Unrecorded Wills, Vol. 6, 325, NJSA; EJD, D:339; Letter of Patrick Falconer to Maurice Trent, October 28, 1684, Whitehead, *East Jersey*, 301; EJD, C:10; NJA, 21:131; NTR, 104 (January 5, 1690/91); George J. Miller, Maxine N. Lurie, and Joanne R. Walroth, eds., *The Minutes of the Board of Proprietors of the Eastern Division of New Jersey* (MBPEDNJ), 4 vols. (Perth Amboy and Newark, NJ, 1949–1985), 1:214 (May 18, 1695).

8. *Heads of Agreement Assented to by the United Ministers in and About London: Formerly Called Presbyterian and Congregational* (London, 1691), 10; Stearns, *First Church in Newark*, 88; Michael P. Winship, *Hot Protestants: A History of Puritanism in England and America* (New Haven, CT: Yale University Press, 2018), 272–279.

9. NTR, 101 (January 2, 1687/88), 101–102 (January 9, 1687/88), 102 (April 30, 1688, and November 19, 1688), 105 (April 2, 1692). See 101 for the names of the fifty-one men; EJD, 2:405; NJA, 21:196. Pierson moved to Killingworth (now Clinton), Connecticut.

10. John Langdon Sibley, *Biographical Sketches of Graduates of Harvard University, in Cambridge, Massachusetts* (New York: Johnson Reprint Corporation, 1967) 2:258–263. Prudden was offered a fifty-pound annual salary (a ten-pound increase over his Jamaica income), free firewood, transportation to Newark, and title to Patrick Falconer's house that the town was in the process of acquiring from Mrs. Falconer, "for his own Proprietie, to him and his Heirs forever" if he made the final two payments. NTR, 105–106 (August 23 and October 28, 1692); Stearns, *First Church in Newark*, 97–101.

11. NTR, 112–113 (January 2, 1698/99, and June 9, 1699); Sibley, *Biographical Sketches*, 2:262–263.

12. NTR, 113–117 (June 9, August 8, and November 16, 1699; April 15, May 9, August 16, and September 30, 1700; November 11, 1701); Stearns, *First Church in Newark*, 106–110; Clifford K. Shipton, ed., *Biographical Sketches of Those Who Attended Harvard College in the Classes 1690–1700* (Cambridge, MA: Harvard University Press, 1933), 391–392.

13. Edwin Hatfield, *History of Elizabeth, New Jersey; Including the Early History of Union County* (New York, 1868), 241–243; "Petition to the King," in *The Grants, Concessions, and Original Constitutions of the Province of New Jersey* (LS), ed. A. Leaming and J. Spicer (Somerville, NJ, 1881), 688–692; Daniel J. Weeks, *Not for Filthy Lucre's Sake: Richard Saltar and the Antiproprietary Movement in East Jersey, 1665–1707* (Bethlehem, PA: Lehigh University Press, 2001), 76–77. William Dockwra, a proprietor based in London, informed Governor Hamilton that agents of New York had been "solliciting again at Court, for an Annexation of both the Jerseys to that Province, but have been frustrated in their designe." Letter of William Dockwra to Andrew Hamilton, April 1, 1693, MG 2, item 3, NJHS.

14. John E. Pomfret, *The Province of East Jersey, 1609–1702* (Princeton, NJ: Princeton University Press, 1962), 318–319; NJA, 2:176–177 (dismissal of Hamilton), 238–241, 244 (*Hester* affair); Joseph Atkinson, *The History of Newark* (Newark, NJ, 1878), 50. The election of deputies took place a few days after the seizure of the *Hester*, NJA, 21:162 (December 1, 1698); NTR, 111 (January 2, 1698/9); Robert Greenhalgh Albion, "New Jersey and the Port of New York," *Proceedings of the New Jersey Historical Society* (1950), 58:84–92.

15. NJA, 13:246–250 (Basse's speech and selection of Harriman), 265 (passage of the act); LS, 376–381 ("An Act for the Redressing a Force of Our Neighbour Province"); Weeks, *Not for Filthy Lucre's Sake*, 95–96.

16. NTR, 113–114 (April 11, 1699).

17. NJA, 2:270–271 (letter from Newark to other towns), 2:273–275 (letter from Newark and three other towns to the Proprietors); NJA, 3:477 (Bergen town meeting), 3:477–479 (Perth Amboy town meeting); Eugene R. Sheridan, *Lewis Morris, 1671–1746: A Study in Early American Politics* (Syracuse, NY: Syracuse University Press, 1981), 28–31; MBPEDNJ, 1:209 (April 20, 1694); Weeks, *Not for Filthy Lucre's Sake*, 96–100; Landsman, *Scotland*, 100, 168, 174–175.

18. NJA, 3:481–482 (order of the Court of Common Right, May 11, 1699), 485–487 (jury presentment against men of Elizabethtown for a riot); Sheridan, *Lewis Morris*, 32–33; F. W. Ricord and W. Nelson, eds., *Journal of the Governor and Council, Volume I: 1682–1714* (JGC), vol. 13 in *Archives of the State of New Jersey* (NJA) (Trenton, NJ, 1890), 269–273 (May 1699); Brendan McConville, *These Daring Disturbers of the Public Peace: The Struggle for Property and Power in Early New Jersey* (Ithaca, NY: Cornell University Press, 1999), 23–24.

19. On May 6, 1700, the Woodbridge town meeting affirmed its support for Hamilton, voting to "acknowledge Coll: Hamilton to Be our present Lawfull Governor." Woodbridge Town Records, Liber A, 261, Rutgers University Special Collections (32907021.1).

20. NJA, 2:313–315 (Essex County Court, March 12, 1699/1700), 315–317 (Middlesex County Court, March 19, 1699/1700), 364–366 (Monmouth County, March 26, 1700 (misdated 1701 in NJA and by Pomfret). Lewis Morris provided these documents to the Council of Trade and Plantations in August 1701, Cecil Headlam, ed., *Calendar of State Papers Colonial, America and West Indies, 1701* (London, 1910), 19:386–399, British History Online, http://www.british-history.ac.uk/cal-state-papers/colonial/america-west-indies/vol19/pp386-399, item 695, accessed February 11, 2024; Weeks, *Not for Filthy Lucre's Sake*, 107–108. Weeks misdates the Piscataway demonstration as March 4.

21. NJA, 2:322–327 (remonstrance and petition to the King, April 1700), 344–352 (response of the proprietors to the remonstrance, December 9, 1700); Cecil Headlam, ed., *Calendar of State Papers Colonial, America and West Indies, 1700* (London, 1910), 18:716–731, British History Online, http://www.british-history.ac.uk/cal-state-papers/colonial/america-west-indies/vol18/pp716-731, item 985, accessed February 11, 2024; Weeks, *Not for Filthy Lucre's Sake*, 109–110; Preston W. Edsall, ed., *Journal of the Courts of Common Right and Chancery of East Jersey* (Philadelphia: The American Legal History Society, 1937), 200; Landsman, *Scotland*, 166–169.

22. NJA, 2:333–339 (minutes of Essex County Court session, September 10, 1700; jury of inquest and depositions, September 12, 1700). A separate eighteen-member grand jury met on September 30 in Newark and brought presentments against the men who had participated in "riottusly Dissturbing" the court during its session on September 10. NJA, 2:339; Lewis Morris explained to the Lords of Trade that many who signed the East Jersey petition had also participated in a court disturbance, including the ones that took place in Newark; he urged that they receive "exemplary punishment." Memorandum of Lewis Morris to the Council of Trade and Plantations, August 5, 1701, NJA, 2:398–403, quotation at 403; Pomfret, *East Jersey*, 340, 356–357. A Court of General Quarter Sessions held in Newark on February 9, 1703/04, formally presented the Elizabethtown men to stand trial for their involvement in the riot. NJA, 3:495–496.

23. Pomfret, *East Jersey*, 360–361; NJA, 2:506–536 (instructions to Lord Cornbury); Patricia U. Bonomi, *The Lord Cornbury Scandal: The Politics of Reputation in British Amer-*

ica (Williamsburg, VA: Omohundro Institute, 1998), 175–177; Thomas L. Purvis, *Proprietors, Patronage, and Paper Money: Legislative Politics in New Jersey, 1703–1776* (New Brunswick, NJ: Rutgers University Press, 1986), 257. Massachusetts abolished its requirement that every voter be a church member when it became a royal colony in 1691.

24. NTR, 118 (October 30, 1705); Purvis, *Proprietors, Patronage, and Paper Money*, 83; *A Narrative of a New and Unusual American Imprisonment of Two Presbyterian Ministers and Prosecution of Mr. Francis Makemie* ([New York?], 1707), epistle to the reader, 4, https://quod.lib.umich.edu/cgi/t/text/text-idx?c=evans;cc=evans;view=toc;idno=N01088.0001.001, accessed February 28, 2024. Makemie was found not guilty but required to pay punitive court costs.

25. Purvis, *Proprietors, Patronage, and Paper Money*, 18–19. In this new political environment, the town focused on recruiting "a Man upon Trial in the work of the Ministry amongst us"; settling a minister was the primary topic at sixteen of the nineteen town meetings held between 1704 and 1711. NTR, 117–123.

CONCLUSION

1. Newark Town Records (NTR), published as *Records of the Town of Newark, New Jersey* (Newark: New Jersey Historical Society [NJHS], 1864, reissued 1966), 283–286 (charter and survey), 123 (February 21, 1711/12, and May 25, 1713, votes to seek a charter and include the costs in the town rate), 124 (April 12, 1714, charter "published" at a town meeting called by the trustees).

2. The text of the Woodbridge charter is Appendix A in Joseph Dally, *Woodbridge and Vicinity* (New Brunswick, NJ, 1873), 298–302. In 1683 and 1684, Woodbridge sought confirmation of its charter (also known as a "patent") from the Twenty-Four Proprietors. Woodbridge Town Records, Liber A, 211 and 214 (April 18, 1683, April 10 and May 22, 1684), Rutgers University Special Collections (32907021.1).

3. NTR, 78 (May 3, 1680). The Woodbridge town meeting continued to make land grants and admit new inhabitants through the end of the proprietary period.

4. NTR, 54 (March 19, 1673/74), 66 (January 1, 1676/77), 87 (January 6, 1681/82), 97 (November 7, 1685).

5. NTR, 61 (January 1, 1675/76), 63 (June 5, 1676), 100 (January 1 and 24, 1686/87), 108 (March 4, 1694/95), 111 (January 1, 1697/98).

6. NTR, 83 (February 25, 1680/81, regulating strangers), 73 (February 12, 1678/79, determining the cost of seating the meetinghouse), 77–78 (February 18, 1679/80, method for seating persons), 79 (July 24, 1680, seating Henry Lyon, a resident of Elizabethtown, so long as he paid proportionally with others toward the minister's salary), 88 (February 24, 1681/82, new committee to handle seating issues), 93 (January 1, 1683/84, attendance), 101 (January 2, 1687/88, contributions to salary). Order by the governor and council, October 24, 1678, Minutes of the Governor and Council of New Jersey (MGC), New Jersey State Archives (NJSA), SEA00001, 40.

7. "Over the Mountain" tract, March 1701/2, deed lost in a fire at Jonathan Pierson's house on March 7, 1744/45, reconstructed March 14, 1744/45, and confirmed by King Quichtoo, King Tishwasqamin, Saphoo, and Yaupis, James Alexander Papers, Box 6, folder 59, Princeton University Library; East Jersey Deeds (EJD), NJSA, SSTSE023, E-3:105–107. The list of subscribers is reproduced in C. T. Berry, *An Historical Survey of the First Presbyterian Church, Caldwell, N.J.* (Newark, NJ, 1871), appendix A; Max K. Vorwerk, *A History of the Horseneck Riots* (Caldwell, NJ: Caldwell Bicentennial Committee, 1976), 11, http://www.rootsweb.ancestry.com/~genepool/njriots1.htm, accessed August 19, 2011; James Hoyt, *"The Mountain Society:" A History of the First Presbyterian Church, Orange, N.J.* (New

York, 1860), 47–48; Brendan McConville, *These Daring Disturbers of the Public Peace: The Struggle for Property and Power in Early New Jersey* (Ithaca, NY: Cornell University Press, 1999), 71.

8. "Indian Deed by the Passaic River Granted to Edward Earle, Jr.," December 31, 1701, James Alexander Papers, Box 6, folder 56, Princeton University Library; West Jersey Deeds, O:145, NJSA.

9. McConville, *These Daring Disturbers*, 2–3.

10. John T. Cunningham, *The East of Jersey: A History of The General Board of Proprietors of the Eastern Division of New Jersey* (Newark: New Jersey Historical Society, 1992), 94–95.

11. *Archives of the State of New Jersey* (NJA), 1st Series, 1–42 (Trenton, NJ, 1880–1949), 6:314–315; Cunningham, *East of Jersey*, 95; McConville, *These Daring Disturbers*, 130.

12. NTR, 185 (1802, report of a committee to make an enquiry into encroachments on public lands and roads); McConville, *These Daring Disturbers*, 141.

13. NJA, 6:351, 400–404; McConville, *These Daring Disturbers*, 158–159.

14. Stevens Family Papers, NJHS, MG 409, Box 42, Folders 4 and 6; *New York Gazette*, February 26, 1749/50; McConville, *These Daring Disturbers*, 147, 168–174; "The Petition of the Subscribers, Inhabitants & Freeholders of Lands in the Township of Newark & Parts Adjacent," filed with the Privy Council on October 23, 1750, Ferdinand John Paris Papers, NJHS, MG 244, Box 4, Folder 5.

Index

Page numbers in italics refer to figures and tables.

About the Author

Timothy J. Crist is a cofounder and president of the Newark History Society. After earning his BA from Yale University and his PhD in history from University of Cambridge, he headed a bibliographical research project at Yale and then held executive positions at Prudential Financial. He has also served as chair of the New Jersey Council for the Humanities and president of the Newark Public Library.

Available titles in the Ceres: Rutgers Studies in History series

James M. Carter, *Rockin' in the Ivory Tower: Rock Music on Campus in the Sixties*
Nicholas P. Ciotola and Gary D. Saretzky, *Grant Castner: The Lost Archive*
Timothy J. Crist, *New Englanders in a New Land: Newark in the Proprietary Period, 1666–1702*
Thomas Gustafson, *American Anti-Pastoral: Brookside, New Jersey and the Garden State of Philip Roth*
Jordan P. Howell, *Garbage in the Garden State*
Aldo A. Lauria Santiago and Ulla D. Berg, eds., *Latinas/os in New Jersey: Histories, Communities, and Cultures*
Maxine N. Lurie, *Taking Sides in Revolutionary New Jersey: Caught in the Crossfire*
Raechel Lutz, ed., *New Jersey's Natures: Environmental Histories of the Garden State*
Jean R. Soderlund, *Separate Paths: Lenapes and Colonists in West New Jersey*
Camilla Townsend and Nicky Kay Michael, eds., *On the Turtle's Back: Stories the Lenape Told Their Grandchildren*
Haruko Wakabayashi and Fernanda Perrone, eds., *Rutgers Meets Japan: A Trans-Pacific Network of the Late Nineteenth Century*
Hettie V. Williams, *The Georgia of the North: Black Women and the Civil Rights Movement in New Jersey*